WITHDRAWN

Illinois Central College
Learning Resources Center

AESCHYLUS

A COLLECTION OF CRITICAL ESSAYS

Edited by

Marsh H. McCall, Jr.

Prentice-Hall, Inc. A SPECTRUM BOOK *Englewood Cliffs, N. J.*

Library of Congress Cataloging in Publication Data
McCall, Marsh H   comp.
    Aeschylus; a collection of critical essays.

    Bibliography: p.
    1. Aeschylus.
PA3829.M27   882'.01   77–178769
ISBN 0–13–018317–2
ISBN 0–13–018309–1 (pbk.)

PA
3829
.M27

To K. McK. T.

10   9   8   7   6   5   4   3   2   1

PRENTICE-HALL INTERNATIONAL, INC. (*London*)
PRENTICE-HALL OF AUSTRALIA, PTY. LTD. (*Sydney*)
PRENTICE-HALL OF CANADA, LTD. (*Toronto*)
PRENTICE-HALL OF INDIA PRIVATE LTD. (*New Delhi*)
PRENTICE-HALL OF JAPAN, INC. (*Tokyo*)

Contents

Introduction

by Marsh H. McCall, Jr.

Aeschylus entered the twentieth century in the stern hands of the textual critics. Scattered, though brilliant, labors on his text during the first centuries of modern scholarship had yielded in the nineteenth to a veritable assault, led by names of such eminence as Schütz, Hermann, Paley, Tucker, and Wecklein. While efforts on the text have continued with ardor in this century—one thinks of Wilamowitz's Weidmann, Weir Smyth's Loeb Library, and Gilbert Murray's two Oxford texts—, it is proper to say that fundamental shifts in Aeschylean studies have taken place, away from strict textual concerns[1] and toward such problems as dramatic purpose, poetic structure, political motivation, and theological beliefs. Some of these areas were touched upon during the nineteenth century, but our era has explored them with far greater intensity and critical sophistication, to the extent that they truly may be said to belong to the twentieth century. It is the purpose of this volume of essays to illustrate something of the range that has marked Aeschylean work. By "range" I mean both the expanse of topics investigated and also the striking diversity of scholarly views on these topics.

A rare statement may be made of Aeschylus: he is a man responsible at once for both the early development and the flowering of an art. No extant tragedian antedates Aeschylus, and we are not at all sure that the word "drama" would be applicable to whatever *did* precede his plays. To be sure, Thespis is the shadowy sixth-century figure credited with the separation of an actor from the dithyrambic chorus. But only when a second actor has been added does drama exist fully, and this essential innovation was ascribed by the Greeks to Aeschylus. He merits Professor Gilbert Murray's subtitle, "the creator of tragedy." Equally impressive is the degree to which the "creator" polished his

---

[1] The following statistic offers a partial explanation for the shift. It has been calculated that approximately 50,000 conjectures have been made on some 8,000 surviving verses of Aeschylus, although perhaps only 400 passages *must* have emendation in order to make minimal sense. The probability, therefore, of any new conjecture hitting the mark more closely than the ten or twenty already proposed for that particular word or line clearly is slight.

1

art. The last of his extant productions, the *Oresteia* and *Prometheus Bound*, have passed far beyond what anyone could call an "early stage" of tragedy. The third actor has been introduced, probably— according to the main ancient tradition—by the young Sophocles, but possibly—according to a few sources—by Aeschylus. In either case, Aeschylus made use of and helped to establish firmly the third actor. And to him alone is assigned the development of the extraordinary stage machinery and pageantry which lent exciting grandeur to that peculiarly Aeschylean dramatic technique, the connected trilogy. Sir Maurice Bowra, in his opening essay, surveys these and other general Aeschylean features with the calm lucidity that marked his scholarship for almost half a century, and amply demonstrates a felicitous truth: an essay which introduces Aeschylus introduces European tragedy.

In 490, when Aeschylus was thirty-five, he fought against the Persians at the battle of Marathon. In his eyes this act of citizenship was the most considerable event of his life, and the epitaph on his grave, said by the ancients to have been composed by Aeschylus himself, speaks of it with pride, omitting any mention whatsoever of his dramas:

> Aeschylus of Athens, Euphorion's son, this tomb
> Covers, who died at wheat-bearing Gela;
> His valor of high repute the grove of Marathon would attest,
> And the long-haired Mede who came to know it well.

The epitaph reflects both Aeschylus' patriotism and the fact that his city-state was one in which patriotism arose easily. The first two generations of Athenian democracy record a glorious era for her citizenry: Marathon, Salamis, Plataea, the growth of an empire. Aeschylus experienced it all, and it was the core of his being. Therefore, now that a recently discovered papyrus fragment has shown that the *Suppliant Women* can no longer be regarded as the earliest extant play but must be redated in the 460s, it is remarkably fitting that Aeschylus' first surviving drama should be the one closest to his own life as a citizen.

The *Persians*, of 472, the only extant historical play from the corpus of Greek tragedy, is not limited in significance to the poetic retelling of the glorious events of 480 and 479; but neither can this function be denied. The Persian messenger's long tale of Salamis forcefully recalls the deeds of Themistocles (now, in 472, in political trouble and, according to one theory, needing all the support that Aeschylus' drama might provide him) and Aristides. The report of the great sea battle also, naturally, sheds luster on the whole city of Athens and on the combined Greek forces, as do the references to Plataea later in the play. Thus, the quality of civic pride is brought to the fore, and we can imagine Aeschylus' excitement in writing this play for his countrymen. Yet it is commonly recognized that the *Persians* goes well beyond celebration, and Gilbert Murray does the theme full justice. After all, the drama is set not in Greece but in Persia; the actors are not Themistocles and Aristides but Xerxes, Atossa the queen mother, and Darius; the play exhibits not the victors but the vanquished. Beyond celebration lies the universal theme of victory and, even more, defeat, whose final cause must be sought not in the human sphere but, as Aeschylus makes clear throughout the play, in the realm of the gods. It is they who have overturned Persian power and have saved Greece. In his earliest extant production, beyond its historical character, Aeschylus has already constructed a tense dialogue between the ways of god and the ways of man, a dialogue that becomes ever more fierce in the succeeding plays.

On one point Murray argues a minority position. He sees plausible thematic connections between the *Persians* and its companion tragedies and satyr play. Most scholars now prefer to regard the *Seven Against Thebes,* of 467, as the earliest extant play belonging to a connected tragic trilogy. It is the final tragedy of a Theban cycle consisting of *Laius, Oedipus, Seven Against Thebes,* and the satyr play *Sphinx,* and it occupies a most enigmatic position in Aeschylus' surviving production. All the other trilogies of which we have some knowledge, the *Danaid* trilogy, the *Oresteia,* and the *Prometheus* trilogy, seem to reflect in their endings a kind of harmony and reconciliation. The *Seven* concludes its trilogy with the mutual slaughter of Eteocles and Polyneices, that is, with the extinction of the male progeny of Oedipus, and with individual and choral lament over the brothers. But if from one view Aeschylus seems here to describe only fulfillment of the family curse and bleak extinction, from another his statement is slightly brighter. Through the play runs a contrapuntal theme of city vs. family, a theme set amidst a war that eventually demands the destruction of one or the other. Although Eteocles' early pronouncements treat the city of Thebes and his own heroic family as a single entity, by the time he accepts the necessity of fighting his own brother the city and the family have moved quite apart. The conclusion to be drawn from their separation, that salvation of one may be achieved only through destruction of the other, is a somber one, but it is stated in a significant and positive order by the messenger who reports the brothers' confrontation: the city has escaped the yoke of slavery, the family curse is completed by the brothers' death. In a highly restrained manner, then, Aeschylus does after all strike a note of resolution in the *Seven,* and thus also in the trilogy, one that stresses the survival of the city against the loss of the heroic family, or in other terms the survival of that which is corporate and democratic against the loss of that which is politically landed and aristocratic.

If the *resolution* rings a political and communal note, the *play* is preeminently individual. It struggles with Eteocles and his painful accommodation to the family curse. And the great central scene, in which the messenger announces one by one the Argive attackers, and Eteocles counters one by one with his Theban defenders, painstakingly reveals what Eteocles is to the play and what the situation of the play does to him. Professor Thomas G. Rosenmeyer carefully analyzes how at the beginning of the long scene (as starkly formal and archaic as any scene in Aeschylus) Eteocles is in kingly control of both the city and the war; at the end, when he recognizes the power of the curse and cries out that he will meet his brother, the city has been lost sight of and the war controls him. War has again provided for Aeschylus his dramatic picture, in this case a picture centering on an individual, but with implications no less universal than in the *Persians.*

In all the manuscripts the *Seven* ends with a puzzling scene in which a herald reports the decree that Eteocles but not Polyneices shall be buried. Antigone, who together with Ismene has been lamenting the brothers, declares she will not abide by the decree; and the chorus exits, half of them resolved to aid Antigone, half to honor the decree. Since the early part of the nineteenth century, when it was recognized that the *Seven* is the last play of its trilogy, this scene, oddly forecasting future action at the end of a trilogy and so strikingly similar to the situation at the beginning of the *Antigone,* has been attacked and expunged as a later, perhaps fourth century B.C. addition, designed as a bridge between the Aeschylean trilogy and the Sophoclean play. The debate continues to rage. The more convincing arguments belong on balance to those who wish to remove the scene; but the defense has by no means been silenced.[2]

Papyrus finds during this century have not contributed as much to Aeschylean studies as to some other areas of Greek literature, such as lyric poetry and New Comedy. Still, their importance for Aeschylus has been far from negligible, and in particular one scrap from Oxyrhynchus has produced spectacular effects. Twenty years ago, a survey of Aeschylus' plays would have started with the *Suppliant Women.* Many factors, but perhaps most especially the prominence of the chorus which in this play is the main actor, had led to the consensus that here was a drama truly reflecting an early stage of the evolution of tragedy out of choral lyric. The play was dated as early as the 490s,

[2] See H. Lloyd-Jones, "The End of the *Seven Against Thebes,*" *Classical Quarterly* 9 (1959) 80–115. For a lively riposte, and condemnation of the scene, see R. D. Dawe, "The End of *Seven Against Thebes,*" *Classical Quarterly* 17 (1967) 16–28.

in any event well before the *Persians* of 472. Then, in 1952, was published (*Oxyrhynchus Papyri* 20, 2256 fr. 3) a fragment of a didascalic notice, a statement of the official circumstances and results of a dramatic contest, which announced that Aeschylus won first prize with his *Danaid* tetralogy (of which the *Suppliant Women* is the opening play) and defeated Sophocles in the process. Sophocles first competed, and won the victory, in 468. Hence, except by special pleading (e.g., the tetralogy was composed early in Aeschylus' career but not produced until the 460s), the *Danaid* trilogy and its satyr play must be put after 468; and a few letters in the fragment suggest the name Archedemides, archon in 463, thus perhaps tying the plays to that precise date, halfway between the *Seven* and *Oresteia*.

The implications of the papyrus administered a severe shock to the vast majority of the scholarly world which had confidently asserted that not only the role of the chorus but also language, metrics, and characterization all pointed to an early date. No less is involved than a total reevaluation of every chronological criterion that has been applied to or derived from Aeschylus' plays. The activity has been brisk, and a new creed has now spread. The prominence of the chorus in the *Suppliant Women* now is seen not as a sign of primitivism but as analogous to the massive choral songs of the *Oresteia*. Statistics have been formulated, or reformulated, to show that stylistically the *Suppliant Women* does actually occupy a position between the *Persians* and *Seven* (which now become the "primitive" plays) and the *Oresteia*. While the new doctrine seems almost certainly correct, the one papyrus fragment raises the specter that another may be unearthed, showing for instance that it was a posthumous production in which the *Danaid* tetralogy bested Sophocles, and throwing the date once more into utter confusion. This is unlikely to happen, but it warns us that perhaps the most salutary feature of the papyrus scrap is its message of the extreme difficulty of classifying and categorizing rigidly the development of a creative artist.

The rich themes and striking movements of the *Suppliant Women* receive rich and striking expression in Professor John H. Finley's essay. The play's conflicts—sanctuary vs. invasion, male vs. female, sex, marriage, the role and character of Zeus—all are truly Aeschylean, some prefigured in the *Persians* and *Seven,* most met head on in the *Oresteia* and *Prometheus*. And, although there is much controversy on this point, it is not reckless to affirm that the lovely fragment from the third play, in which Aphrodite proclaims a union of heaven and earth, provides a key to the trilogy. After two plays of violence and counterviolence, Hypermestra, the one Danaid who spares her husband and is probably brought to trial for her act of clemency, somehow becomes Aeschylus' vehicle for an eventual reconciliation between

the sexes and a deeper understanding of Zeus's purpose throughout
the saga's long generations.

The essays on the *Oresteia* by Professors Richmond Lattimore,
N. G. L. Hammond, and Robert F. Goheen illustrate impressively
the challenging magnificence of the trilogy. Let it suffice here to mention some of the benefits and dangers that arise from the bare existence of the trilogy, the single one that survives whole (though the
satyr play, *Proteus,* has not survived). Without it we would have no,
or very little, concept of a vast range of things Aeschylean. The
Oresteia shows us a spaciousness of dramatic and poetic structure
which we could not surmise from the single plays. It displays a
dazzling complex of imagery, both within the plays and stretching
from one play to the next. And Aeschylus, more than Sophocles or
Euripides, blurs but thereby intensifies his imagery by shifting repeatedly between object as real and object as image. The role played
by figures of hunting and nets, particularly in the *Agamemnon* and
Libation Bearers, is perhaps the sharpest instance of this duality of
language. The *Oresteia* shows how Aeschylus' absorption with inherited guilt can be played out, and worked out, through a family's
generations, and how during the process the individuals of that family,
no matter how powerfully delineated, are subsumed in part within
the larger entity and destiny of the house.

All these, and other, staples of Aeschylean interpretation *are* staples
because they are documented by the *Oresteia.* Another—potentially
subversive—form of authority also looms. Whatever appears in the
Oresteia is likely to become dogma in our attempt to comprehend the
single plays. The *Oresteia* trilogy *exists* and therefore becomes the
canon. Thus, to invoke one of the broadest issues, the trilogy ends by
dissolving the chain of murder and countermurder that has lasted for
three generations, replacing it with reconciliation between the infernal
deities of retribution, the Furies, and the Olympian representative of
Zeus's higher justice, Athena. Violence yields in the long course of
time to harmony. This *exists* in the *Oresteia,* and most scholars conclude that some similar statement of harmony must have marked the
lost third plays of the *Danaid* and *Prometheus* trilogies. It is nearly
impossible to withhold one's fervent assent. And yet is it not just conceivable that we are making the *fact* of the *Oresteia's* existence a basis
for demanding that its structure be the norm for other Aeschylean
trilogies? The third play of the *Danaid* trilogy, as we have seen, is
thought to have contained a trial scene in which the clemency of
Hypermestra is vindicated through the testimony of Aphrodite. But
on what is this belief founded? In part, on statements of later my-
thographers which seem to suggest it. In part, in rather too large part,

on the *fact* that there *is* a trial involving divine personages in the *Eumenides,* the third play of the *Oresteia.*

No one would wish the *Oresteia* to vanish. But it is so monumental, so existential, that it threatens at every moment our critical independence in viewing the rest of Aeschylus. The predicament is an exquisite agony, arising as it does from our very real possession of a complete trilogy. But it is there.

The *Seven Against Thebes* may be enigmatic. *Prometheus Bound* is plainly impossible. Its date is unknown (it has been placed from before the *Persians* to after the *Oresteia*), and no illuminating papyrus has yet appeared. Even worse, since the middle of the nineteenth century its very genuineness has been attacked, most elaborately in a 1929 monograph by Wilhelm Schmid. There are few scholars today who uncompromisingly deny the play to Aeschylus, but this does not mean that the various arguments—the reduced role of the chorus, linguistic and metrical oddities—can be ignored, or indeed satisfactorily answered. One can retort that where we have only seven plays out of an original corpus of more than seventy it is difficult to know what apparent technical anomalies might be paralleled several times over in a substantially larger selection. But the central situation of the *Prometheus,* which also provides the central argument against authenticity, is so strange, so shattering, that one can hardly imagine a parallel anywhere in the lost plays. For here is a drama enacted not among humans but among gods, in which the moral base of the world seems overturned. Zeus, the Homeric "father of men and gods," the prime mover of the natural universe, the dispenser of justice, is here portrayed in his early years of rule as an enemy and would-be destroyer of man and of man's true benefactor, Prometheus. In all the Aeschylean plays, from the *Persians* onward, the gods, and Zeus above all, are inherent. Their purpose, and Zeus's purpose, may be obscure or may entail violence and suffering, but in either event they are not far distant. Now comes a play in which Zeus is starkly alienated from mankind, and intent only on complete control of all other gods. The whole vision does indeed appear so un-Aeschylean as possibly to be non-Aeschylean.

It need not be so, however, and the many scholars who have spoken firmly for an Aeschylean *Prometheus,* written most probably after the *Oresteia* in the last years of his life, in the main have followed two paths. One centers on the figure of the protagonist. Prometheus is, almost more than Oedipus, all things to all people. For one scholar his torment is "the crucifixion of intellectual man." In Professor George Thomson's interpretation he is the revolutionary savior of the proletariat. *Alii alia.* For these scholars, the literally titanic character of Prometheus makes the play and makes it indubitably Aeschylean. The other approach centers on the antagonist. Professor C. J. Herington's essay illustrates this focus on Zeus and boldly advances to a general theory of the late trilogies, in which Aeschylus gathered together his most innovative strengths for a final assault on the nature of Zeus and divine governance. Despite the worrisome questions raised over *Prometheus* and its trilogy, in the end we must surely respond sympathetically to those who defend and interpret it as supremely Aeschylean. Both the mammoth figure of Prometheus and the mammoth scope of a trilogy which confronts a "cosmic split" and looks to have resolved it cry out for identification with the creator of Eteocles and Clytemestra and with the creator of the encompassing trilogy form.

The *Prometheus Bound,* with all its problems, belongs to Aeschylus. In the *Persians,* the gods stand behind the human actions; in *Prometheus,* Zeus may be distant from humans, but he is not distant from the play. From beginning to end of his surviving production, Aeschylus' dramas contain Zeus, the gods, god. The nature of his "theology" has long been open to contention and is currently receiving close scrutiny. A generation ago Aeschylus was hailed, particularly in the English speaking world by such scholars as Gilbert Murray, as the brightest example of Greek theological progressivism. On the basis chiefly of the structure of the *Oresteia* and such lines as the famous choral appeal to Zeus in the *Agamemnon,* 160 ff., "Zeus, whoever he is . . . ," Murray and others projected a view of Aeschylus' theology, which was widely received, as moving far beyond the Homeric and Hesiodic worlds, almost all the way to an enlightened, pre-Christian monotheism. In 1956, Professor Hugh Lloyd-Jones delivered a stinging attack on this view,[3] and argued instead that Aeschylus has advanced hardly a whit beyond Homer and Hesiod, that his dramas and characters are populated by and subject to the same demonic forces, that his Zeus and other Olympians are as capricious and willful, and that his presentation of *dikē,* justice, is as archaic and retributive as anything in the *Iliad* or *Theogony.* The battle was joined and has continued unabated since.

There is no denying the validity of several of Lloyd-Jones's arguments, and he has soundly countered Murray's slightly beatific approach. On the other hand, he and those who agree with him seem loath to venture beyond precise analysis of certain key passages to the admittedly vague realms in which one talks of the "feeling" or "tone" or "movement" of a trilogy. But in poetry such ventures must be

---

[3] H. Lloyd-Jones, "Zeus in Aeschylus," *Journal of Hellenic Studies* 76 (1956) 55–67. For a recent statement, and some modifications, of Lloyd-Jones's position, see Chapter IV of his *The Justice of Zeus* (University of California Press: Berkeley, Los Angeles, London, 1971).

braved if we are to reach the poet, and in Aeschylus' poetry the venture leads us back at least part way to Murray. Who on reflection will not be perfectly ready to see the Aeschylean plays full of archaic forms of expression and archaic forces? He is an early artist working in a religious medium, whose direct mythological and theological antecedents are Homer and Hesiod. It would be most remarkable to see anything else. Indeed, this very fact makes all the more stunning those parts of Aeschylus which have no real precedent and *are* radically novel: trilogic composition, the repeated expression of ultimate resolution emerging from a long past of violence, a magnificent grappling on a quite non-Hesiodic scale with the ineluctable problem of cosmic strife. Aeschylus was not five centuries ahead of his time. But he did experience a range of events unknown to Homer and Hesiod: the birth of Athenian democracy; the miraculous turning back of the Persians at Marathon, Salamis, and Plataea; the first flush of Athenian empire; the doctrines of Orphism; the intellectual force of Anaxagoras; the verses of Simonides, Bacchylides, and Pindar. We need not attempt to depict him as more than a man of his time, only as what he was in his time, its most profound artist, in order to sense the theological extent of his drama.

Those who know Aeschylus and feel braced by the proud air of his poetry do not wish to possess him jealously. He reaches out to all, and deserves heralding. Herein lies a final dilemma of Aeschylean studies. Professor Peter Green aptly recalls the era in which some Greek was the property of all educated men, and a translator's intent usually was to write *his own* version of Aeschylus, confident that readers could always return to the Greek text. No such confidence is possible today, and the translator has become very probably the most important force, for good and bad, in preserving and fostering the classics. Green's essay demonstrates how divergent the theories of translation have been and are likely to be and, therefore, in what an unstable and fallible condition this lifeline of the classics continues. It is a sobering final theme, made tolerable only by a belief, unabashedly Aeschylean, that the frustrations and halfsteps natural to a constant succession of translations and translators will lead us closer step by step to that poet of lofty word and thought whom we seek.[4]

[4] I should like to thank George Goold, Bernard M. W. Knox, and Henry T. Rowell for their interest and advice in the preparation of this volume.

The Tragic Vision

by C. M. Bowra

The Greek word *tragôidia*, from which our own word "tragedy" is derived, means nothing more than "goat-song." The Greeks disputed whether this was because a goat was the prize for the best song or because a goat was sacrificed when songs were sung, and modern speculations have added an alternative theory that the goat embodied Dionysus and the song was sung at his annual, ritual death. From a mass of obscure facts and ingenious theories a few solid facts emerge. All drama has its beginnings in mimetic dances in which the dancers identify themselves with certain characters and dress or daub or mask themselves to sustain the illusion. Their aim is religious or magical, a wish to enter into a closer relation with supernatural beings and usually to get them to do something. Such dances were common in Greece, and vases from the sixth century onwards have many pictures of men dancing in disguise. In Athens some dances were connected with Dionysus, the god, not only of wine, but of fertility and ecstatic excitement. To him songs were sung, accompanied by dances, and the whole complex, known as the Dithyramb, was at an early date standardized as an art-form, which told a story and no doubt illustrated it with action. The public performance of Dithyrambs was prominent in the second part of the sixth century, and in the first half of the fifth Simonides, Bacchylides, and Pindar composed them. Though they were performed at the spring festival of Dionysus, their contents did not necessarily have much connection with him. On the one hand this kind of song became a special kind of choral lyric, but before it had reached its final form as such, it engendered a new and different form, which turned into tragedy. Soon after the middle of the sixth century a choir-leader called Thespis inserted into the performance pieces of spoken verse in which he assumed the part of one of the characters told of in the song. In 534 BC this art had developed sufficiently to be recognized officially at Athens and to have annual performances in the spring. At the start tragedy contained a large element of song and dance and a small element of acting done by a single actor, and no doubt closely related to the main theme of the song.

Of Thespis' work not a word has survived, and we know nothing at all about it. Even of his immediate successors we are equally ignorant, but it is clear that in the next fifty years the form of tragedy, helped by official approval from Peisistratus, was rapidly developed and more or less established. The number of actors was increased from one to two and eventually to three and four, but never to more, while the chorus was fixed at fifteen. The performance was held on a circular space, an orchestra or dancing-place, probably once a threshing-floor, from which at one end a thin slice was cut off and included in a tangential area to provide the equivalent of a stage, though it is not certain that an actual stage was regularly used. Behind this was a simple, conventional scene of a palace-front, with a large central door and entrances or exits at the sides. The performance was held under the open sky in a theatre, carved like a horse-shoe from the side of a hill, and the acoustics were excellent. Some of the acting, as well as the songs and dances, took place in the orchestra and to this extent the performance was "in the round." The use of masks and elaborate clothing need not have hampered the actors in a free play of gesture, and there is no reason to think that Greek acting was stiff or formalized. In the fifth century the guaranteed life of a play was a single performance in a series which lasted from dawn to dusk. Each dramatist produced four plays, of which the first three were tragedies, and the fourth was a satyric drama, that is, a less serious piece in which the chorus was played by Satyrs, the traditional companions of Dionysus. The dramatist whose play was adjudged best was awarded a prize. In these conditions tragedy kept its first features unimpaired. Though the speaking portions were continuously increased as the actors became more important, the chorus never ceased to have a central importance and almost to hold the play together. Just because originally events were narrated and not acted, much of importance takes place off stage and is reported by a messenger. A play often begins with a monologue by a god or goddess or chief character who sets out the situation, and almost equally often it ends with the epiphany of a divine being who tidies up the action and passes some judgment on it. Though Greek tragedy does not always obey the unities of time, place, and action as they were formulated by Boileau after Aristotle, it preserves a simplicity of structure which is quite unlike the generous and varied scope of Elizabethan drama. All the parts were taken by men or boys, and a single actor might often have to take two or three quite different parts in the same play.

It is hard to see how so serious a form as tragedy could have been born from the Dithyramb. It is true that, unlike modern tragedy, Greek need not have an unhappy ending, but that does not prevent it from dealing in a most searching spirit with problems that concern the relations of men with the gods. Most of the early dances, as we see them depicted on vases, are either boisterous or phallic or comic, and from them we can easily imagine how the antithetical art of comedy came into existence. Nor has extant tragedy much to do with Dionysus, except in the remarkable case of Euripides' *Bacchants*, in which Dionysus is the chief character and the chorus consists of his votaries. Euripides, who was something of an antiquarian, may possibly have gone back to the beginnings of his art in this last burst of his remarkable genius, but if he did, it is hard to see where he got his knowledge, and still harder to explain why in all other Attic tragedies Dionysus has almost no part at all. The answer is probably to be found in the special character which the Dithyramb had taken at Athens. From being a rowdy, improvised song it had developed a special dignity and told stories of high events from the heroic past. Almost by accident the cult of Dionysus was deeply infused with an epic tone, and this in its turn was applied to contemporary problems in a lofty spirit. Myths and legends were used to present in concrete form large issues which troubled the Athenian mind and called for a clear presentation in this dramatic way. Greek tragedy deals with conflict and confusion, but this may be resolved either by annihilation or by the restoration of order, and both solutions were common. What matters is the universal importance of the issues raised. With the single exception of Aeschylus' *Persians* the plots of extant Greek tragedies are taken from myth, but each myth is told, not simply for its own sake, in the epic way but for its implicit questions and lessons. It presents its problem from more than one angle and is fully aware of their dramatic character and the thrill of their episodes, but these take a deeper significance because they are made to illustrate vexed issues in the human state.

Greek tragedy belongs to Athens, and to Athens alone. If it was sometimes performed elsewhere, we know very little of it, but at Athens it incarnates the spirit of the fifth century from the defeat of the Persian invaders in 490 BC and 480–479 BC till the surrender to Sparta in 404 BC. This art is characteristic of Athens in that it keeps the fine sense of style and the lively curiosity of the aristocratic age and at the same time derives an adventurous strength from the new democracy, not least from its concern with ambition and power, and the belief that Athens had a civilizing mission to all Hellas. The abounding vitality of these years finds in tragedy an outlet, which is at once a fulfilment and a criticism of the Athenian outlook and provides a searching commentary on what Athenians thought about fundamental matters in their exuberant heyday and in the approaching shadows of their decline. Of its first fifty or so years we know next to nothing, and for us Greek tragedy is embodied in the surviving plays of the three dramatists whose work weathered the centuries successfully enough for a small proportion of it to be studied in the schools of Constantinople. Aeschylus (526–456 BC) grew up before Athens expelled its tyrants, and at the age of thirty-five fought against the Persians at Marathon, a fact recorded on his tomb to the exclusion of any mention of his poetry. He lived through the most glorious days of Athens after the democracy had reached its logical limit by making all free citizens take part in the government. His earliest surviving play, the *Persians,* was produced in 472 BC and his latest, the three plays of the *Oresteia,* in 458 BC, and this means that of his early work we know almost nothing. Yet, we can hardly doubt that he, more than anyone, laid the true foundations of tragedy and established the forms and the spirit which marked it out from other kinds of poetry. What survives from his work belongs to the years in which Athens established herself as a sea-power with an empire, reformed her constitution, and secured her system of liberty guaranteed by law. Sophocles (495–406 BC) was fortunate in that his life almost coincided with the great days of Athens. As a boy of fifteen he took part in a choir, which celebrated the victory of Salamis, and he died before the capitulation of his country to Sparta. Of the more than a hundred plays which he wrote seven survive and, though his first prize was won in 468 BC, when he defeated Aeschylus with his *Triptolemus,* his earliest surviving play, the *Ajax,* probably comes from the forties, and the other plays come at intervals up to the *Philoctetes* in 409 BC and the *Oedipus at Colonus,* which he finished just before his death. Thus what we have of his work comes from his mature years, and even when he wrote the *Ajax,* he may have been older than Shakespeare when he retired to silence and death at Stratford. Euripides (480–406 BC) wrote ninety-two plays, of which nineteen survive, ranging from the *Alcestis* in 438 BC to the *Iphigeneia in Aulis,* which he left unfinished to be completed by another hand. Each poet speaks for a different generation. Aeschylus, despite his concern with grave and enigmatic issues, is the veteran of Marathon, who believes that in the end most questions can be answered and that the darkest catastrophes have the promise of some comforting light. Sophocles, the friend of Pericles, reflects his seriousness and his interest in primary principles. He is more detached than Aeschylus from the contemporary scene and examines it with a more searching insight. Euripides speaks for more troubling forces, for the questions and doubts and uncertainties which were in the air before the Peloponnesian War and much aggravated by it. While Aeschylus and Sophocles are at home in their generations, Euripides sometimes seems to be a misfit or an oddity, but, despite this, he was in later times more widely read and quoted than they, and, even in his own time, he enjoyed an enormous, if critical, popularity. Enough has survived from these three poets to reveal typical qualities of their art, even if we cannot but lament the vast amount that has been lost and may have contained much of which we have no inkling. We must make the best of what we have, and this leaves no doubt about the extraordinary level of achievement of which these three men, with their quite different gifts, were capable, and the astonishing judgment of the Athenian people, who both expected such works to be written and understood them when they were.

Though the three tragedians differ greatly from one another in outlook and manner of technique, they are all controlled by the conditions of dramatic performance and have to conform to certain rules. These settled the length of a play, which may vary from about 1,100 to 1,700 lines, and is usually nearer the first than the second, and no play would take more than two hours to perform. This means that the dramatist must exercise economy and discrimination in deciding what he may put in and what he must leave out, and this is all the more insistent since a certain part of the play must be taken up with choral songs, which in their very nature are different from speeches and dialogue and limit even further the space allowed to these. The result is that any Greek tragedy not only operates with a small number of characters, but confines its action almost to a single crisis, which has indeed its preliminaries and its aftermath but is in itself complete and unelaborate. It cannot allow anything comparable to the wide sweep of persons and actions with which Shakespeare, for instance, builds up the first two acts of *Antony and Cleopatra*. Moreover, even economy of characters and action is not enough. To cram the full force of his drama into so short a space the Greek tragedian has to concentrate as much as possible into his words. There is no room for diversions, no matter how splendid, and the words spoken by the characters are directed immediately to the development of the action. This is assisted by a device, which may come from the beginnings of Greek tragedy. When characters converse on the stage, they often speak to one another by interchanging single complete lines. Less than a single line is very rare, and a normal method for conversation is this stately, formal intercourse. It looks archaic and may well be, but for the dramatist it has the advantage that he is almost forced to distil his words into a very short space. Each line caps or completes or contradicts the line before it, and, despite the obvious formality, this means a quick, rapidly changing, highly dramatic process by which the action develops through the shifts of thought and feeling in the actors. Even when the poet goes to the other extreme and makes a messenger tell a full and varied story, he must still see that every word is on the point. In its very nature Greek tragedy practises selection and exclusion, and this calls for a high degree of attention in watching it. If the spectator allows his mind to wander, he will miss something indispensable to the whole development of the action.

Secondly, tradition laid down that every tragedy must have in it a Chorus, whose task was to sing about the action, to play some part in it, and in general to provide some kind of continuity since it is always present from soon after the beginning to the end, when it usually has the last word. The Chorus represents some suitable general role, such as old men or captive women or in special cases Oceanids or Bacchants. As tragedy developed through the fifth century, there was a tendency, not only to reduce the time given to choral songs, but to relate the Chorus more closely to the action, but throughout it has a central part, and its importance may be gauged from the fact that four plays of Aeschylus, one of Sophocles, and five of Euripides are named after it. It is not an entirely impersonal body, but it is not very fully individualized and it can vary from expressing the poet's own ideas to saying what ordinary people might feel in an extraordinary situation, or even, as in Aeschylus' *Eumenides* or Euripides' *Bacchants,* to presenting an unusual point of view. What happens to the other characters must be judged against the background of the Chorus, which provides a setting for it, passes comments and judgments, and often sets an emotional tone, which affects our response to the actual events. Sometimes it is the central actor in a play, as in Aeschylus' *Suppliant Women,* and this may be an inheritance from the first days of tragedy. The mere existence of the Chorus means that the dramatic action is set in a certain perspective and hardly ever moves in a self-sufficient world of its own as it does in Shakespeare and Racine. However strongly we respond to the actual events of a play, we must take them in conjunction with what the Chorus says about them. It gives to them a greater depth and a richer significance by relating them to other issues, even if these issues are no more than the usual thoughts of men on such subjects, and the Chorus is certainly not meant to give final answers on any matter. The degree of this relation may vary from play to play even in the works of a single dramatist, but it is always there and must be reckoned with in any attempt to understand Greek tragedy. The Chorus is not an appendage to the other actors but, like them, part of a single design. We are right to see it as belonging to the whole imaginary world in which the dramatic action takes place, and just because it is so little individualized it suggests all the more forcibly what reactions are possible to the striking and disturbing episodes of tragic action.

Thirdly, we must not expect to find in Greek drama characters so

fully personal as those of Shakespeare. This is impossible, partly because of the much smaller scale on which the Greek poets work, but
also because they were primarily concerned with depicting human
destinies as what might happen to anyone through his human nature
and his place in the world. Tragedy speaks, as Aristotle saw, of universal matters, and to these a high degree of personality and minor
idiosyncracies are alien. This general character was enhanced by the
use of masks. Even if a character changed his mask during a play, as
Oedipus may have done after blinding himself, the mere wearing of
it imposes a permanence on a character and makes us look at him from
a single angle and not expect anything discordant with it in what he
says or does. In the Greek theatre the mask is almost the man, but not
quite. After all, he speaks, and his words, though not inconsistent
with such a part as a mask suggests, certainly amplify and enrich it.
Yet, when we compare the characters of Greek tragedy with those of
modern drama, still more with those of novelists who work on a
large scale like Tolstoy or Proust, we feel that what concerns us is
not so much their personalities, as their destinies, not what they are,
but what they do and have done to them. The top moments of Greek
tragedy come when through the force of circumstances men and
women represent in their single selves a whole human destiny and,
even if they have brought it on themselves, their motives are like
those of other human beings and remarkable more for their strength
than for their subtlety. They are presented as examples of behaviour
seen from without rather than from within and, though this sooner or
later invites us to discern special characteristics, we may doubt whether
their creators were much concerned with them. So, far from acting
on the principle of Heraclitus that "character is destiny," the Greek
tragedians almost insist that destiny is character.

   This does not mean that the persons of tragedy are mere abstrac-
tions, but it does mean that they are highly simplified and that their
special kind of vitality comes from the omission of much that we take
for granted in human beings. This simplification strengthens their impact on us and concentrates our attention on those few qualities
which are indispensable to their fate. They are far from being types
of the kind favoured by the comedy of manners; for a type is created
by a different kind of simplification, in which everything is dominated
and determined by a single quality, visible in a character's every action and infused through his whole being. In Greek tragic characters
something is needed to explain why they are in their actual situations
and why they act or suffer as they do. They have qualities, which we
know in ourselves and others, and these keep them alive before us,
but we do not have to look for cryptic or complex motives or take
notice of irrelevant, if engaging, superfluities. The tragedian's task

is to show men and women in their universal characteristics as crisis tests and reveals them. When we see a Greek play acted, we interpret the actions of the characters by the familiar rules of human nature, and we are right to do so, but we need not look for anything paradoxical or unfamiliar. The tragedian's task is to illuminate the familiar, recurrent, recognizable situation, not to seek out unexplored recesses in the soul. In the end this is a great strength. Because tragedy eschews the odd and the unusual and gives its full powers to matters with which we are all acquainted, it makes special exertions to keep to the truth and to make it more impressive even to those who think that they are well acquainted with it.

Aeschylus differs from Sophocles and Euripides in making his unit of composition not the single play, but the trilogy, or three plays in succession on a comprehensive subject. This gives him a remarkable breadth and scope in his main design and enables him to show unseen powers at work in more than one generation. Though he seems to have composed almost entirely in trilogies, only one complete example survives, the *Oresteia,* which consists of the *Agamemnon, Libation Bearers,* and *Eumenides.* From this it is clear that a trilogy is not a long, three-act play but three separate plays, united by a single dominating theme. Each play is a well-conceived unit, which can be acted quite satisfactorily by itself, but between them they tell a single story at three stages, the murder of Agamemnon by his wife, Clytaemestra, the vengeance which their son, Orestes, takes by killing her, his final acquittal from the crime of murder in the eyes of gods and men. From this single example we must surmise as best we can how his other surviving plays were fitted into similarly grandiose schemes. *The Suppliant Women,* which survives, was the first play of a trilogy and tells how Danaüs and his fifty daughters have escaped from Egypt to Argos, and are in peril from their suitors coming in pursuit. They are finally welcomed in Argos, and the play catches the excitement, uncertainty, and fear of their reception there. The second play, the *Egyptians,* told of the arrival of the Egyptian suitors, their battle with the Argives, whose king was killed, and their taking to marriage the daughters of Danaüs. The daughters, then, at their father's command kill their husbands, with the exception of Hypermestra who accepts the marriage. In the third play, the *Daughters of Danaüs,* Hypermestra, who has disobeyed her father, and invited trouble by her disobedience, seems to have been tried and acquitted through the intervention of Aphrodite. On the other hand the *Seven Against Thebes* in the last play of a trilogy, which turns on the doom of the house of Laius. In the first play, the *Laius,* Laius hearing that he will be killed by his son, has him exposed, but the child none the less survives. He is Oedipus, who in the play called after him has grown up and accidentally kills Laius, not knowing who he is. The hideous truth comes out, and at the end of the play Oedipus curses his children for their harsh treatment of him. In the *Seven Against Thebes* the curse is at work. One son, Polynices, has attacked Thebes, which is ruled by his brother, Eteocles. They meet in battle, and both are killed, and the play ends with prognostications of evil for the other members of the house of Laius.

The *Prometheus Bound* presents more complex problems. It deals with the punishment of Prometheus, himself a divine being, by Zeus for having stolen fire from Olympus and given it to men. It was followed by the lost *Prometheus Delivered*, in which Prometheus was freed by Zeus because he knew a secret, that, if Zeus married Thetis, they would have a son who would overthrow him. But the rest is almost hopelessly obscure. It is possible that there was a third play, *Prometheus the Fire-bearer*, which may have brought the action to earth and told of the establishment of fire-festivals, but almost all that we know of it is that in it Aeschylus said that Prometheus had been chained for thirty thousand years. It is even possible that the third play was never completed, and that this accounts for our ignorance of it. What we do know is that the two plays, of which we have the first and some information on the second, told of the punishment of Prometheus and then of his deliverance, and were certainly parts of a single plan. On the other hand the *Persians* was written as a single play and, though it was produced with two others, the *Phineus* and the *Glaucus Potnieus*, its connection with both cannot have been related to its subject, since this was contemporary and theirs was mythical. They may of course have touched on some superficial connections, but it is hard to say how they can have, and not necessary to think that they did.

From the little that we can construct from these imperfect trilogies and from the extant *Oresteia* certain points emerge. Since a trilogy can extend beyond a single generation and can make each play deal with a self-contained topic, it is free to develop a theme on a large scale, and in this it differs from a single play. The individual plays were independent and complete wholes in themselves, comparable with the single plays of the other two dramatists, but the trilogy held them together by some large, uniting concept. In the *Oresteia* the question is of vengeance for murder in a family. Clytaemestra kills Agamemnon for sacrificing their daughter, Iphigeneia; Orestes kills Clytaemestra; what then should happen to Orestes? By the old rules, embodied in the Furies, blood calls for blood, and Orestes should be killed. But Aeschylus in the *Eumenides* has Orestes acquitted of murder and a new rule of order established under law. The Laius trilogy dramatized a curse which visits the sins of the fathers upon the children to the third generation. The idea was at least as old as Solon, and Aeschylus shows how it worked in practice. In the three plays on the daughters of Danaüs the central theme seems to be built on the relations between the sexes and to claim that a woman has a right to marry the man she loves. No doubt there was much more than this, including a conflict between filial obedience and personal passion, but that is about all that we can say. The central theme of the Prometheus plays was certainly the conflict between Prometheus and Zeus, which began in the punishment of Prometheus by Zeus but seems to have ended in some sort of reconciliation, though how this came we can only guess. It is at least not impossible that Zeus was displayed as growing milder as he grew older. The scale of structure in the trilogy corresponds with the sweep of Aeschylus' dramatic vision. He sees events in a large outline and detects divine laws at work in them, and for this the trilogy is a more capacious field than the single play.

Though Aeschylus builds his trilogies on a single dominating theme, this is only part of their structure, and he must not be treated as a philosopher or a theologian. His ideas are transformed into drama and poetry and make their effect through the individual, concrete shapes which they take. What engages us is not the mere idea but its significance in special situations, which have their own fascinating appeal. Thus, though the theme of vengeance runs through the three plays of the *Oresteia,* what is really significant is the actual sequence of events, the murder of Agamemnon, the madness of Orestes, the uncertainty whether he will in the end be acquitted. In the *Persians,* where the punishment of pride is amply displayed, we see what it means not merely to Xerxes himself in his humiliation but to his aged mother and to the Ghost of his father, who stand for wiser policies and convey almost historical lessons as they deplore the excesses of their son. In the *Prometheus Bound* what first concerns us is the fate of Prometheus, which is presented almost entirely from his point of view, so that we cannot but sympathize with him and admire him. In the *Seven Against Thebes* Eteocles may indeed be doomed to die, but before his death he is magnificently in control of his people and, when he goes out to battle, it is with a truly heroic ardour and desperation. Whatever Aeschylus' own processes of composition may have been the effect which he makes on us is to feel the impact of his dramatic events first and then to ask what interpretation, if any, he offers of them. And indeed the same may have been true of his own processes. When he chose a myth for a drama, he seems first to have felt its claims on the emotions and then to have shaped these into some guiding but never very interfering plan. He certainly does not use his dramatic persons to embody abstract situations or to illus-

trate lessons. They have their own extraordinary life and appeal
to us by their own natures, which may well run counter to the designs
of the gods and the laws of men but are none the less human and
enthralling in their own right. Even Clytaemestra, who lives with a
paramour and has long plotted her husband's murder before she com-
mits it on his return from Troy, has an everwhelming splendour in
the force of her hatred and the brazen effrontery of her speech. Zeus
may have his own reasons for having Prometheus nailed to a rock
in the Caucasus, but the scene of the nailing, with which the play
begins, spares nothing of its cruelty or of the silent fortitude with
which Prometheus endures it. The first appeal is to our human feelings, and through these we are eventually led to think about the
vast issues involved in the action.

Aeschylus reinforces this method by using the Chorus to raise questions which are relevant to his drama. We must not assume that his
Chorus always speaks for himself. It certainly does not in the *Suppliant Women,* where the Chorus are important actors in the drama,
and the comments made by the Oceanids to Prometheus throw a new
light on Prometheus' fate but are not necessarily final. But in the
Agamemnon the long choral songs, which deal with large abstract
conceptions, have been thought to be the poet's own comment on the
events. So, to a considerable extent, they are, but these comments are
not the exegesis of an abstract thinker but the imaginative musings
of a poet at full stretch. The dark forces of doom and heredity, of
pride and humiliation, which he sees at work fill him with awe and
wonder, and he is less concerned to make them clear than to convey
their mysterious power. They belong to an order halfway between
gods and men, and they are relevant to both. Aeschylus presents
their strange movements and gives to them a mythological reality,
but his first interest is to catch their nature from more than one angle
and to convey their character through a rich array of symbols and
metaphors. They add to the drama by enhancing its less intelligible
sides and make us look at the events in the knowledge that far more
is at work than meets the immediate eye. They are indeed highly
intellectual poetry in the sense that much hard thought has gone
into them, but this thought is not explanatory but pictorial, not
analytical but impressionist, not factual but imaginative. Though there
are moments when Aeschylus by his sheer visual power reminds us of
Dante, he differs from him in making us form our own conclusions
from the many hints which he throws out and does not throughout
assume a single, consistent system in which everything is clear.

Aeschylus' notion of dramatic action is not the same as our own.
In some plays he might even seem, by modern standards, to be unduly
undramatic. In the *Prometheus Bound,* the actual drama is confined to

the beginning, when Prometheus is nailed to the rock, and the end, when he is engulfed by an earthquake. But the rest of the play consists of conversations between him and first Oceanus, then Io, and finally Hermes, and of these only the last has any dramatic results, since Prometheus' refusal to tell Hermes his terrific secret leads to his being swallowed under the earth. In the *Seven Against Thebes* the larger part of the play consists of speeches in which Eteocles hears in turn of his main opponents and learns about their appearance and their characters. It is only after this that he moves into action and displays his full being. Much of the *Suppliant Women* consists of songs and debates, and it is not till the end that a real crisis emerges. Yet, despite the lack of action on the stage and even of descriptions of it off, these long passages are certainly not dull nor, strictly speaking, static. What they do is to present with much force and imagination states of consciousness, both mental and emotional, and present issues which cannot fail to catch our attention. Their dramatic quality lies in the play and counterplay of vivid prospects and retrospects, of fears and hopes equally uncertain and unfulfilled, of large controversies reduced to individual discussions and yet alike far-ranging and inexorably present. The fascination of these long discussions lies in their rich and loaded poetry which transforms everything that it touches and raises it to an exalted, visionary level, in which every theme is at once clairvoyantly vivid and yet rich in vast associations beyond itself. Aeschylus does not need to fill his plays with obviously dramatic moments; there is drama enough in his shifts of mood and his brilliant presentation of them to engage all our attention.

At the same time Aeschylus can, when he chooses, present scenes of an unusually dramatic power, firmly conceived and economically worked out. His bold, confident imagination finds no difficulty in giving verisimilitude to the strange creations of myth but thrives on making them at once striking and plausible, or perhaps so striking that they become plausible in their own world. When, in the *Persians*, the ghost of Darius is summoned at his tomb, there is no attempt to enforce the unearthly character of his appearance. He speaks as the great conqueror, the king of kings, who recalls with pride his own achievements and condemns the reckless effrontery of Xerxes. When Hephaestus helps to nail Prometheus to his rock, he does so unwillingly, but there is a relentless determination in his performance of his duty. When at the beginning of the *Eumenides* the Furies wait outside Apollo's temple to snatch Orestes as their victim, they are indeed true children of Hell and bestially convincing as the agents of the old rule that blood calls for blood. But it is not only the supernatural which sets Aeschylus' finest powers to work. In dealing with a purely human situation he displays powers no less formidable and exalts his scenes to a superhuman simplicity and power. In the *Agamemnon*, which abounds in dramatic episodes, one of the most striking is that in which Clytaemestra compels her husband to walk on a purple carpet and thus to show an arrogance which he would gladly avoid. She does it by pure power of will and shows that he is even at this moment her victim. A little later Cassandra, whom Agamemnon has brought from Troy to be his concubine and who has hitherto kept a complete silence, bursts into words and tells of the butcheries which haunt the house of Atreus, until Clytaemestra summons her into the palace. Then to our surprise she refuses to go, and Clytaemestra leaves her outside. But Cassandra knows that she is doomed, and soon goes of her own accord, a predestined victim, to her death. Aeschylus is keenly aware of the advantages of surprise and knows how to exploit them. When, in the *Libation Bearers,* Orestes is about to kill his mother, he falters and asks whether he should have pity on her, but he is kept to his task by his friend Pylades, who says:

> Where then shall be Apollo's oracles,
> The solemn covenants giv'n at his shrine?
> Let all men hate you rather than the gods.
>
> (900–2, translated by George Thomson)

These are the only words spoken by Pylades in the whole play, and for that reason all the more impressive and terrible. When, in the *Seven Against Thebes,* Eteocles has heard the long accounts of the warriors who await battle against him, he makes up his mind to fight them, but at this moment he is filled with a savage desperation and knows that the doom of the House of Laius is on him:

> Now that a god mightily drives things on,
> Let all of Laius' breed, that Phoebus hates,
> Drive with the wind into Cocytus' waves.
>
> (689–91)

There is a sudden change both in the action of the play and in the mood of Eteocles. The crisis has come with irresistible suddenness and the whole play reveals its essential shape. Yet here too what counts is the powerful, poetical impact, by which words, straining to their limit, convey the full meaning of this moment of decision. In Aeschylus the poetry holds everything together and blends the moments of high crisis with the mental conflicts and preparations of which they are the culmination.

In his concentration on this all-important point Aeschylus may seem to pay insufficient attention to the actual details of his plots. We might of course surmise that, since he was largely the creator of tragedy and was among the first to give it a plot, he had not divined how much is gained by making this clear and convincing. But this does not seem to be the case, for, when he chooses, as in the carpet-scene in the *Agamemnon*, he provides an entirely satisfying episode. It is more likely that in his concentration on the changing moods in his drama, he chose to sacrifice the secondary interest of dramatic intrigue. Thus, in the *Eumenides*, Orestes is tried for matricide, of which he is unquestionably guilty, and we might expect that he would be acquitted because he is the only man who can exact vengeance for his father's murder. But this is not what Aeschylus says. Orestes is acquitted by the single vote of Athene on the strength of Apollo's argument that a man's mother is not really his parent, and, therefore, it was not wrong to kill Clytaemestra. This is in itself unsatisfying and neglects much that has been said in this and the previous plays. But Aeschylus seems to do it because he wishes above all to show that the gods approve of Orestes' action and must protect him from the dark powers which pursue him. In a similar spirit Aeschylus deals unexpectedly with the recognition of one another by Orestes and his sister, Electra, in the *Libation Bearers*. The Greek tragedians excelled at such scenes, and Aristotle thought of them as one of the essential points in a tragedy. But Aeschylus treats this one in what seems almost too artless a way. Electra finds a lock of hair on her father's tomb and says that it is very like that of Orestes, whom in fact she has not seen for many years. Her suspicion is confirmed when she finds footprints, which are of the same shape and size as her own. On the strength of these two rather scanty pieces of evidence she concludes that Orestes is about, and before long she is united to him. As a recognition-scene this does not compare with some far more skilful scenes in Euripides, but Aeschylus has something else in mind than the mere excitement of a brother and sister recognizing each other. The hair and the footmarks are signs of the unbreakable ties which bind Orestes and Electra together and of the common task which awaits them. This calls for emphasis and he secures it by a rather artless device.

Aeschylus enforced his effects with a generous use of spectacle, on which he relies much more than Sophocles and Euripides. In the *Suppliant Women* the fifty daughters of Danaüs are pursued by an army of Egyptian slaves. The daughters flee, and the Egyptians are put to flight by an Argive army. This must have called for a large number on the scene at the same time, and the soldiers would presumably be equipped with glittering military accoutrements. In the *Prometheus Bound* the action takes place, not before the usual palace, but on a rocky crag. The daughters of Ocean, who form the Chorus, arrive on chariots at a higher level and descend from them to speak to Prometheus; Ocean himself arrives on a four-legged bird, and Io comes pursued by a monstrous gad-fly. All this called for inventive ingenuity in the stage-craftsmen and enhanced the effect of remoteness and strangeness. In the *Agamemnon* the victorious king comes home with a following worthy of his triumph. He himself rides in a chariot and is followed by his men-at-arms, who are presumably on foot, and by the prophetess Cassandra in a second chariot. The *Eumenides* opens at the temple of Apollo. By it are the Furies, black and ugly, who make weird unintelligible noises and display their lust for blood in their dripping eyes and drooling mouths. Soon afterwards the ghost of Clytaemestra appears and with a savagery worthy of her living self calls on the Furies to do their fell task, and they reply with suitable grunts. To be able to present such scenes Aeschylus must have had rich patrons, and they are notable evidence for the wealth of Athens after the Persian Wars. Though convention limited him to three actors with speaking parts, he employed a large number of mutes who at times must have filled the whole orchestra as well as the tangential area which served as the stage. The spectacle dazzled the eyes, while the words caught and held the ear, but the spectacle was essentially secondary to the words.

With Aeschylus it is the poetry that counts. Like Pindar, he writes in a rich metaphorical style, which makes no concessions to vulgar realism. It is this which sets the distance between his subjects and the common world and places them in their own majestic sphere of the imagination. Yet, though his language is always rich and elaborate, it has an extraordinary variety of temper and effect. Aeschylus proves what we might otherwise find hard to believe, that the consciously grand style can adapt itself to a whole range of different needs without losing any of its grandeur. Though he is magnificiently eloquent, he is not rhetorical, and his words do not try to say more than they really mean. When later writers tried to imitate him, they fell into bombast, but he himself is in full control of his adventurous and amazing speech. Its range may be illustrated from three small cases in the *Agamemnon*. First, when the play opens, the Watchman on the roof of the palace is on duty waiting for the bonfire to tell that Troy has been captured. To his enormous surprise he suddenly sees it, and he expresses his delight in words which are homely and yet vastly expressive:

> And I will dance the overture myself.
> My master's dice have fallen well, and I
> For this night's work shall score a treble six.
> (31–3, translated by George Thomson)

The images suit the Watchman's humble station, but they are not the less lively for that. Next, when Cassandra goes to her death, her last words are about her doom which she sees as an example of the whole human state:

> Ah, for the life of man! in happiness
> It may be like a shadow—in unhappiness
> A wet sponge drips and rubs the picture out.
>
> (1327–9)

The image is again simple and even humble, but just for this reason it stresses the futility of life, which is no more important than a casual action of this kind. Thirdly, when Clytaemestra comes out of the palace, having killed her husband and glorying in it, she says:

> There he lay prostrate, gasping out his soul,
> And pouring forth a sudden spurt of blood
> Rained thick these drops of deathly dew upon me,
> While I rejoiced like cornfields at the flow
> Of heavenly moisture in birth-pangs of the bud.
>
> (1388–92, translated by George Thomson)

The murderess exults in what she has done and feels that life revives in her as it does in the earth in spring time.

Though imagery is central to Aeschylus' language and enables him to catch the precise tone and temper of almost any occasion, there are moments when he uses a much simpler statement and yet maintains his habitual majesty. When Clytaemestra brushes aside Agamemnon's doubts about walking on a purple carpet, she argues for it in a spirit of reckless extravagance on the grounds that there is plenty more purple dye where it came from:

> There is the sea, and who shall drain it dry?
>
> (958)

When Prometheus is left alone by his gaolers to whom he has said nothing, he bursts into speech and addresses the whole wide world around him:

> O holy sky, and breezes swift of wing,
> O river-springs, and multitudinous laughter
> Of ocean waves, and you, all-mother Earth,
> And on the Sun's all-seeing orb I call:
> See what, a god, I suffer from the gods.
>
> (*Prometheus Bound*, 88–92)

Imagery plays a part in this, but the whole effect is of a boundless simplicity and spaciousness, worthy of the vast solitude in which Prometheus is imprisoned. At the opposite end of the scale we may set words which Orestes' old nurse speaks when she has heard a false

rumour of his death and recalls his childhood and what it meant
to her:

> A child in swaddling clothes cannot declare
> His wants, that he would eat, or drink, or make
> Water, and childish bellies will not wait
> Upon attendance.
>
> (*Libation Bearers*, 755–7, translated by George Thomson)

This is innocent and touching and entirely true to life. So too in a
fragment of *The Net-Haulers*, which is a satyric play and might be
expected not to maintain the high Aeschylean manner, there is a
charming scene in which Silenus, seeing Danaë and the infant Perseus
thrown on land from the sea in their chest, tries to cheer the child:

> Don't be afraid. Why are you whimpering?
> Over here to my sons let us go,
> And you can come, my pretty one,
> To my protecting arms—I'll be kind to you,
> You'll delight in the martens and fawns,
> And the young of the porcupines.
>
> (*Oxyrhynchus Papyri*, 2161, col. ii, 6–11)

Though Aeschylus' language is remarkably his own, it is surprisingly
adaptable and able to express a whole gamut of moods and effects.
Once we have assimilated its commanding tone, we see of what variations it is capable. If we say that it has something archaic about it,
this is true only in the sense that it is always experimenting and finding its way and that it takes risks which a more mature or more so-
phisticated art might avoid. In its own realm it is in complete command, and it has the great advantage that it is doing many things for
the first time. Though Aeschylus has something in common with
Pindar, he goes far beyond him in his use of words, for drama called
for a more adventurous style than choral song and had to maintain
it on a much larger scale.

Aeschylus was consciously proud of being an Athenian at a time
when Athens had begun to dominate Greece. His patriotism is confidently to the fore in the *Persians*, when the queen Atossa asks the
Chorus about whom Xerxes is attacking and hears only about Athens.
Even when the Chorus sings of the many places which have been
liberated from the Persians, they are precisely those which had at the
time of the play's production joined the Delian League under Athens.
But Aeschylus is also a Panhellenic poet, and the account of the Persian defeat at Plataea does ample honour to the other Greek states,
who took part. Nor are contemporary references lacking in other
plays, though we must be careful of reading too much into them.

The most notable is the reference in the *Eumenides,* produced in 458 BC, to the court of the Areopagus at Athens, which had two years earlier been transformed from a last stronghold of the aristocracy into a high court of justice, and there is no doubt that Aeschylus' sympathies are with the reformers. Indeed the whole conclusion of the play is like an Athenian festival in which the gods, especially Athene, display their love for Athens, and the reformed Furies, now become guardians of law and order, sing as they march in a torchlit procession of the happy prospects which await the city:

> Joy to you, joy of your justly appointed riches,
> Joy to all the people blest
> With the Virgin's love, who sits
> Next beside her Father's throne.
> Wisdom ye have learned at last.
> Folded under Pallas' wing,
> Yours at last the grace of Zeus.
>
> (996–1002, translated by George Thomson)

Even here high politics are transformed and transcended in far more important issues, and this, outside the *Persians,* is as near as Aeschylus gets to speaking of contemporary events. It is conceivable that the *Suppliant Women,* in which the action takes place in Argos, comes from a time about 464 BC when Athens was encouraging Argos to abandon her neutrality and support Athens against Sparta, but there is no sign that the main issue of the trilogy is political. In the *Prometheus Bound* the conflict between Zeus and Prometheus may possibly have been suggested by the sudden growth of Athenian power after the Persian Wars and by the problems which it raised, but, if so, these are seen from an exalted, universal standpoint with no references to the present. Aeschylus may have found some of his starting-points in contemporary events but he looked far beyond them to the lasting principles which they illustrated and which could best be presented in a mythical form without any distracting local or ephemeral details. If Pindar illuminates the events of his own time by myths, Aeschylus goes further and makes myths illustrate matters which pass far beyond the present and are often everlasting principles behind the changing scene.

Aeschylus' conception of tragedy can to some extent be deduced from his practice of it. No more for him than for Sophocles and Euripides is it an art which necessarily ends in disaster and death. Rather it tries to grasp the main issues of life and death and to face the problems of human fortune with its contrasts of good and evil, of prosperity and disaster. Its main material is conflict, which is usually between human beings, but can be, as in the *Prometheus Bound,*

between a greater and a lesser immortal, and in all such conflicts the
gods are in some way at work. Aeschylus suggests explanations for his
conflicts at two levels. The human actors behave in accordance with
their human nature, and what they do is perfectly intelligible to
anyone. But behind them are darker forces, which compel them to
act as they do, through a hereditary curse as in the house of Laius
or through the claims of blood for blood as in the house of Agamemnon. Aeschylus thus presents us with the familiar paradox that, though
men think themselves to be acting by free choice, their actual decisions are determined by forces beyond their control and almost beyond their knowledge. Aeschylus was not worried any more than
most Greeks by attempts to distinguish between free will and determinism, and assumes that, though men make their own decisions,
they are largely forced to do so by divine powers. In this there is of
course an ultimate inconsistency, but most of us are not troubled
by it, and it need not trouble us in Aeschylus. What it does is to
show human actions from two points of view, in their immediate
character and in their remoter significance. In this way Aeschylus
builds up his plots and makes them both individual and universal,
though they always keep the particularity of presentation which is
necessary to true art. Having built up his complex patterns of dramatic
action he comes to a conclusion, and in the *Eumenides* it is not merely
happy but radiantly positive and constructive. Out of much evil even
greater good will come. We may suspect that if there was a third
play in the trilogy of Prometheus the end was similarly satisfying,
while in what we know of the *Daughters of Danaüs* doubts were dispelled and quarrels healed. Aeschylus seems to have welcomed the
idea that tragic actions could end in some grand restoration of life
and order. This enabled him to show the gods in a beneficent light
and to favour the Hesiodic rather than the Homeric view of them.
On our scanty evidence the only exception to this rule is the *Seven
Against Thebes,* which ends with the extinction of the House of Laius.
Yet even this has its own kind of consolation. The curse started by
Laius himself was deserved, and, even though it passed to his grand-
children, the Greeks would have accepted this as right enough. When
at last it is worked out, we have a sense of relief because the gods'
will is done and there is nothing more to fear. More than this, Eteocles
dies heroically in battle, and no end is more honourable than that.

The *Persae*

by Gilbert Murray

The *Persae* is not only a play: it is a direct historical record of one of the great events that have decided the destiny of Europe, the repulse of the invasion of Greece by Xerxes. It gives a detailed account of a great sea-battle fought more than two thousand four hundred years ago by one who was not only an eyewitness but a combatant, and one who, besides his Greek sense of poetry, had also the peculiar Greek power of describing what he saw. In some ways his account of the actual Battle of Salamis is better even than that of the historian Herodotus, writing forty years later with an abundance of carefully sifted material. True, the details of the long Persian retreat are much vaguer; Aeschylus knew them only by report. The account of previous Persian history shows how very little was known in 472 even by the best-informed Athenians about the great empire which had almost become their master. Aeschylus knew nothing apparently about Astyages and Cyaxares, he had little of the information at the disposal of Herodotus; but his account of Salamis, the night before, the morning, and the day, and the look of the shores and shallows on the day after, is that of an eyewitness of the sort the Greeks called *alêthês*—"one who does not forget."

We have also some details about the performance. The Didascalia, or official record of the performance at Athens, is in part preserved. The date was the archonship of Menon, 473–472 BC; and since the Great Dionysia took place in the spring, that clearly takes us to the spring of 472. The *chorêgus*, that is, the citizen responsible for the expenses, was Pericles. Aeschylus obtained the first prize with the four plays *Phineus, Persae, Glaucus of Potniae,* and *Prometheus the Firekindler.* We learn further that Aeschylus produced the *Persae* a year or two later at Syracuse, on the invitation of the Tyrant Hiero.

The list of four plays raises a problem. It was the custom of Aeschylus to produce a proper trilogy of continuous plays on the same subject, followed by a satyr-play. It was so in the *Prometheus* trilogy, the Theban trilogy, the Danaid trilogy, and finally in the *Oresteia*. Indeed, Suidas tells us that it was Sophocles who began the practice of competing with separate plays which did not form a continuous story. This practice had its obvious advantages, and one would not be surprised to find that in some of his later work Aeschylus had followed the younger playwright's example. But the *Persae* is a very early play. Consequently one cannot but suspect that the four plays *Phineus, Persae, Glaucus of Potniae,* and *Prometheus the Firekindler* really form some sort of continuous story.

For this last a quite good connexion suggests itself. For when the Greeks returned to their cities after the Battle of Plataea, they had to purify the sacred places which had been polluted by the Persians, and to do this they put out all the fires in the country and had them relit from the sacred hearth at Delphi.[1] That great ceremonial of firekindling would be a good subject for the final play of a tetralogy.

As to the first of the four, *Phineus,* that blind prophet is chiefly known for his meeting with the Argonauts, when he was delivered from the harpies by the two Sons of the North Wind. Now Herodotus treats the Argonaut expedition as an invasion of Asia by Europe, duly repaid in course of time by the invasion of Europe by Asia under the Persians.[2] On this view, the *Phineus* would give us the blind prophet foretelling to the Argonauts the retributory war which their bold adventure must bring about: the *Persae* would show the prophecy fulfilled. The third play, *Glaucus of Potniae,*[3] fits in less well. This Glaucus was a hero of the vegetation type, like Dionysus, Osiris, Pentheus, Orpheus, who died by a *sparagmos*; like Hippolytus, he suffered it from his own horses. He fed his horses on flesh, as the Thracian Lycurgus did, and they went mad and devoured him at the village of Potniae. One can see no direct connexion with the *Persae,* though it is curious that Potniae was close by the site of the Battle of Plataea and was perhaps actually covered by the preliminary skirmish in which the general of the Persian cavalry, Masistios, was killed by the action of his horse. Struck by an arrow, the animal reared and fell on him, and he was then cut to pieces by the enemy.[4] A horse and a *sparagmos*: it is just possible therefore that the *Persae* did form the second play of a connected trilogy and that we can accept Suidas'

---

[1] Plutarch *Aristides,* 20; *Numa,* 9.
[2] Herodotus i. 2.
[3] The word *Potnieus* is omitted in the best MS. There was another play by Aeschylus, *Glaucus of the Sea, Pontius,* which, however, seems from the scanty evidence to have been a satyr-play, not a tragedy.
[4] Herodotus ix. 20, 24.

statement as true. But the connexion was clearly far less close and
cóntinuous than in the other Aeschylean trilogies known to us.

The *Persae* is generally described as the first historical play in European literature, and to some extent the description obviously fits.
The Battle of Salamis was fought in 480, Plataea in 479; the Athenians
rebuilt their ruined city in 478, and soon afterwards celebrated their
victory, or rather their deliverance, in a tragedy, the *Persae* of Phrynichus. In 472, i.e. four or five years later, came the *Persae* of Aeschylus,
with the same subject and title and, so we are informed by a very
ancient authority,[5] a general similarity of treatment. One would like
to know if there had been a regular celebration of the same theme at
the Great Dionysia every year between 478 and 472. It seems quite
likely, though evidently the institution was not permanent. There was
certainly a regular celebration every four years at the Panathenaea,
where the epic of Choirilos on the Persian War was, for a time, allowed
the unique privilege of being recited along with the works of Homer.
There was an annual celebration of the Victory of Salamis at the
Aianteia, or festival in honour of Ajax, the Salaminian hero, on Mu-
nychion 16, about a month after the Dionysia. It seems therefore a
little misleading to speak of the *Persae* as an historical play. It is
rather a national celebration. It is not so much to be compared with
a modern play about, say, Mary, Queen of Scots, as with a Thanks-
giving Service at Westminster Abbey to commemorate the Armistice
of 1918 . . . except that the service would of course be a service and
the *Persae* is, after all, a drama.

The construction is extremely simple. It needs only a Chorus and
two actors, and falls into three distinct parts. At the opening the Persian Elders, "The Faithful," are at their Council Chamber waiting for
news, long delayed, of the vast armies that have gone overseas to
subdue Hellas. We hear of the long array of Persian and Median
nobles, of vassal kings from Memphis and Egyptian Thebes; Lydian
princes, gay with golden armour and four-horsed and even six-horsed
chariots, followed by subject tribes from the mountains; and lastly
the golden Babylon with her motley multitude of nations, marshmen
and rivermen, terrible archers, and "all the long-knived multitude"
from the hidden valleys of Asia. Their hearts rise as they sing. Who
could ever stand against such a flood of armed men? War has been
from of old the birthright of the Persian; the thunder of the horsemen
and the overthrowing of towers and the trampling of cities in the dust.
And now, the dry land being conquered, they have turned conquering
to the sea.

---

[5] Glaucus of Rhegium, *floruit c.* 400 BC.

> We have seen the waves whiten in the fury of the wind,
> We have faced the holy places of the deep.

And yet . . . the inscrutable craft of God, is Man ever safe from it? It is strange in this empty land; with no news; only the old men and the women left, and the women often weeping for the men who have gone. They are about to take counsel together when there enters to them the Queen Mother, Atossa—who, as Herodotus tells us, "held at that time all the power." She has been disturbed by strange dreams and asks for advice. The Elders advise her to pray to her dead husband, Darius, the old and good King, who had visited her in the dream, and are answering her questions about Athens and the Greeks, what armies they have, what resources, how, with no master over them, they can ever face an angry foe, when there rushes in a Messenger from Xerxes to announce that all is lost. Salamis—hated name—is crowded with Persian dead.

The Messenger is at first wild and inarticulate with grief; then in answer to Atossa's questions he becomes coherent. Xerxes himself still lives.

> That word is joy to all my house, a bright
> Gleam as of morning after starless night.

But the others—Artembares, Dadochas the chiliarch, Tenagon the Bactrian are dead; there was a little island full of wild pigeons where the bodies were floating. Name after great name we hear of them, slain some one way and some another. Atossa questions further: What were the numbers? Is Athens still unbroken? "Yes," says the Messenger; "while her men live she has an unbroken wall." As a matter of fact, the town and acropolis had been sacked and burnt; all Athens was now in the ships. At last the Messenger tells his full story of the battle: how a pretended traitor came secretly to Xerxes to warn him that the Greeks intended to fly as soon as night fell. Xerxes was delighted and made his plans for surrounding them; all the outlets were guarded, ships sent round to the other side of Salamis, and all the Persian fleet kept at work, rowing up and down, so that no Greek vessel should escape. But nothing happened. No sign came from the Greeks at their anchorage.

> Not till the wild white horses of the Morn
> Took all the earth with glory; then was borne
> A sound across the sea, a voice, a strong
> Clamour exultant like a leaping song,
> And Echo answering from the island rock
> Cried "Battle."

The Persians had been enticed into the narrows, where the sea-craft of the Greeks had more scope to crowd them and drive them on one another till their oars were broken by the brazen rams and ship after ship went over. The few escaped who could.

And even that was not the end. Xerxes had taken possession of a little island, Psyttaleia, between Salamis and the mainland, and landed a body of chosen troops there. When the sea-fight was lost, this island became a trap. The Greeks surrounded it and charged

>   till no more
> Breathed any life of man upon that shore
> And Xerxes groaned, looking upon that deep
> Of misery. For a throne he had, a steep
> And towering crest, hard by the open sea,
> Commanding all the field.

He groaned, rent his robes, sent orders of retreat to the land army, and fled. The retreat was long and painful. Command of the sea being lost, there were no means of feeding adequately such large numbers; winter storms came prematurely, and of course the route lay mostly through hostile country.

Atossa goes to prepare her offerings, and after a great imaginative lyric by the Chorus, wailing for the men who are "torn by the awful sea, gnawed by the voiceless children of the Undefiled," returns in sad garb and without her train of attendants, to pour the libations to Darius. We find that we are now at his grave—which was, as a matter of fact, at Persepolis, some hundreds of miles away from Susa. Early tragedy paid little attention to such minutiae. There follows an impassioned scene of Invocation, full of strange words and oriental colour, till out of the Tomb arises the ghost or spirit of the Great King. "Why have they called him?" The Elders for very dread cannot speak. He turns to Atossa, who, with the same dignity and courage that she shows all through the play, tells him without shrinking the whole tale of disaster.

It is news to him and yet not news. For he recognizes in it the fulfilment of an oracle which he had hoped would be long postponed, but which had now been precipitated upon Persia by the Hubris of Xerxes. And the end is not yet. The crown of suffering is still to come for

> Those godless, those of pride infatuate,
> Who made of Greece their prey, nor held it shame
> To rob her gods and give her shrines to flame.
> Altars lie wrecked and images of God

O'erthrown, disbased, and down in rubbish trod.
For which dire sin, dire suffering now is theirs,
And direr yet shall be. . . .
An oozing crust Plataea's field shall know
Of mire blood-soaked beneath the Dorian lance;
And piles of dead dumb warning shall advance,
Even to our children's children, that the eye
Of mortal man lift not his hopes too high.

Hubris against his fellow man, and sacrilege against the gods: the two sins for which *Moira* and *Dikê* inevitably exact atonement. Darius takes his way again to the darkness, after bidding Atossa go to meet Xerxes, who is returning in discomfiture, his rent garments scarcely covering his body. "He shall have robes meet for a King!" cries his mother, and goes.

A strange Chorus of dreams and memory follows, about the greatness and peace of the Persian Empire in Darius' day; the Greek cities and islands which are now lost to Persia—or from another point of view, now free and in alliance with Athens; the great armies of Persia and the allies from unnumbered lands, now brought to nothing, "scourged by the conquering sea."

Xerxes enters in lamentation, humiliated yet still dignified and even generous. He is met by the Elders with bitter reproaches: Where are those he took with him, the youth of the land, the friends who fought at the King's side, where has he left them, he, the "Crowder of Hades with Persian dead?" He accepts the full blame.

I left them dying;
Fallen I left them,
From a Tyrian galley
Fallen and lost.

Yâwân, the despised Ionian, had taken them in his conquering "ship-wallèd battle

As he swept the dark of the waters
And the desolate shore."

The sad procession moves towards the Palace—the scene is before the Palace again, not at Darius' Tomb—through the long streets:

Xer. O ye that walked so softly, raise your head,
              Let your grief roam.
Cho. O soil of Persia, thou art hard to tread!
Xer. O trireme ships, O shoals of Persian dead!
Cho. With sobs that scarce find voice I lead thee home.

Why is the *Persae* a great tragedy? It has little plot and not much study of character; it was apparently a performance written to order for a public celebration; it was not original—in the ordinary sense at least—but modelled on a previous play of the same title and subject by another author; and lastly, it is a celebration of national victory, one of the very worst fields for good poetry. How can it be a great tragedy?

To take the last point first, patriotic poetry as a class is not usually good: it is poetry written not to express an essentially poetical impulse or intuition, but poetry used as a vehicle for expressing an alien emotion. It suffers from the same dangers as political or argumentative poetry. The emotion of patriotism may no doubt include highly dramatic and poetical elements; but conquering patriotism hardly ever makes good poetry. One may think of Drayton's *Agincourt,* Dryden's *Annus Mirabilis,* or the long persecution of the Muse which eventually produced Addison's poem on the Battle of Blenheim. The fact is that the emotions of victory—the self-satisfaction of success, the triumphing over opponents, the exultation, the almost inevitable blindness to deeper issues—militate against true poetry. If the victory is felt as an escape or deliverance, the case is different; but otherwise defeat is a deeper experience than victory, as being wounded involves stronger sensations than wounding some one else. Consequently, it is defeat, not victory, that has produced most of the great epics. Shakespeare did well not to write about the defeat of the Armada.

In our time there has been much fine literature generated by the Napoleonic Wars, from Stendhal and Erckmann-Chatrian to Thackeray and Tolstoy. But none are celebrations of mere victory; all are studies of the experiences of the human soul in times of great trial, and this is most markedly true in the greatest of them, *War and Peace.* I am disposed to think that, except possibly the *Song of Deborah,* a lyrical outburst of primitive emotion, the *Persae* is the only celebration of a victory in war which reaches the rank of the highest poetry. Here again, Aeschylus has shown his power of creating tragedy. As he made the *Prometheus* tragedy out of a folk-tale, so here he makes high poetry out of a public celebration of victory. If once we can really grasp this quality in Aeschylus, the quality of deepening and making great all the issues that he touches, we can see why the *Persae* has overcome—or at least is not injured by—the other points which might be expected to tell against it. If it has little plot or study of character, those are qualities which make an average play or story interesting and clever; they are not wanted in the highest imaginative work and, if present, tend rather to belittle it. In the mood of high contemplation one does not want to have the attention diverted to ingenuities. If it was "written to order for a public celebration," so apparently was the *Iliad*. We must accept the strange fact that an ancient city could be a beloved and beautiful thing, a thing not necessarily better than a modern municipality, but different in atmosphere. In the security of modern life we have outgrown the sanctity of the walled city, as we have outgrown that of the tribe or family, and cannot any longer feel about them as the ancients felt. When man lived surrounded by enemies, his family were the people who would fight for him while living and avenge him when dead; his city was the ringed wall within which he could breathe in peace and pursue happiness. And as for the *Persae* being largely modelled on a previous play by another writer, that, one might almost say, is the normal condition of most great poetry. The true poet loves the tradition and rehandles it as his own special love suggests; the demand that a poet should be original is one of the eccentricities of modernism. The writer of a detective story ought to give us "something new," but a poet should mostly deal with things that are not new but eternal.

It is all very well, however, to prove, or at least to argue, that certain qualities which would certainly be bad in a modern novel need not be so in the *Persae*. It is more difficult to show in what ways Aeschylus has in the *Persae* transfigured his subject and "created tragedy" out of the story of a battle not yet ten years old, just as he did out of folk-tales about the Danaids and Prometheus.

In the first place, we must remember that the subject of Greek tragedy is always the heroic saga. It is never an invented story, and it is never the history of ordinary human beings. I should doubt if there was any named character in an Attic tragedy who was not actually in some way an object of worship: a god or hero or at least the possessor of some taboo tomb or oracle or ritual. One of the things that roused such strong criticism against some of the works of Euripides was not that he was too "realistic" in the ordinary sense: he was certainly not so. It was precisely that he carried a little farther the natural work of any dramatist handling traditional religious material. While keeping the heroic names, he seemed to make the possessors of those names speak and feel like normal human beings. Now when Aeschylus, or Phrynichus before him, put on the stage the story of a contemporary war, there must have been a question whether he would bring down tragedy from its heroic level to that of common life, or exalt the contemporary story to a legendary greatness. We cannot say what Phrynichus did, but Aeschylus certainly did the latter. There is a speech of Themistocles recorded by Herodotus (viii. 109) after the Battle of Salamis: "It is not we who have done these things! It is the gods and heroes, who grudged that the sovranty of Asia and Europe should be in the hands of one proud and impious man." "It is not we who have done these things!" That is the expression of the

emotion of a great moment. The Greeks were delivered; the deliverance was a thing incredible; it must be the work of God, not of Man.
The first secret of the *Persae* is that Aeschylus preserves that emotion
from beginning to end.

It is the work of the gods, not of man: not of Aristides, nor Themistocles, nor Pausanias, not even of the Spartans or Athenians. Consequently not a single Greek individual is mentioned in the *Persae*.
This was clearly right. If one Greek general had been named the
play would have become modern and been exposed to all the small
temporary emotions of the immediate present, the gratified vanity,
the jealousy, the annoyance, the inevitable criticism. Even the gods
that fight for Hellas are anonymous, save Zeus himself and—once only
—the mail-clad Virgin of the Acropolis.[6]

With the Persians it is different. Persian names abound, and make
a large element of colour in the piece. Persians are strange, far-off
beings, exotic, and, if need be, heroic. There is no danger of bringing
the action down to an everyday level by making the Elders ask the
returning King:

> Why is Pharnouchos not with thee?
> And Ariomardos, where is he?
> Where is the Lord Seualkes gone?
> Lilaios where, the faithful son?
> Memphis, Tharybis and Masistras,
> And Artembar and Hystaichmas?
> I ask these things.

Evidently the outlandish and sonorous names seemed to the contemporary Greeks, as they seem to us, far enough removed from the
common to be suitable in tragedy. There are altogether fifty-five;
forty-two of these are said by philologists to be genuine Iranian; ten
are either of Greek form or somewhat transmuted by Greek analogy;
only three have no visible etymology in Greek or Persian.

Further, the Persians are treated in the heroic spirit. They are
terrible men; full of pride, insatiable in their claims, and—as was
natural in a practically monotheist nation—impious in their neglect
of the gods. But there is no hatred of them; no remotest suggestion
of what we now call "war propaganda." No Persian is in any way
base: none is other than brave and chivalrous. The Elders are grave
and fine; their grief is respected. Atossa is magnificent; not a word
escapes her that is unworthy of a great Queen. Darius is a type of
the old and good King, Father of his people. Xerxes himself, no

---

[6] Zeus 740, 762, 827; in exclamations 532, 915; Athena 347. (Pan is mentioned in
passing, 449.)

doubt, as a contrast to Darius, has been wild and reckless, but even there the contrast is not between Persian and Greek; only between the Old King and the Young.

This greatness of spirit in Aeschylus' treatment of the enemy is remarkable. There is a similar fairness of judgement in Herodotus and of course in Thucydides. It was not a universal ancient convention, as we can see from the Old Testament or the history of Livy; or again by turning to the Persian dithyramb of Timotheos. But to read the *Persae* during the Great War did indeed fill one with some shame at the contrast between ancient Hellas and modern Europe.

I have spoken before of the scene and the diction. The scene is merely the heart of Persia; the Greek poet does not care to be consistent about topography or to inquire exactly where the Council Chamber is situated with regard to the Tomb of Darius. It is not in the manner of ancient Greek art to trouble about such details. One may perhaps ask why the scene is not somewhere in Hellas among the victors who rejoice rather than the vanquished who lament: but the answer is simple. Aeschylus was producing a tragedy, a *Trauerspiel*. So the scene had to be among those who grieved, not those who rejoiced.

There is one point more which we may notice; the spirit in which the victory is to be taken and the moral to be drawn from it. It is the inevitable lesson of Greek tragedy, that pride leads to downfall. It is the moralizing of the processes of Nature; the Year waxes and then wanes: the corn and the vine reach their fullness and are then destroyed: man also grows great and then weakens and dies. Therefore let him walk humbly and not transgress.

The lesson is taught, in the first instance, at the expense of the Persians. They have not learnt the wisdom of *Mêden agan*. They are conquerors on land from of old; now they must attack the sea. They are the masters of Asia; now they must have Europe. In particular the Persians had committed one particular sin on which antiquity felt strongly. They had destroyed temples and burned images of the gods. Very likely they had partly been moved by a spirit of conscientious monotheism; they had destroyed idols as Cromwell's troopers destroyed church carvings; but to the Greeks the act seemed to be mere wanton impiety. The memory of it remained for centuries. Alexander when he invaded Persia gave strict orders that no sacred object whatever was to be injured, and Polybius writing about 400 years after the event still remembers what the Persians had done.

Why, then, after all their Hubris and sacrilege, does one like the Persians and feel such sympathy for them? It is partly that their names sound so grand, partly that they all fight fairly and "die game"; but I think it is chiefly because Aeschylus has steeped his verses in such charming colour and made us believe it to be Persian. Whether the colour is really Persian or only Lydian or Phrygian is a question we need not wait to ask. To Aeschylus and his audience the Persians were the East, and it is the colour and music of the East that he gives us. The effect is produced partly, as we saw above, by the use of strange words with barbaric sounds; partly by a most skilful handling of Ionian or oriental metres—based on a foot of two short followed by two long, like "by the grāve mōūnd of Atrīdēs" with a variant "by the mōūnd of grēāt Atrīdēs"—and the combination of them with lyrical anapaests. There is no other play which makes such use of the resolved anapaest with two short syllables in place of the final long; or of a metre which is really the ordinary anapaestic dimeter minus the first foot. Such technical explanations can give little impression of the real music in these lyrics, so frail, so delicate, which has nevertheless preserved its magic for these two thousand five hundred years.

Seven Against Thebes: The Tragedy of War

by Thomas G. Rosenmeyer

This is a play about war, a play "full of Ares" as an ancient critic
put it. Perhaps we should say: a play about *a* war, for the attack
of the Argive champions on Thebes, the struggle of Greek against
Greek, brother against brother, is a particular chapter in history.
Aeschylus does all he can to remind us of the uniqueness of the
event. But the nature of war is such that the chroniclers of particular
wars always transcend their immediate focus and touch upon the
archetype. . . .

How, then, does one go about writing a play about war? One way
is that of Shakespeare, in whose Histories war is presented as an
extension of diplomacy, the busyness and chicanery of royal intercourse brought to a boil. Political intrigue, council sessions, duels,
flourishes, and soldiers groping in darkness: the panoramic range of
the Elizabethan stage delights us with the sheer beauty of effort, of
vital force clashing with vital force. What tragedy there is is almost
forgotten over the bluster and the strainings on the field of battle.
Homer provides us with the closest Greek analogue. Yet there is this
difference that in the *Iliad* fighting is not only a thing of beauty but
carries its own tragic moral. For Shakespeare, war is an extension, a
pinpointing, and also a catharsis of the tragedy of human relationships; for Homer, war is the proof and authorization of life itself.

Another way is that of some recent playwrights who portray the
fears and the miseries and the desperate gentleness of the common
soldier. E. M. Remarque's *Im Westen Nichts Neues,* conceived as a
novel but experienced as drama, set the tone. The mood is unheroic,
candid, lyrical, an Archilochean mixture of grossness and sensibility.
In the film version of Remarque's book the hero dies while watching
a butterfly. In this kind of play life stands still and death takes control. . . . There are no heroes in this war, only sufferers; their
pleasures are such as can be eked out from death, the small inglorious

"Seven Against Thebes: The Tragedy of War" by Thomas G. Rosenmeyer.
From *Arion,* I, No. 1 (Spring 1962), 48–78. Copyright © 1962 by *Arion.* Reprinted
by permission of *Arion.* The pages reprinted here are only a part of the chapter
entitled "*Seven Against Thebes:* The Tragedy of War."

pleasures of men condemned to die. Of this perspective brief flashes
are to be caught here and there in Greek drama. Take, for example,
the herald's speech in the *Agamemnon* (555ff., tr. Lattimore):

> Were I to tell you of the hard work done, the nights
> exposed, the cramped sea-quarters, the foul beds . . .
>   We lay
> against the ramparts of our enemies, and from
> the sky, and from the ground, the meadow dews came out
> to soak our clothes and fill our hair with lice.

The herald goes on to recall the dying of the birds, the sea paralyzed
into wavelessness, the dead men fixed in their graves. Hopelessness,
revulsion, and death are the keynotes of this formulation of war.

Then there is the war lampooned by Aristophanes. His thoughtful
clowns are brothers in the flesh to the Achaean soldiers encamped
below Troy and fighting against dew and vermin. But in comedy it
becomes possible for the sufferers to change into scoffers, to turn
back death with a flick of the wrist and laugh him off the scene.
Aristophanes achieves this by domesticating war; in the place of
swords and helmets and breastplates, the paraphernalia of a heroic
delusion, the comic heroes use cooking utensils to make battle. Thus
war becomes both manageable and funny. Yet its horror continues
to be felt, for the domestication remains a device, open for all to see.
The device produces a moral, by posing a question: why not use the
pots and pans for making porridge or soup? Why not use iron for
ploughshares, atomic power for cancer research? It is the triumph of
comedy that now and then, using the kind of material which informs
tragedy, it can, by means of comic distortions and inversions, prompt
the asking of specific questions and generate a directed response.

In most plays about war, it appears, the treatment is unified. War
is visualized in a certain way, and the actions and responses of the
characters are brought into line with that particular emphasis. It is
not to be expected that Coriolanus feels about fighting as Virgilia
does. For Agamemnon the Trojan War means one thing, to Clytemnestra it means something quite different. But within the imagination of the audience each play that deals with a war establishes a
recognizable pattern, a unique impression of the specific quality and
meaning of that war. . . . The status and appeal of the war are
clearly defined, for a very good reason. For war, in these plays, is to
serve as a matrix for the action or inaction of the tragic hero. The
brighter, the better defined the foil, the more mysterious and affecting
the individual heroism pictured against it.

The *Seven Against Thebes* of Aeschylus deviates from this norm,
as it deviates from the attitudes toward war lightly sketched above.

In this drama war and the hero are not related to each other as the field of action and the agent. There is between them a reciprocal relationship, a mutually quickening involvement, which reduces the traditional schemes of free will, fate, and responsibility to irrelevance. The war shapes Eteocles, and Eteocles in turn shapes the war. What is more, the war itself is developed in terms of a daring counterpoint. Toward the beginning of the drama it is an impersonal mechanism, an irresistible brutal assault on the weakness of man, a senseless grinding pressure from abroad. Under its aegis beauty takes refuge in despair and heroism is cast out. Toward the end of the play, on the other hand, the machine aspect of war is long forgotten, beauty has reentered with the engagement of the leader, and heroism saves the day. Between the beginning and the end there is much subtle manipulation of the contrapuntal themes of tanks versus bayonets, of logistics versus courage, of Ares versus the Curse. As against Shakespeare's panorama of blood and fuss and thunder, against Remarque's portrayal of human frailty sustaining senseless bombardment, Aeschylus' image of war in the *Seven* is more complex and more comprehensive. It is also more real because it partakes of the ambivalence and the mystery which attach to the heroic achievement.

It will be useful to recall the facts. Laius king of Thebes was told that Thebes would flourish only if he had no sons. He flouts the oracle, begets Oedipus, exposes him after his birth, and is ultimately killed by him. The flouting of the oracle in combination with the parricide produces a curse which settles heavily on the royal house. Oedipus himself, crushed by the curse, revitalizes the Fury by cursing his own sons before he dies. Against this compounded curse the brothers, Eteocles and Polyneices, attempt the feeble protection of a political settlement. Eteocles, the older, is to remain and rule in Thebes. Polyneices, the younger, is to go south and seek a kingdom of his own. Polyneices is lucky; on the strength of a dynastic marriage in Argos he gains influence and persuades Adrastus, the king of Argos, to march against Thebes and challenge his brother. As the play opens the siege has begun. Eteocles selects seven leaders from the Theban army to engage seven champions of the Argive forces at the seven gates of Thebes, arranging for himself to take up the position opposite Polyneices. The brothers kill each other, the city is saved, and the play ends with the sons of Oedipus being laid alongside their father in a holy grave.[1]

It is often said that Aeschylus delights in spectacle, in violent action on the stage, in vivid colors and extravagant gestures. The present

---

[1] In spite of some recent objections, most scholars are today agreed that the play originally ended with line 1004. What follows in the traditional text are subsequent additions inspired by Sophocles' *Antigone*.

play forms an exception to this rule. The setting is simple. At the back of the stage stands a large stepped altar adorned with seven divine statues, each of them representing the divinity presiding over one of the seven gates of Thebes. It is these seven images, clearly characterized as belonging to Athena, Ares, Poseidon, and so forth, which determine the stage action. Both the chorus and the actors focus their attention, as the progress of the play requires, now on this and now on that divinity, or on all of them jointly. . . . The constant referral to the gods clothes the proceedings in severity. The public character and the grandeur of the issues, at least so we are led to believe from the beginning, rule out intimacy and sentiment. Apparently they also rule out flamboyance and baroqueness. The stage is simple, the movements on it deliberate and repetitious, masks and costumes purposely subdued in color and design. . . .

II

As the play opens, we face a public situation. Thebes is under attack, and the question is whether and how the salvation of the city can be worked out. Eteocles, the king, is charged with finding a solution to the problem. In this task he is disturbed by the presence of the chorus of Theban women. They break in on his calm and reasoned dispositions with an almost prophetic fervor, born from fear. In their excitement they visualize the enemy spilling over the city walls although the battle has not yet begun. Eteocles, the confident organizer, manages to break the hysteria of the women. Actually, . . . he strikes a compromise with them. He suggests that they go home. . . . But of course they cannot take his advice, for a chorus must remain on the scene. As women imperiled by war they symbolize the endangered city as a whole; and in this capacity they must be present to frame the composure of the king, and to justify his decisions.

Eteocles, it appears, simultaneously faces two different fronts. On the one hand there are the attackers, beyond the stage, outside of the city. They are the enemy, and his position as leader requires that he devote his undivided attention to counteracting that threat. At the same time, however, his mind is distracted, and his function complicated, by the women who are on the stage, within the city, visible to the audience. Standing between the two blocks he forms a connecting link between them; he finds out that he may have as much to fear from the one as from the other. In the end, in spite of some brave maneuvering to protect his rear, he is crushed between them. But this will not happen until the play has run its course. For the present we do not see the disaster, but take our visual cues from the king. By alternately focusing on the aggressors outside the city and on the sufferers within, Aeschylus permits us to recognize the gulf which separates the two. In this we are helped along by the poetic elaboration of a network of crucial antinomies. On the stage we witness a segment of Greek culture, with its altars, its gods, and its demonstrations of freedom; beyond, there are barbaric rites, Titans invoked, and the threat of slavery. . . . On the stage we review solid fighters, relying on courage and modesty and little else; beyond, the instruments of actions are beasts and emblems and idle boasts. Here, soft women conveying the suffering that comes with war; there, shields and chariots and brazen bells, the glossy impenetrable impersonal equipment of battle. In Thebes, a reliance on Earth, the great mother, the giver of food and the shaper of feelings; outside, blood and fire and rootless barren monstrosity.

Let us look at some of the details of this antiphonal system of references. The conception that the Thebans are Greeks while their enemies are barbarians has of course no foundation in history or reason. What is more, for an Athenian playwright in the fifth century to intimate that an Argive army was less Greek than the Thebans is a diplomatic faux pas of the first order. And yet Aeschylus dares to risk the displeasure of an Athenian ally, and to fly in the face of familiar history, by unmistakably contrasting Thebes (71),

> a city which pours forth the speech of Greece

with (170)

> an army of another tongue.

For Aeschylus is a dramatist, not a historian. To point up the viciousness of war, and to deepen the gulf between the city and the forces beyond, he does not scruple to practice a deception and to paint his Argives with the colors of the Persians of recent historical memory. The result, at least to begin with, is a clearer drawing of the lines, a more crystalline hardening of opposites.

One reason why the enemies have to be barbarian in speech and character is their lack of a home. To be Greek, within the world of this play, means to be tied to the soil which your fathers have cultivated. . . . The loss of Thebes, beyond all else, would mean the loss of a living hoard of Greek tradition. The opponents do not share in this earth-bound culture; uprooted, uncommitted as they are, they are shown to practice a vain and vicious self-reliance, an *autarky* such as is exhibited by fools, villains, and barbarians. . . .

The Thebans have freedom, the opponents offer slavery. This constant theme, struck whenever the issue between Greeks and barbarians is raised, forms one of the major motifs developed in the choral songs.

The women fear enslavement, ending in concubinage. With vivid and pathetic colors they paint scene after scene of subjugation and humiliation. But at this point Aeschylus introduces a jarring note. Eteocles, at pains to calm their fears, suggests to the women that it is they, by their own behavior, who are liable to bring about their enslavement (254). . . . Perhaps he means to say only that their lack of control is interfering with an effective defense of Thebes. But I believe there is more in this than the forecast of a dreaded outcome. . . . Their behavior shows that they are unfree, they are jettisoning the dignity and the spiritual strength, the *sophrosyne,* which they should have absorbed. . . . Eteocles reminds them of their birthright and their obligations as free citizens. For the members of the chorus *are* citizens, whatever the status of women in Greek politics.

In this fashion Aeschylus averts what might have been a fatal flaw in his design. There is nothing more dangerous to the successful planning of a tragedy than a moral situation which is all black and all white. The treatment by antinomies which pervades the play brings it very close indeed to the line after which tragedy resolves into melodrama and audiences may hiss in comfort. . . . But this is, after all, a tragedy, and it can be that only because the antinomies are not allowed to stand without some subtle adjustment. Hence the characterization of the women who are not entirely free. The absence of Polyneices from the stage is a further touch to blunt the edge of the melodrama. It is true, of course, that he could have come on the scene only under the protection of a truce; and that would have meant proliferating the action in a way which Aeschylus, unlike Euripides, avoids. Polyneices, at any rate, does not appear; and a villain off stage can never be quite so effective in drawing upon himself the hatred of the audience as an adversary who faces the hero visibly and concretely.

But these are rather superficial measures. There are other, more incisive means whereby Aeschylus arranges to prevent the set contrarieties from degenerating into a moral paradigm. They are, principally, the dynamics of the selection scene, and the gradual self-revelation, completely unexpected, of Eteocles who in the end turns out to be and to have been quite different from what we had a right to expect. For, and this is part of the irony which restores to the action its tragic dimension, Eteocles winds up as one who "would seem rather than be."

The initial role of Eteocles is highlighted by one of those nautical metaphors which recur in many parts of the play (1):

> He must speak to the point
> who watches the course from the city's deck,
> his hand on the tiller and his eyes unsoothed by sleep.

Eteocles is the pilot of the state. There is no reason to doubt, during
the first part of the play, that his chief business is to guide his crew.
. . . About his soul, his private feelings, his hopes and fears as a
human being we learn nothing at all. The public crisis requires a
public official to cope with it according to the lights of his profes-
sion. . . .

The language of political authority has a ring all its own. It makes
statements, it shouts commands, it never hedges or wavers or falters.
Above all, it works through speech. Eteocles has no lyrics. His iambic
trimeters consistently reflect the rational calm of his public commitment. The king, as king, has no music. Contrast the women; their
utterance exhausts itself in exclamations and interjections and rhetorical questions. Theirs is the language of despair, or terror, of the imagination. . . . They sing and dance out their experiences, and the
varying curve of their passions finds audible expression in the intricate texture of their musical rhythms. . . . Only toward the end,
when Eteocles reverses himself, the shock causes the chorus to inter-
rupt the continuity of this musical pattern and to lapse into speech.
But this is a deviation which proves the rule. The antithetical posi-
tions of the leader and his flock are acted out through the antithesis
between music and the spoken word. Particularly when they turn
toward each other, to persuade or beseech, the "epirrhematic" alternation of song and speech (203ff.) carries an obvious moral.

We have noted that the mind of Eteocles works on the level of
reason, while the women give themselves over to their emotions and
their violent fancies. This is only another way of saying that it is
Eteocles' role to think of others and for others, whereas the members
of the chorus are wrapped up in their own fears and specters. At any
rate this is true of the Eteocles and the chorus who are presented to
us in the first half of the play. That the women should be so concerned with their own fate and their own sufferings, instead of helping
to support high strategy, is only to be expected. It is not for nothing
that the chorus consists of women. This is a play about war, and war's
destructive power is felt most sharply by the women. Men brave the
war, they enter into a partnership with it, the terms of the partnership being that if they win, they have the glory, and if they are killed,
they have neither shame nor suffering. But women are the losers
whatever the outcome. Driven by restless fancies the chorus con-
templates only the worst, and some of Aeschylus' formulations have
the keen edge of collective memories of pain . . . (333):

> Weep upon girls freshly plucked who, even before
> the cruel harvest of marriage rites, leave
> their home on an odious path.

> Nay, I say that the dead
> have a fate better than this. . . .

The picture is one of women wasted, violently and at random. Aeschylus merges this with another picture, a vision of foodstuffs recklessly spilled (357ff.). . . . As a portrayer of women's thoughts and feelings Aeschylus has few equals among the great writers of tragedy. He does not set out to create lifelike characters, to copy the bundle of significances and irrelevancies which constitute a specific personality. But he understands the important differences between the world of men and the world of women. This prevents him from ever conceiving his women as mere negations or parodies of masculinity, such as are occasionally found in the plays of Sophocles and Euripides. The dramatic situation is often contrived or abstract, but the variety of human responses which Aeschylus builds into his situations is drawn from a fountain of sympathy and discrimination. . . .

When the chorus, in their characteristic hallucinations, see the enemy vaulting the wall, the objects on which their inner eye dwells are many: horses, chariots, helmets, plumes, spears, bridles, shields small and large, and disembodied crashes and thunderings (100ff.). . . . Behind this imposing front of armor and equipment the men themselves are barely noticed. The concentration on the war machine, on the gear and the artillery, is deliberate. For it communicates the hard impersonality of war which Aeschylus wishes us to accept as the initial thesis of the play. Above all, there is the accent on the shields. The symbolic function of the shields in the selection sequence will be discussed directly. But long before that phase of the play, . . . the shield asserts itself as the principal image of the vision of war we have been discussing: war as a meaningless mechanism, as crude physical necessity and violence, as the impact of mass on mass. We need not rely on our own sense of metaphor to see how fitting the image is; archaic vase painting furnishes us with independent evidence. When the artist paints a duel, the contortions of the limbs, the tautness of the facial muscles are sharply individualized. Each fighter has his own posture and his own momentum; the contest is one in which two souls meet and clash. The arms, though an important part of the artistic design, are largely decorative, or at any rate subordinate to the contours of the heroic physique. But then there are the vases with serried ranks of fighters moving into battle or engaging an enemy host. In such scenes of mass fighting the soldiers are, as a rule, barely differentiated as men; their movements and their facial expressions form a repetitive design. Only their shields, reaching from chin to knee and allowing only the smallest margin to heads and extremities, are grandly distinguished, by their blazons. These

blazons—snakes and eagles and bull's heads and Gorgons and boars
—form the real personalities, the true entities engaged in the battle.
It is a battle of shields, not of men.

This is the formulation which Aeschylus uses in the first half of his
play. The conception is essentially visual, invented by painters for
their panels of mass war. Because it appeals to the eye, its use by
Aeschylus is particularly effective. For it is important that a playwright should, at the beginning of a tragic action, supply his audience
with a firm visual anchoring. The image of the shield permits us to
follow the development of the theme with a full perception of the
distance we are traveling. . . .

III

At the end of the *stretta* which concludes the exchange between the
king and his people (245ff.) there is a momentary reconciliation. It
marks the end of the exposition, of the setting of the stage for the
tragic action that is to follow. The women are impressed with the
warnings of Eteocles; they promise to behave themselves, to subject
their anxieties to the military-political-philosophical discipline recommended by him (263):

> I hold my tongue; and bear the general fortune.

There are some critics who argue that Aeschylean *stichomythia*, the
stiff alternation of single lines of dialogue, does not give us an insight
into the shifting personal relations of the characters. It is their opinion
that *stichomythia* serves only to further the plot. It is at best difficult
to make so rigid a distinction between the development of the plot and
the realignment of the characters. In any case, the *Seven Against
Thebes* furnishes us with the prize example of a *stichomythia* in the
brief course of which the relationships of the characters are significantly changed. At the end of the passage the chorus are launched
on their slow road to political and personal salvation. There will be
lapses into their old nervousness and trepidation, notably in the ode
which follows immediately upon their apparent adjustment to the
policy of Eteocles, after the king exits from the stage and leaves them
to themselves. . . . But the first flash of a new spirit has been glimpsed,
a token of the strength and the freedom which the women are to
achieve before the play comes to an end.

More important, at precisely the same moment Eteocles begins to
travel in the opposite direction. The reconciliation is no one-sided
affair. To pacify the chorus and give them the confidence they need for
their conversion, the king promises to relinquish his generalship and
to become a fighting soldier. This decision to fight—though Adrastus,

the leader of the opposition, does not—is a concession won from Eteocles in his contest with the women. Ostensibly the move is not out of keeping with the military preparedness for which he stands. In reality it is in the nature of an abdication. Earlier, before the force of the choral frenzy exacted its toll, he had asked (208):

> How now, does the skipper, when his ship
> wearies against the sea swell, find a means
> of safety by leaving the stern for the bow?

With his announcement that he will share in the fighting (282), . . . he himself turns into a captain who leaves the stern, who gives up his post of command and joins the sailors in their undirected efforts throughout the length of the ship. The detached leader, the organizer, begins to be personally involved. At first the involvement is only on the surface; his fighting is to be primarily for show, to convince the women that there is nothing to fear. . . . He continues to regard himself as the pilot of the city, as if such doubling in brass were possible in the world of the city state. But administrative discipline is not the stuff from which heroes are made.

The chorus is calmed, Eteocles leaves. Now we expect the battle. But Greek drama shows no battles on the stage, just as it is reluctant to show deaths. Perhaps the writers feel that an enactment of dying, particularly of blood and wounds, would strain the nice tension between truth and illusion which is demanded in the theater. . . . Some suggest that the religious setting of the performance, the Dionysiac background, must be held partly responsible. Whatever the reason, the battle cannot be staged. It must be reshaped to fit the bounds of the tragedy.

Now what is a heroic battle? It is the measuring up of two men against each other. What counts is the comparative standing of the two parties. . . . Significantly in Homer the great duels are fought through the medium of oratory before they are decided by means of arms. Often we are made to feel that the fight is won when one of the heroes has managed to deflate the ego of his opponent through his superior art of boasting. The wounds inflicted afterward are merely the natural consequence of the power arrangement which the speeches of the men have rehearsed before our eyes. Thus, if we could look into the hearts of the people as they confront each other, . . . we might perhaps be able to catch the quintessence of the duel. We should perceive the form or idea rather than the phenomenon, which is stunted and disfigured by accidental detail. The confrontation of vital components is to be found already in the antiphonal symbolism discussed earlier. But now we need more than a thematic counterpoint. We need a concrete clash. . . . To furnish this is the purpose of the selection sequence. We cannot have the paltry reality of a genuine battle; so the formal organization of speeches and counterspeeches, stately and deliberate and richly colored, gives us what we need to know about each of the fighters, to judge or to applaud. The sequence permits us not only to see the duels, as we might in a proper war, but to assess their worth and to reflect on the rights and wrongs of the fighters. Above all, it saves the duels from appearing either ludicrous or obscure. . . .

The sequence consists of seven double panels, each separated from its neighbor by a brief choral interlude in which the enduring fears of the women continue to be voiced. Each of the seven panels consists of two speeches; in the first the messenger describes the preparations of an attacker; in the second Eteocles arranges for a defendant to repel the enemy. At the end of Eteocles' final rejoinder the chorus does not add its usual sung comment but adopts the blank verse of the speakers. For once they respond with a remonstrance rather than a sentiment or apprehension. This suggests that the last panel is different from the others, and that perhaps it is the one which the others are meant to prepare. Indeed, before the choral ode which concludes the sequence there is an exchange between Eteocles and the chorus, parallel to the exchange which prompted the earlier reconciliation and obviously conceived as a complement to it. By purely formal means, therefore, we are given to understand that at the end of the selection sequence the king and the chorus once more find themselves at opposite poles, but in reverse, and that a new solution of their difference must be worked out. The reason for the new constellation of attitudes is supplied by the sequence itself. It turns out to be the dramatist's chief instrument for refashioning our vista of war, for guiding us from the impersonal horror of the machine and its extensions to the moral and spiritual substance of the heroic encounter.

If we compare the attackers listed by the messenger with the defendants sent against them by Eteocles, the latter are, for the most part, a colorless lot. They have to be, for color in this play is linked with wrong. The colorfulness of the enemies is part of their barbarism, their Orientalism; it is the visual confirmation of their boastful preening. Color is, as it were, the accompaniment of emptiness. Solidity and substance are persuasive enough without the surface thrill of an optic illusion. . . .

The aggressors are all the more interesting. First there is Tydeus. He is a beast; more particularly he is the proverbially roaring beast. He roars like a serpent—the context suggests that the bellow of a dragon rather than the hiss of a snake is intended. . . . The beast imagery and the impression of vocal compulsiveness carry us beyond the limits of good and evil. Tydeus lacks the moral dimension which makes of a man a responsible human agent. He is part of the animated machine; through the turbulence of Aeschylus' verse we experience some of the terror spread by the inhuman howl of the monster.

Capaneus, the next man from Argos, though differently conceived, is of the same stuff: like Tydeus and all the other attackers but one he is a blasphemer (427). . . . But with him blasphemy is not merely an attitude, a partial symptom of his villainy; it is his very nature. His "gigantic" frame brooks no commerce with the gods; the lightning bolts of Zeus are to him only a mild discomfort to be shrugged off along with the midday heat. He is, or fancies himself, an irresistible and unfeeling bulk, an engine destined to hurl firebolts of its own and burn the city. Like Tydeus, then, Capaneus perpetuates the vision of war as a compulsive mechanical threat which is the play's point of departure.

Roughly the same is true also of the portrait of the third Argive warrior, Eteoclus, except that in his case the emphasis is less on the unfeeling mechanism than on the irrational nature of the monster (461):

> He wheels his mares snorting in their muzzle
> straps, eager to dash against the gate.
> The muzzles whistle with a barbaric ring,
> filled with a nostril-sniffing insolence.

This is all we learn about the person of Eteoclus (the embarrassing closeness of the name to that of Eteocles must mean that the myth on which Aeschylus draws is based on historical memories, however dim). . . . The personality of Eteoclus disappears behind the vicious energy of his horses. Once more we find ourselves stationed in a moral desert, in a fierce devilish stamping ground where good and evil have no meaning.

The horses of Eteoclus duplicate, with an increase in the brutality of it, the neighing of Tydeus. Similarly Hippomedon, the next aggressor to be described, may be called a doublet of Capaneus. But now the governing idea of automatic bulk is fully realized; the description comes to be completely divorced from the anatomy of the human body. . . . We gather that the eyes of the messenger are not fixed on the person of the man, or even on his "frame and huge design" (488), but on the shield. The shield, the symbol of mechanical war, has come to cover and hide the lineaments of the fighter behind it. . . . This enlargement and self-assertion of what should be an instrument in human hands contains an element of humor. Bergson reminds us that human beings who are shown behaving like machines are funny. Aeschylus, with characteristic courage and with a minimum of subterfuge, exploits the humor where it presents itself (489):

> I shuddered as he wheeled his vast threshing-floor—
> I mean, the round of his shield.

. . . The fact remains that the shield has now become an autonomous substance. As an image it is no longer merely basic, but also terminal. No further development of the initial conception of war is possible, unless the drama is to bog down in the species of humor which feeds on insistence and hyperbole. . . . The joke of the messenger, therefore, heralds a turn.

The first thing to be noted about the messenger's description of Parthenopaeus is its anonymity. He withholds the name till almost the end of his speech. . . . True, near the beginning of the passage there are certain pointers—"mountain-dwelling mother," "man-boy," and others—which an audience learned in mythology will interpret correctly. But it is a matter of interpretation, and for most of us, as for the majority of the ancient audience, the speech is a protracted riddle, whose solution, in this case the name, is held off until the personality has been cast into full relief. For now, for the first time, the messenger gives us a man, a complex human being, rather than a monster or a machine. Like the others he is a blasphemer (529):

> He swears by the spear he holds, prizing it more
> than a god, nay, higher than his eyes . . .

The terms of the comparison are revealing. He worships his spear; in fact he resembles the others. But in his vanity he makes reference to his eyes, and it so happens that these eyes belong to an unusually pretty face. The warrior has, we are told, an adolescent, girlish look—and in fact that is the meaning of the name as yet unannounced. But his spirit is by no means girlish, and his eye, set in a lovely ephebic face, is a true mirror of his spirit: a grim Gorgon eye. In short, Parthenopaeus is an angelic miscreant; charming without and rotten within, he exhibits a gross disparity between character and looks. . . .

It is clear that with the appearance of this man we have entered a new arena. He is not a beast, or a colossus, or a shield, or one of the other unnatural concretions which take us beyond the pale of pity and fear. He interests us as a person, for we know his type. . . . We have left the machines and the beasts behind us; from now on we shall be looking at men.

With the next messenger report, . . . the leap is complete. The sixth aggressor is Amphiaraus, a prophet. . . . He knows that the expedition will fail and that he himself will, by his death, enhance the power of Thebes (587). . . . He opposes the whole war and along with it the men who have carried it to the gates of Thebes. This is what we would expect from a hero who resembles Eteocles in being temperate and controlled (568), who holds his shield quietly instead of whirling it (590), and who carries no design on the shield. For (592)

> he means not to seem best, but to be,
> and gather fruit from the deep furrow ploughed
> in his mind where noble counsels grow and thrive. . . .

Amphiaraus is not easy to understand. The unorthodoxy of his position answers to the tension in his mind. His name-calling of Polyneices . . . points to a harsh sense of frustration. We should remember also that he is a prophet, a "man of curses" as his name says. His abuse has the force of crushing souls. After he has finished with Polyneices we can no longer believe that Polyneices has any justice on his side, or that he will be victorious. A good man who curses the aggressors; an enemy who helps to secure the salvation of Thebes: no wonder that Eteocles bursts out in sorrow and perplexity at the spectacle of Amphiaraus conjured up by the messenger. For the anomalousness of the position of Amphiaraus closely resembles his own. He also has found himself at odds with his friends; he also is in danger of being (614)

> pulled down and smashed along with the rest, God willing. . . .

The goodness of Amphiaraus does something else. Earlier we commented on the artistic precariousness of a dramatic situation which is morally all white and all black. The presence of the prophet among the villains is yet another means of mitigating the risk. It appears that the attackers are wicked but not unexceptionally so. Eteocles has been inserted into the ranks of the aggressors, under another name, to redistribute the light and the shade, and to save the tragedy from becoming an open book. At the same time the device cannot fail to suggest that the comparison works also the other way round. Because Eteocles is like Amphiaraus we must be prepared for the possibility of his defeat. For the doom of the prophet shows that the good is not necessarily victorious.

But, to turn now to the last panel, Polyneices is a moral agent, a man, not part of the machine. He prays to Justice, and carries her image on his shield. To be sure, she is *his* justice, a fragmentary portion of justice of which Heraclitus would say that it is illusory like a dream. It is worse than illusory; being a relativist distortion of true justice it is more evil than moral indifference. . . . The audience knows that his departure from Thebes was voluntary and sanctioned by usage. He is in the wrong; but instead of simply drawing him as a villain Aeschylus has him indulge in a flight of ethical fancy which prompts us to reflect on the justice or injustice of his enterprise. . . .

And finally, the moral complexion of his character, itself prefigured by the virtues of Amphiaraus, helps ˌto prepare the eventual shift of Eteocles. Thus the selection sequence turns out to have an important function in shifting our focus from mass war to personal engagement and the question of right and wrong, and in setting the stage for Eteocles' liberation from his role as detached manipulator.

IV

Through most of the selection sequence, Eteocles remains the master strategist. Each of the attackers, we are told, carries a shield with a telling blazon, all except Amphiaraus who prefers being to seeming. That is to say, the shields are conceived as outgrowths and manifestations of the hollowness of the aggressors. They need shields, and colorful and articulate shields at that, to conceal their own lack of substance and to frighten their opponents. Such shield magic, like the boasting speeches that precede a duel, serve the purpose of psychological warfare. It is up to Eteocles, in his capacity of general, to oppose the magic and to devise countercharms. The answers of Eteocles to the messenger's descriptions, therefore, constitute a display of magic at work. But this particular magic, unlike that exercised by the shields, is a magic of words, a protective wall of remedial oratory raised up in the face of monstrous shapes and blasphemous images. . . .

The shield of Tydeus carries a flaming sky with stars and a bright full moon. Eteocles' answer (403):

> If he should die, and night descend on his eyes,
> this arrogant device would rightly prove
> its nature and its name for him who bears it.

. . . Capaneus displays a naked man with a lighted torch in his hands and the legend: "I shall burn the city." Eteocles contrasts this torch with its divine counterpart (444):

> I believe he will be struck, inescapably,
> by the burning thunderbolt.

. . . Eteoclus' shield shows a fully armed man ascending the rungs of a ladder toward an enemy battlement, with the legend: Not even Ares will cast me from the ramparts. Eteocles' answer has the ring of a Socratic whimsy (478): the device will enable the defender Megareus to capture two men and a citadel. Hippomedon, the fourth attacker, has on his shield a picture of Typhon spewing black smoke from a fiery mouth. On this occasion Eteocles' rebuttal is ready-made: father Zeus, flaming weapon in hand, will fight on the side of Hyperbius and win his ancient victory all over again. The refutation is so obvious that for once, and perhaps also for the sake of variety, rhetoric descends to the level of iconography, and Zeus is shown enthroned on the defendant's shield (512). But the next adversary, Parthenopaeus, is once more neutralized with the proper refinement and wit. His device, even more baroque than those of the others, is the voracious Sphinx holding in her talons a single Theban man (544). . . . The notion is that the Theban soldiers, faced with the prospect of injuring one of their own, would be reluctant to fight. Eteocles deftly exposes the ambivalence of the implied argument (560): it is the Sphinx herself, the arch enemy of Thebes, who will have cause to complain, for she will be much buffeted when she gets close to the citadel.

And so the battle is dramatized as a series of magic pretensions on one side and counter-arguments on the other. Both the magic and the dialectic are used toward an artistic objective, to let us see the power and the limits of the personalities posted for battle, to create and in turn unmake the characters participating in the attack. . . . H. D. F. Kitto reminds us that the characters in a Greek tragedy are constructive; that is to say, the Greek dramatic writers, instead of aiming at the flexible naturalism usually found on the modern stage, conceived of their characters as aggregates of significant features and behavior patterns required by the action of the play. The selection sequence grants us a glimpse into a workshop in which such characters are manufactured. . . .

Amphiaraus carries no shield design, hence no rebuttal is needed, only sorrow which comes from the reflection that good men perish indiscriminately with the bad (597). . . . Here, just before the curse begins to move him, in the very teeth of war, Eteocles injects a last and most emphatic note of human sympathy. . . . As suggested earlier, he senses in the fate of Amphiaraus a parallel to his own. The elegiac mood . . . is not the kind of thing we should have expected from the confident leader of the earlier part of the play. . . . In fact the whole speech of Eteocles, with its somber contemplation on the fate of man and with its formal division into general examples and specific application, has a decidedly choral quality. Eteocles has undergone a change. By itself the present scene is not sufficient to reveal the precise nature of the change. This much is clear, however, that the public function of the general has become overshadowed by the private ponderings of the man, and that his former sanguine assurance has given way to a new humor, to worry and despair. From a leader manipulating war he is turning into a man experiencing the war in himself. . . .

But there is one more shield-carrying enemy: Polyneices. His device is not symbolic in the same way as those of his associates. Rather it conforms more closely to the reality with which we are already familiar. The image shows a woman decently leading a man in full armor (644); the legend says that she is Justice conducting her champion back to regain his native city. . . . By putting himself into the picture Polyneices shows it for what it is, a pictorial design which directly communicates the spoken announcement which it is meant to convey. . . . In the eyes of Eteocles this type of blazon must be the most dangerous of all. He has no countermagic, no deflecting whimsy, no refutation. All he can do is deny the claim. Simple negation is the only instrument left to him when an ethical claim takes the place of brute force. As it will turn out, negation is not enough.

In the case of Amphiaraus no magic was necessary because the prophet already knew his destruction; he had no need to have it invoked against him. In the case of Polyneices magic is equally out of place. . . . For now, at the end of the sequence, the contest is between two moral agents locked in meaningful combat. The stress is no longer on the device but on the men themselves and on their intentions. The men are seen as products of a development, as characters with a past; each has his upbringing and his achievements, almost in the Sophoclean manner. We note the biographical dimension of Eteocles' answer (662):

> If Justice, the maiden child of Zeus, had stood
> by him, in his deeds and thoughts, this might well be.
> But no, not when he escaped from his mother's darkness
> nor in his childhood nor in later youth
> nor even when his chin collected down
> did Justice glance on him or judge him just.

We cannot miss the undertone of regret and disappointment at a life of promise steered in the wrong path. . . . With the other aggressors, from Tydeus to Parthenopaeus, he has nothing in common. With Amphiaraus he is connected only by the tenuous link of a moral understanding. With Polyneices he shares a life, and a curse.

V

> Alas, the god-crazed towering hatred of heaven;
> alas, my clan, the tear-drenched clan of Oedipus;
> alas, my father's curses now fulfilled!

This is Eteocles' reformulation of the curse, of the divine hatred under which his family has labored for generations (653). A curse is something constant, a stain which cannot be expunged except under the most unusual circumstances. And yet, so that it may retain its full force in the hearts of men, it has to be re-evoked periodically from generation to generation. This, at any rate, is what we find in Aeschylean and Sophoclean tragedy. A curse once pronounced goes into effect unto the third and fourth generation; the men affected by it turn into spontaneous victims, reasserting at crucial junctures their commitment to the curse. . . . With Eteocles' outburst we are thrust back into the living domain of the curse. No longer does the city occupy his thoughts; the war machine has vanished from the scene. Eteocles has ceased to be a general, sovereign and efficient, and turned into a hero, involved, committed, obsessed. To be a hero, whether on the Homeric battlefield or in Attic tragedy, means to be unreasoning, self-centered, surrendering oneself headlong to the needs and demands of an engrossing mission. . . . For such a man a curse presents a challenge and a scope.

The chorus recognize the shift (677):

> Do not, child of Oedipus, break our hearts
> by raving like an evil-spoken zealot.

Here we have an extraordinary development. The mention of Oedipus shows that the chorus perceive the workings of the curse. Moreover, in their judgment the brothers are now as one, for there can be little doubt that Polyneices is precisely such an "ill-spoken zealot." . . . Finally, as Eteocles rejects his public status and concentrates on his own person, on his needs and his fate, the chorus give up their own self-centeredness and begin to take thought of the hero. By an unparalleled crossing of lines the chorus assume the earlier role of Eteocles, the role of the unselfish warner. Formally also they authenticate their new position, for these lines are spoken rather than sung. Each of the preceding six tableaux of the selection sequence is terminated by a choral lyric; now, at the end of the final tableau, . . . the leader of the chorus takes over with a small speech of his own.

> Let not madness, filling the heart,
> spear-crazed, carry you away!

So sing the chorus, resuming their traditional lyric medium (686). And Eteocles answers (689):

> Since it is the god who activates the event,
> let it sail before the wind, straight to Cocytus,
> the whole Apollo-hated clan of Laius.

Such subservience to the gods . . . had once been the preserve of the chorus. Now Eteocles has adopted the perspective for his own. There is more yet. A few moments before he rushes into the battle he states (710):

> Too true the visions of nightmarish dreams . . .

We had hardly dared to suspect that Eteocles, like the chorus, might have his own hallucinations. His Platonizing homage to the intellect, his strictures on the women's turmoil, have proved a sham. Given the proper setting, in this case the catalyzing effect of war, man, whatever his position, will betray himself as the simple, raw, vulnerable organism that he is. . . . And vulnerability is the first condition of heroism. An administrator cannot be heroic, only an undisguised and unsheltered human being can, a man reduced to his essential condition by the curse.

The liveliness of the action has perhaps caused us to forget that there is a curse. The picture of a commander in chief issuing orders is not liable to remind us of the Furies hovering over the clan. And yet Aeschylus, in his own careful manner, does not mean us to forget. In Eteocles' second speech, near the beginning of the play, when the king calls on his divinities to protect the land and the city, . . . he prays to Zeus, Earth, the city's gods, and the (70)

> Omnipotent Curse, the Fury of my father.

This first appeal to the curse is contemplative, almost gentle, quietly edged in. From then on each mention of Oedipus, each mention of the family of which Eteocles is a member, should prepare the audience with cumulative explicitness for the final explosion. Nothing else is to be expected in this third play of the Theban trilogy. A king is tied to his community; it glories and suffers with him. Laius had failed to do his duty and thereby brought ruin on city and house. The city remains in danger; she cannot be saved except by deflecting the curse so that it will come to rest entirely on the house. Only by meeting the curse head on, by identifying his fate with it, . . . can Eteocles hope to eliminate it. This is not to say that Eteocles recognizes the need for saving the city as he prepares to meet his brother. . . . But by allowing the curse to operate at full strength, by challenging its potency into the limited area of the fratricide, he makes possible the survival of the city. The achievement remains his, no matter that his original perspective, his concern for the community, has been cut off.

Sophocles, a generation or so later, was to show in his *Oedipus Tyrannus* that the evasion of a curse makes for an intensification of the doom. Conversely he demonstrated, yet another generation later, in his *Oedipus Coloneus,* that a man could, by submitting to the curse and uniting it to himself and his career, bring about an eventual release. Just so Eteocles, by rekindling and embracing the curse, brings about the great cleansing and liberation with which the trilogy ends. Even with the fragmentary evidence available to us it is quite apparent that the proper ending of a trilogy is one in which conflicts are resolved and passion stories terminated. It does not matter whether the resolution is profound or superficial, whether it is achieved by reconciliation or adjudication or, as in our case, sacrifice. Sometimes, as in the *Oresteia,* the ending is happy; sometimes it hinges on a death. The important thing is that by the end of the third play the tensions and conflicts which are set up and manipulated in the trilogy have ceased to operate. . . . This resolution is usually climactic; it coincides with an act of heroism or a similarly impressive event underscoring the power or the littleness of man. In the present play the curse has produced a war, and both curse and war are terminated when Eteocles allows the Fury to seize him up and deliver him to certain death.

The curse is the theme of the choral song which follows after the exit of Eteocles. The ode begins and ends with the picture of hardened steel in the hands of the brothers (727ff. and 788ff.). . . . The iron is the special tool and substance of the curse, now fully materialized after more than a lifetime of hints and threats. More particularly the iron succeeds to the shield. Before personal involvement and private impulse undermined the relentless workings of the machine, the shield had served as the chief image of the war and of the attitudes taken toward the war. As such, characteristically, the shield was visualized as an autonomous entity, not suspended from the shoulder or held on the lower arm but, as it were, dwarfing the bearer and obeying an action or motion of its own. By way of contrast the steel rests in the brothers' hands. We can watch the physical effort, the specific turn of the body which gives to the weapon its aim and success. Thus once more the imagery helps us to follow the shift from the machine to the soul. . . .

The King is killed, but the city is saved. The two outcomes are reported and accepted side by side, in the order of their importance to the reporter and his audience. Both the messenger who enters to announce the events and the chorus who respond to the news first emphasize the salvation of the city (792ff. and 822ff.). . . . Only after this first spontaneous cry of happiness over the deliverance of the city do messenger and chorus turn to consider the death of the brothers, and to allow grief a place beside their joy. This grief, an unintricate, noble, calming grief is not for Eteocles alone but jointly for the brothers. With their death the curse has fulfilled itself and the community is restored to health. Hence the death emerges as a beneficent thing, and the question of justice or injustice pales before the simple act of self-sacrifice in which brothers share to an equal degree, no

matter what the intentions that lay behind it. The curse had set the
brothers at each other's throats; the curse had drawn forth Eteocles
from his isolation and made him come to grips with the war on terms
of intimacy and wrath. Now the curse has bound the brothers together
in a new union and wiped out the scores of guilt and resentment.

In their great hymn to the curse the women predict (734):

> When they die killing their own,
> their own victims,
> and the earth's dust drinks
> black-clotted murder-blood . . .

Earth, the giver of life and freedom and culture, is to be the arena of
the final torture, the recipient of the sacrifice. But earth is to be something more than that. By an old magical Greek tradition the burial
of a sinner, of a polluted man makes for a hallowed spot. . . . Just so
the fratricide, in itself a monstrous act, is now absorbed by the earth
and metamorphosed into an asset (947ff.). . . . In this manner the
earth, "the demon having ceased" (960), contributes her own time-
honored magic to help along with the "happy ending," the restoration
of balance and the cleansing which we expect at the end of the play
and the trilogy.

The exorcizing of the curse is above all the result of Eteocles' conversion. This is a fact; but the fact needs to be confirmed, ritually
and aesthetically. Hence the dirge. The curse is rescinded once and
for all by the lament of the chorus which follows upon the first shout
of triumph for the delivery of the city, and which stretches over more
than 150 lines to the end of the play. Its inordinate length and its
lack of poetic interest have caused much dismay. It will help to remember, however, that the dirge was sung and danced, that the ritual
exigencies of a funeral song rule out poetic venturesomeness, that the
lament is designed to conclude the whole trilogy rather than merely
one play, and, finally, that it serves a special function: it is a kind of
binding song, analogous to the sorcerers' chant with which the Furies
in the *Eumenides* try to overcome the resistance of Orestes. The bury-
ing of the brothers, vicariously enacted in the dirge, also becomes a
burial of the curse, and thereby a storing up of pregnant treasure. To
ensure all this the dirge must allow liberally for the repetitive for-
mulae native to prayer. . . . Without an appreciation of the religious
cast of the lament we cannot hope to understand the emphatic
terminalism of the last scene.

Still, we cannot be entirely persuaded that the curse has been neutralized. In the course of the play we have seen the terror and grue-
someness and unintelligibility of war subjected to a process of refinement and subversion until only heroism and tragedy and finally

sacred blessings remain. Aeschylus asks us to pay tribute to war and to carry away the illusion . . . that war is manageable, that even at its worst it allows a man to exercise his most personal aspirations, to struggle for heroism and glory. But the terror, the brutal shock of the barbaric shield, the desolation of the sacked city are not completely muted. In spite of the resolution and of the allaying of the family curse, the antiphonal arrangement of the theme of war continues to echo in our ears and to release its ration of fear and disgust. The satyr play which followed—it is no longer extant but we know that it dealt with the Sphinx—would of course erase this echo, or cushion it with a soothing dose of harmless laughter. But the palliative is short-lived. When the whole tetralogy has been played through the sanguine finale is soon forgotten, and the tragic mood of the earlier plays is recalled in full. That this mood is not all terror and futility, that the dramatization of war which the play gives us leaves room for glory and dignity as well as horror: this is the special achievement of Aeschylus, an achievement equalled only perhaps by Homer's *Iliad*.

It is tempting to suggest that in mood, style, and objective the *Seven Against Thebes* is cast in the epic mould. Homer made it the business of the epic to formulate the manifold nature of war, to point up its beauty and its ugliness, its significance and its pettiness, its grandeur and its bestiality. But in the *Iliad* the complexity of the experience emerges from the successive highlighting of various isolated perspectives. Now we see the war through the eyes of Priam, now through the eyes of Achilles, now of Hector. Each one of the key figures catches the meaning and the spirit of the war from a specific angle which, despite minor variations depending on the situation in which the witness finds himself, is on the whole constant. . . . Everyone in the *Iliad* takes the war for granted and accepts the part in it which destiny has allotted him.

In the *Seven* the relation between men and war is not similarly fixed. For one, war is not seen as a necessary or normal thing, to be dealt with as best one can. It is an enormity, an aberration from the settled ideals of peace and culture and domesticity. More important, however, the view of war is not, as in the epic, a totality of singular views each of which admits of some sort of definition by itself. . . . Our play develops a portrait of war which is not a composite of perspectives at all, but an organic experience, growing under our very eyes. From the moment when Eteocles begins his address to the citizenry, with his cool appraisal of the military contingencies, to the point when the chorus lyrically re-enact the fratricidal duel, the picture of war undergoes a constant shifting. Its outlines never grow sufficiently firm to allow the picture to harden into a set of perspectives. E. Staiger has said about the lyric that in contrast to the drama and the epic it does not deal with "objects" and therefore does not operate with perspective. The poet and his world are not sufficiently distinct to require the help of a perspective. Aeschylus' tragedy verges upon the lyric mood; the picture of war which it distills into us, to use a term of Staiger's, is a feeling rather than an image, an experience rather than the fruit of an illumination.

Neither Eteocles nor the chorus can be said to offer us a single identifiable formulation of what war means to them. Above all, the gradual incubus-like growth of war in the soul of Eteocles, the transformation of the planner into the enthusiast, permits us to focus on war in its full extent through the lens of a single life and a single commitment. This is an act of compression which cannot but enhance the power of the communication. In the epic, the understanding of war is fragmented; the audience is asked to bring the fragments together and weld them into a response of their own. In the *Seven* the representation of war is whole, evolving, natural. Driven by the vigor of Aeschylus' verse the audience must surrender itself to the comprehensive truth generated on the stage. To this extent, then, the play goes far beyond the epic, in spite of the epic touches of its language, and in spite of its echoes of the Homeric world of heroes. Unlike the *Iliad* it does not describe a succession of battles, it creates a war. It plants its disharmonies into our very hearts, with an urgency and a pathos which only tragedy can accomplish, and which is the special hallmark of the art of Aeschylus.

The *Suppliants*

by *John H. Finley, Jr.*

The *Suppliants* opens a trilogy of which the last two plays, the *Egyptians* and the *Danaides,* are known only conjecturally and in outline. Because the chorus consisting of the fifty daughters of Danaus has by far the chief part and its lyric and corporate tone contrasts sharply to the developed characterization of the *Agamemnon,* the play has been thought the first extant tragedy and from Aeschylus' early period. But this criterion which makes characterization the mark of his growth suggests nineteenth-century rather than Greek feeling. It is incompatible with the abstractness of the *Prometheus,* which has been argued to be the latest of the plays, and even with the *Eumenides,* which merges the individualism of the *Agamemnon* in the corporate light of the Areopagus and an ideal Athens. It is by no means clear that in his middle or late years Aeschylus could not have given chief weight in the older manner to the chorus, as he comes near doing in the *Eumenides.* A recently published papyrus[1] fragment of an hypothesis to the trilogy, stating that Aeschylus won with it over Sophocles, is likely to force revision of the older view.

The hatred for their cousins, the sons of Aegyptus, which drove the suppliant Danaids from Egypt to Argos and gives the setting for the first play, did not persist in one of them, Hypermnestra. The sons of Aegyptus, who are off shore at the end of the first play, landed in the second. Apparently after a battle in which the king of Argos was killed, Danaus expounded his famous scheme whereby his daughters shall marry their cousins and murder them on their wedding night. All do so except Hypermnestra, who spares her bridegroom Lynceus through love and is tried before a court in the third play, or possibly in the Argive assembly. The trilogy ended with her acquittal after a defense by the goddess Aphrodite herself,[2] part of whose speech is

[1] E. Lobel, E. P. Wegener, C. H. Roberts, *The Oxyrinchus Papyri* (London, 1952) XVI 2256, fg. 4.

[2] [Cf. A. F. Garvie, *Aeschylus'* Supplices: *Play and Trilogy* (Cambridge, 1969), 233—J. H. F., Jr.]

preserved. "Pure heaven yearns to wed the earth and love solicits earth
to meet his wooing. The rain descending from the bridegroom sky
impregnates earth, and she bears for mankind pasturing flocks and
the life-giving grain. Green-fronded springtime from the showery
union is wrought, and I of all this am part cause" (fg. 44). Hypermnestra's love for Lynceus thus signifies the love which frees earth
from her sterile isolation, uniting her with the sky and giving her a
fruitfulness which attests the gods. The point to be noted here is that
this conclusion of the trilogy in a new and divinely sanctioned order
is close in spirit to the conclusion of the *Oresteia* and, so far as we
can imagine, of the Promethean trilogy. In the *Prometheus Bound*
(869) the Titan predicts the happy results of Io's sufferings which will
come after generations when her descendants return to Argos and
from their line will spring the demigods Perseus and Heracles. The
present trilogy shows a step in a similar progress. The king Pelasgus
having died in battle, Danaus, and from him Lynceus and Hypermnestra, will rule in Argos, and the new line will contain through Io
the blood of Zeus. Hypermnestra's love for Lynceus initiates a state
radically distinct from the mood of fear and flight in the first play.
This better state stands clear of two equally unhappy possibilities: of
a rooted localism which contains nothing of the divine scope, and of
a wandering and search which contains nothing of localism. Hypermnestra dissolved both defective choices by a commitment through
love which, in Aphrodite's speech, is itself the bond of the free gods
with earth. If the *Suppliants* is part of an early trilogy, one could only
conclude that Aeschylus' thought emerged nearly full-grown. But the
questions of date are secondary, and what is notable in this trilogy is
that, despite a lyric tone in the *Suppliants* quite distinct from the
dramatic clarity of the *Agamemnon,* the movement of Aeschylus' mind
toward resolution of conflict in harmony is the same.

The opening lines announce the conflicting themes of placelessness
and place which are resolved only at the end of the trilogy. "May Zeus
who protects arrivals look mercifully on our ship-borne troupe, that
put to sea from the smooth sands of the mouths of the Nile. We
flee forsaking the sacred country bordered of Syria.—What happier
land than this could we reach, bearing our wool-decked suppliant
branches? O city, o soil, o water clear, o gods of heaven and vengeful
gods who inhabit tombs underneath earth, and third, o saving Zeus,
who watchest righteous men's houses, look with the land's sweet influence on our fugitive band" (vv. 1–5, 19–29). The wide sea and remote places of Egypt and Syria are balanced by the security of Argos,
the former evoking space and movement, the latter fixity and rest.
The girls' motives in their flight remain obscure after much discussion. They say that they left Egypt for no crime, but in what they

call "kindred man-flight" (v. 8) namely, from their cousins, the sons
of Aegyptus, whose intentions they call impious. A later dialogue
with the king, Pelasgus, somewhat illuminates their minds. "Why do
you say you seek these gathered gods, proffering newly-plucked your
white-wreathed garlands?" "To flee subjection to Aegyptus' sons."
"From hate or do you mean it is unholy?" "Who could enjoy connections which possess them?" "But this is how the strength of
families grows." "Yes, and divorce is easy when they founder" (vv.
333–339). The girls evade the question whether such a marriage with
first cousins is illegal, as it was not in Attic law. A textual difficulty
slightly obscures their reply, and they ask either who could enjoy or
who would buy connections which own them (v. 337). In either case
they foresee servitude to their husbands' financial authority, and when
Pelasgus answers that this is the way by which a family's property
is kept intact (i.e., by kinsmen marrying heiresses), they reiterate that
a woman is then helpless when her husband wants to divorce her. It
has been argued from this passage that Aeschylus understood the freer
position of women in a tribal society which was destroyed by male
control of property in the mercantile age.[3] He obviously felt a cleft
of interest between the sexes, and it is reasonable that legend and
popular memory should have conveyed to him a sense of happier
times before the competitive present. Throughout the plays male ambition is dangerous even when it is heroic, and the Egyptians' menace
for the Danaids resembles that of the conquering Agamemnon for
the peaceful Iphigeneia or of the warlike Eteocles for the pious women
of Thebes. Aeschylus wants a community in which female peace and
abundance shall not fall prey to male will and intellect, and the
luxuriant blessings which the Danaids presently invoke on Argos are
similar to those which the Eumenides bring Athens at the end of the
Oresteia. But Aeschylus' interest is hardly antiquarian. If the Danaids
evoke a bygone age in rejecting marriage customs currently sanctioned,
they do so because they express the deeper question of freedom and
commitment. As descendants of Io, who had herself been uprooted by
Zeus and carried to a higher if harder destiny, they will not willingly
relapse into a fate even more bounded than hers before her change.
Their dislike for their cousins is a dislike for dull and servile limits.
In their trailing clothes and sunburnt skin they are several times
likened to Oriental women (vv. 71, 234, 279), but they are Greeks at
heart and their Greekness is their passion for scope. Aeschylus manages
to forget, at least in this first play, that the sons of Aegyptus are
likewise descended from Zeus by Io. Their name made them foreign,
and they have become Egyptians as the Danaids have not. Hence the

---

[3] G. Thomson, *Aeschylus and Athens* (London, 1941) 304.

conflict between the girls and their suitors is a conflict between Greek liberty and Oriental subjection, and liberty carries implications of the wider mind which is Zeus. The paradox of the play is that the character of the girls as women conflicts with their character as fugitives and descendants of Zeus. As women they ultimately imply commitment and love, the traits which are vindicated in Hypermnestra by Aphrodite and which resolve the trilogy. Yet as fugitives they seek at the beginning an entire uncommitment, and their hatred of the Egyptians drives them to a mood of flight which shares the spirit of Io's wanderings but lacks that of her final release.

The question, like all the main questions in Aeschylus, involves Zeus's will for mankind, and the Danaids presently break into a superb and deeply agitated hymn to Zeus. They have returned to Io's haunts; one who heard their cry would think it the sad nightingale's who killed her son (their later murder of their husbands speaks in this lament, which is that of placelessness and lost ties); yet the gods hate violence; "even for the oppressed of war there is an altar, refuge for war's fugitives, the awe of heaven" (vv. 40–85, here speaks the justice of their claim to resist subjection). Their hope both for the safety that they seek and for the deeper accord which they do not yet understand is Zeus's will. "It blazes on all sides, even from night, with issue dim for men. Tangled stretch the pathways of his mind and shadowy, invisible to eyes. He hurls men ruined from their high-towered hopes, yet wears no violence. Effortless is all that is the gods'. Seated, he yet from where he is fulfills his will, from his untouched repose" (vv. 88–103). Their cry resembles the famous prayer to Zeus in the *Agamemnon* (160–183) both in language and in position just after the king's half-right, half-wrong decision for the army and against Iphigeneia has been presented. So here the Danaids' isolation which was in their likeness to the nightingale conflicts with their just search for freedom, and only the incalculable mind of Zeus will find the solution. They are consciously praying that their own wishes be enacted, and they go on to describe the violence of the Egyptians and to invoke Athene as the protectress of girlhood. But time to Aeschylus begets the unforeseen, and their conscious hopes are not the end. Even they subconsciously know this, and the incalculability which they ascribe to Zeus contains, like the comparable lines of the *Agamemnon,* a dim awareness of the further state which Hypermnestra, like Orestes, will reach through pain. This evolution was revealed in Io, to whom they revert at the end of the ode. Her suffering was inseparable from her destiny as bride of Zeus, but though they know her final rest, they cannot conceive a like mood for themselves, understanding as yet only flight and rejection.

Danaus now announces the approach of the Argives, and all the warlike masculinity which Aristophanes later felt in Aeschylus is in this description of dust, shrieking wheels, spears, and marching men. In this passage and in the speeches of the king, Pelasgus, is a quality of unspoiled native force descriptive of a people who had not yet felt the complexity of the world. The Danaids gather by the images of the gods which adorn the precinct where they have taken refuge, and Pelasgus, after marveling at the girls' barbaric clothes, explains himself, his city, and the wide extent of his early kingdom. They reply by expounding their claim through Io on Argos, recalling how she was wooed by Zeus, hated by Hera, changed into a heifer, driven over much of the earth by a gadfly, and finally in Egypt was delivered of a son, Epaphus. By Libya he in turn had a son Belus, who had two sons, Danaus and Aegyptus, the fathers respectively of the girls and their pursuers. At this point occurs the dialogue quoted earlier in which the king tries to discover the girls' motives for flight. But though they prove to lack clear grounds in law, they have the authority of the shrine in which they stand, and their interchange with the king becomes a conflict between worldly and religious claims. Pelasgus is entirely Greek in feeling both claims acutely. Though the girls insist that as king he has authority to decide in their favor, he protests that he cannot act without appeal to the people. Aeschylus is evidently describing early Greece in him, and if the picture is anachronistic, it conveys both native force and native sense of liberty. In its political aspect, the trilogy will show how these virtues emerge on a wider stage. Sensible as the king is of the girls' religious appeals, he is equally horrified at the prospect of war in Argos if he heeds them. "The judgment is not clear. Call me not judge. I have already said, without the people I cannot act, though sovereign, lest with time citizens murmur if disaster fall, 'Honoring strangers you destroyed the state'" (vv. 397–401). He stands at the lonely moment of decision which all Aeschylus' heroes face and in which Hypermnestra will follow him (vv. 407–417): "Now must the seeing and undrunken gaze of deep remedial intellect descend bottomwards like a diver, so that first the city be undamaged and events ensue benign for us, and yet that strife seize not on you as victims nor by shunning fugitives to these sacred images we plant among us the pursuing god who still in Hades remits not the dead. Think you I have no need for saving thought?"

What then do the Danaids bring Argos? The answer is rather implied than stated in this first play of the trilogy. In describing himself and his kingdom, Pelasgus made no claim of divine descent. The Greece over which he rules, though vigorous and uncorrupted, is parochial. Zeus's love for Io was the hand of divinity touching Argos, and the destiny which it imported was at once higher and harder. The

sense of space which was in the Danaids' opening lines returns in all
references to Io, and something of the placelessness of Zeus himself
surrounds her. In the question whether to repatriate her descendants,
Argos confronts an element of immensity in things which endangers
its earlier security, and the troubling destiny which had been Io's
alone now touches the city. Similarly in the *Oresteia* the Trojan expedition, while great and partly just, disrupts the life of Mycenae and
leads eventually to a new view of the state. Pelasgus is so disturbed by
these dangerous prospects that after the troubled speech just quoted
he ends by disclaiming responsibility. Wealth, he says, can be restored,
but life cannot. "I'd rather be untutored in disasters than expert"
(v. 453). The turning point in the simple action of the play comes as
the girls threaten to hang themselves in the sacred precinct if they are
rejected. Pelasgus is horrified. "The words I hear are lashes to my
heart" (v. 466). He sees the future now as deeply uncertain, but feels
no choice but to avoid the worse evil of sacrilege (vv. 472–477):
"Unless I pay you our indebtedness, no arrow can outshoot the curse
you utter. And yet if stationed at the wall I try issue of battle with
Aegyptus' sons, your cousins, is it not a bitter price that men for
women's sake corrupt the earth?" The statement of conflict between
the sexes well expresses what the Danaids have to offer Argos. It was
noted that they have a double character, as fugitives and as women.
The one side of their nature conveys the disturbing quality of Io's
wanderings. They disrupt security much as Helen disrupts the peace
of Greece and Troy, though they are not guilty as Helen is guilty.
They are figures of unrest, partly through their own timorous and
emotional natures, but partly also because Zeus has shown his hand in
history through them and they in turn are more sensitive to his will.
But in their second aspect they resemble Penelope rather than Helen
and imply rest rather than unrest. This side of the Danaids appears
only indirectly in the present play, which nevertheless looks to it as a
solution. The Danaids' quality of unrest is ended in Hypermnestra,
whose act of commitment replaces their mood of wandering. Three
states or stages of mind thus emerge: first, the confident and masculine
but limited and even youthful security of Argos before the Danaids'
arrival (a state corresponding to Io's before she was loved by Zeus);
second, the loss of this security by awareness of remote places and peo-
ples and even of the hitherto remote gods (the condition corresponding to Io's wanderings); and third, the recovery of something like the
first peaceful stage, but after events which have brought much deeper
understanding of the world and the gods and which consequently
force a new definition of place and peace. Pelasgus' reluctance to en-
danger men on behalf of women is his reluctance to surrender the
order and intelligibility of the first stage for the uncertainties of the

second. The tone of vigorous and martial confidence which was in the description of the Argive army has been made less secure in his lonely choice.

The Danaids have in effect won their point, and the action verges toward its consequences in the later plays of the trilogy. But as Pelasgus could not avoid endangering Argos' first state of sheltered peace, so the Danaids cannot linger, as they hope to do, in the second state of flight and negation. Two fine odes express their mood, the one sung after Pelasgus leaves to urge the people on the girls' behalf, the other after Danaus returns to announce a favorable decision. They sing the first ode, about Io, while some uncertainty still remains. They fervently seek Zeus's protection both as Io's descendants and as women. "Lord of lords, of blessed most blessed, power perfectest of perfections, serene Zeus, heed and may it be. Fend in loathing off the lust of men; cast in the purple sea their black-benched folly. Look on our storied breed, the women's cause, and happily renew our forebear's praise, the woman thou didst love" (vv. 524–534). They describe her wide travels and the reverence which she received in Egypt, then come to her deliverance. "By his unwounding strength and breath divine her trial subsided and she welled away her tears' sad shame. She took a burden justly named of Zeus and bore a blameless son. . . . What god then may I fitly hail for righter acts? By his mere touch our sire, progenitor, and lord, our breed's great builder brooding anciently, Zeus of fair winds, in all remedial. Enthroned beneath no other's rule, he the greater sways the less. None seated higher heeds he from below. His acts are as a word, to bring to pass his pondering mind's intent" (vv. 576–581, 590–599). All Aeschylus' distances are in this ode: geographical in the reaches of Io's travel, speculative in the reverence for Zeus's creative will, temporal since he reveals himself darkly and at his own pace. From the point of view of the action, the girls' claim through Io on Zeus is their claim on Argos as suppliants, but as in the earlier ode, their sense of Zeus's vastness gives their thoughts a wider dimension. They convey a kind of listening for Zeus's will, and their character as women fits this role, in that their impressionability intuitively rejects both the harsh authority of the Egyptians and the secure prudence of Pelasgus. The conflict between male and female widens into that between place and placelessness, and the claim which the girls make on Argos is a demand that the state, however fixed and rooted, somehow accommodate itself to the freedom and change which are Zeus.

In announcing on his return that the assembly has acted favorably, Danaus quotes the king as foretelling immense disasters if the rights of suppliants are neglected (vv. 616–620). These evils resemble the wasting sickness with which Apollo in the *Choephoroe* (269–296) threatens Orestes if he shall fail to avenge his father. Both threats express the impossibility of refusing change and of lingering in a sheltered state when the painful time has come to leave it. The vote of the assembly confirms the earlier impression of the Argives' native strength and sense of freedom, and these virtues are about to emerge into history. At this point the Danaids sing the second of the odes just mentioned, invoking blessings on Argos. This is the ode that closely resembles the brilliant closing passages of the *Oresteia* in which the Eumenides in the presence of Athene pour out blessings on Athens. There these benefits are the culmination of Orestes' painful act, at last healed and translated into a new order. Here the end has not yet come, but the peaceful fruitfulness of land and people which the Danaids invoke is precisely that which Aphrodite sees in Hypermnestra's love for Lynceus. The ode is a vision of the solution, though the Danaids themselves have not reached it. And as the Eumenides are women who until their final conversion had fiercely upheld Clytemnestra's cause against Orestes, so the Danaids' blessings convey a final harmony between the sexes, and Pelasgus' acceptance of the Danaids implies Hypermnestra's union. "They did not set their vote with males, dishonoring women's pleas, but spied pursuant Zeus, watcherlike, incontestable. What house is glad with him against its roof? He presses heavy. . . . Therefore prodigal blessings shall take wing from our bough-shaded lips. Never may plague drain from this state her men, nor civil war corrupt her fields with tumbled sons. Unharvested be flowering youth, nor may harsh Ares, Aphrodite's bridegroom, reap its bloom down" (vv. 643–651, 656–666). They pray for smoking altars, fruitful fields, herds, music and singing, justice at home and abroad, and piety.

Yet the Danaids have not themselves inwardly reached the state of peace corresponding to these prayers, and the end of the play casts them back into their original agitation. When Danaus sights the Egyptian ships off shore and goes for help, leaving his daughters alone, their fears show themselves again in images of space and flight (vv. 792–799): "How could I find some skyey seat where drift the dank clouds into snow, or some precipitous hanging cliff outranging goats, beyond sight, lonely-thoughted, where vultures haunt, that it could witness to my sinking leap before I violently meet heart-cutting marriage?" They repeat their cry to Zeus. "The males of Aegyptus' lewd outrageous breed hunt me with shouting follies as I run, to clutch me with their strength. But thine the scales are balanced over all. What for mankind is wrought apart from thee?" (vv. 817–824). There is obvious provocation for these fears, which nevertheless contain something excessive, and it is this excess which will end in the murder of their husbands. The sexual conflict has bred an emotional

disturbance hostile to the harmony of Zeus, to whom they at the same
time pray. Hence the political problem confronting Argos is matched
by an inward problem confronting the Danaids, and neither will be
solved without the other. In this interpenetration of public by private
states is the deep source of Aeschylus' power. Egyptian heralds, though
not the pursuers themselves, finally enter talking a wild half-Greek,
and they are dragging the girls off when Pelasgus and Danaus return.
When the king states the city's will to protect them and the heralds
threaten war, the situation of the next play is presented. Danaus
directs the girls to Argos with minute advice about their behavior, a
passage which amusingly shows the contrast between idea and detail
in the late-archaic style. In the choral odes Aeschylus had presented
the Danaids as almost pure idea, figures sensitive to Zeus, deeply inward, associated with space and change, but here they are simply
eligible girls. In the same way, the Oceanids are partly seen in the
Prometheus as sympathetic spirits of earth and sea but partly also as
the hero's young sisters-in-law. As the Danaids leave with prayers to
the virgin Artemis, their servants have the last word. "But this glad
song shuns not the Cyprian. With Hera she holds power most near to
Zeus, devious goddess honored for sacred acts. Jointly on their mother
wait Desire and winning Persuasion undenied and Harmony partakes
from Aphrodite the whisper and the touch of love" (vv. 1034–1042).
Though the suppliants protest their continuing hatred of the Egyptians, the suggestion has been made that leads beyond the murder of
their husbands to Hypermnestra's act of love. Alone she will outweigh
the others and prove Io's true heir by bringing flight to rest and
changing loss to possession. As for the city, the return of Zeus's line
will inaugurate its destined greatness. Through the touch of Zeus
place and fixity will lose their boundedness by harboring the unbound
traits of justice and mercy. As for the quarrel between the sexes, it
will have been solved in favor of the male, yet with a harmony which
alone can produce the blessings invoked in the Danaids' prophetic
song.

To make a brief comparison with Pindar, the flaring night-fire of
Zeus's will which the Danaids proclaim in the first ode is both like
and unlike the night-fire of heroism in *Olympian* 1. Both men see in
the divine the same blazing vitality, but whereas for Pindar it shines
from the night of common life in the flash of joy and glory, to Aeschylus it is the blaze of justice guiding to the future. Insofar as it acts
for him in the present, scattering, for example, the darkness of the
Egyptians, it has the violence of lightning, and even the Danaids who
invoke it cannot grasp its power, which will singe them in their
resort to murder. This is only to say that Aeschylus' blazing vision of
justice wakens proportionately black shadows, blacker even than those

in Plato's cave, because the light of justice shines directly against the
passions of the world. Pindar, because he lacks this ardor for justice,
is able to see finality already about him. He is the visionary of the
present, Aeschylus of the future. A similar difference colors their
feeling for women. Cyrene and Evadne in *Pythian* 9 and *Olympian* 6
resemble Io to the extent that their fixity in earth and place is likewise broken by the intruding god. Yet in Cyrene there was a willingness for his coming, and for both women the intrusion soon brings a
bright completion beyond their hopes. Only Thetis in the sorrowing
Isthmian 8, written just after the Persian invasion, conveys the tragedy
which haunts the union of mortal with immortal, in that her glorious
son Achilles must die. But the emphasis is different there; Thetis is
the immortal who by her union with the mortal Peleus sacrifices something of her bright permanence. From the opposite point of view,
Peleus reaches his highest happiness in her, as do Cyrene and Evadne
in Apollo. The gods for Pindar complete rather than jostle the actual
world, which thus from the first shows a latent harmony with them.
In Aphrodite's speech Hypermnestra's marriage also finally reveals
this harmony, but only after the sufferings of Io, the Danaids, Argos,
and herself. The Danaids perpetuate the spirit of Io's unrest because
Zeus for both was of scope too vast for common limits. The destiny
which he implants corresponds to Aeschylus' vision of wide space; it
bursts rooted ties and leads to remoteness. It is true that a second and
ultimately stronger side of Aeschylus' mind accepted place, fearing
the limitless horizons on which the divine presence opens. His problem was therefore to conceive a return to mortal limits which would
yet be compatible with boundless space. This return comes near being
his definition of freedom. It is a state like Hypermnestra's which is
finally able to recognize the unbounded and divine in the bounded
and mortal. But the difficulty of reaching this state is to be felt in the
initial conflict between space and earth. Place and commitment do
not, as they do in Pindar, find ready and natural fulfillment in the
pure being of the gods, but accord between earth and sky follows a
chastening tuition.

Introduction to the *Oresteia*

by *Richmond Lattimore*

Agamemnon

Agamemnon is, first of all, a domestic tragedy. The dominant figure, Clytaemestra, is a wife estranged through the wrong her husband
committed on their daughter; love for Iphigeneia, acting through
the murder of Agamemnon, is on its way toward driving her to fight
her love for her surviving daughter and for her son. Her paramour
and partner is her husband's cousin. Behind them all is the figure
of Helen, Clytaemestra's sister, wife of Agamemnon's brother, whose
treachery caused the Trojan War, Iphigeneia's death, and all the
estrangement and broken faith that followed. The theme here is the
philos-aphilos or hate-in-love; its drive is the dynamic force of contradiction.

Behind the domestic tragedy lies the tragedy of war. For the sake of
Helen, whose beauty was unforgettable but whose worth could not be
demonstrated by reason or defended by argument, Agamemnon
drained Greece of its manhood and involved the innocent in the
miseries of a bitter campaign. The Trojans welcomed Helen and her
captor and so were guilty; but their punishment—the total destruction
of their city, their temples, and their men; the enslavement and
defiling of their women and children—was out of all proportion to
any harm they had done to Greece. Neither Troy nor Greece deserved
what the idea of Helen made Agamemnon do to them. For he destroyed his own country as well as Troy; many died in the years before
Ilium, the survivors were drowned or scattered in the great storm on
the way back; and the pomp of his entrance thinly disguises the fact
that he brought home the crew of a single ship.

Because of this, with the war tragedy goes political tragedy as well.
The means by which this is communicated is through the chorus,

"Introduction to the *Oresteia*." From *The Complete Greek Tragedies: Volume
I, Aeschylus,* edited by David Grene and Richmond Lattimore. Copyright © 1953
by The University of Chicago. Reprinted by permission of The University of
Chicago. The pages reprinted here are only a part of the section entitled "Introduction to the *Oresteia*," by Richmond Lattimore.

who, in so far as they function as characters in the play, represent the solid elders of Argos. These are king's men, since the king in the heroic period stands for lawful authority; they have seen that Agamemnon's expedition was wrong, and they tell him so (799–804), but they would still be loyal to him if he were a much worse man than he is. It is these sturdy citizens who tell how, as the death reports and the urns full of ashes came in from the front, the people at home began to mutter against the king and ask why the war was fought; and, though the chorus cannot take their part, they cannot deny that there is cause for such mutterings. But the people did find a champion, or so they thought, at least a leader, Aegisthus, the king's cousin. He took advantage of the disaffection among those who hated the king he hated, and so returned from exile; he won the throne by winning the queen, confirmed his seizure by contriving the murder of Agamemnon, and defended it with his tyrant's personal bodyguard. . . .

On the personal level, *Agamemnon* works through a complex of collisions, not so much right against wrong as right against right, each person insisting on his right with the force of passion. Agamemnon, the king, with a king's power and pride in arms, appears briefly and is relatively simple. Pride would have driven him without hesitation to undertake the recovery of Helen, and this decision sets in motion a chain of events which becomes increasingly inescapable. The sacrifice of Iphigeneia, the persistence in besieging Troy, even the intrigue with Cassandra, follow necessarily; his pride grows on its own acts, until just before death he is a swollen vanity. He himself began the series of acts which pile up to overwhelm him, but, looking back, one cannot see where a proud king could have chosen otherwise. Clytaemestra's motives are far more complex. Homer had made her act in simple surrender and consequent betrayal. But Pindar speculated on motives which would, if admitted by Homer, have spoiled the cast of his version:

> Was it Iphigeneia, who at the Euripos crossing
> was slaughtered far from home,
> that vexed her to drive in anger the hand of violence?
> Or was it couching in a strange bed
> by night that broke her will and set her awry—for young wives
> a sin most vile.
>
> (Pindar *Pythian* 11.22–25, trans. Lattimore)

Two motives to choose from: Iphigeneia or Aegisthus. But Pindar has already mentioned Cassandra and so implied a third alternative, mother-resentment, guilty love, or jealousy. After Pindar, we could choose A or B or C. Aeschylus ignores the "or" and takes them all. Clytaemestra has loved Agamemnon, Iphigeneia has made her hate him, she loves Aegisthus. But her love for Agamemnon was real, and enough of that love remains to waken perfectly real jealousy at the sight of Agamemnon's lovely captive. This also moves her enormous pride, which amounts to unprecedented ambition for dynastic power. The women of the heroic age are represented as people of character, with will and temper of their own; but if their men insist, they must give way. Force them and they love. Cassandra, Clytaemestra's foil and rival, has seen her city and people wiped out by Agamemnon, her father and brothers butchered by his followers, but she clings to him. So Briseis in the *Iliad* clings to Achilles, who has personally killed her husband, and so Sophocles makes his Tecmessa protest to Aias that she loves him, for she has no one else, since he has destroyed her home. Not so Clytaemestra, who, like Helen her sister, chooses her own loves. Again, the code obviously allowed the warlord, married or unmarried, to have the comforts of a captive mistress on campaign. But if Clytaemestra did not like a code, she would smash it. With her "male strength of heart in its high confidence," she steps boldly from the sphere of women's action into that of men;[1] like a king, she handles the city in her lord's absence, and to her the hostile and suspicious chorus turns with unwilling admiration. When the chorus doubts her intelligences, again when after the murder they openly challenge her, she faces them down and silences them; and it is only on the appearance of Aegisthus, whom they despise as they cannot despise Clytaemestra, that they break out rebelliously again. Even in deceit, as in shameless defiance, she is stately (855–88, 1667). She is the born aristocrat, heiress by birth as by marriage to the power and wealth of kings, and so contemptuous of the *nouveau riche* (1042–46). Everything she does and says is in the grand manner. The chain of beacon fires linking Argos and Troy, defeating distance and time, is a characteristically grand gesture, and worthy of it are the arrogant lines in which she concludes her story of relayed signal flares (315–16):

> By such proof and such symbol I announce to you
> my lord at Troy has sent his messengers to me.

Such is the spirit of her grandiose welcome to Agamemnon, the purple carpet on which he is forced to walk to his butchery, and the words in which such lavish outlay is defended, "the sea is there," with its plain implication that "the sea is ours."

[1] When she refers to herself as "a mere woman," it is with massive sarcasm (348, 590–97, 1661).

Such characteristics give Clytaemestra stature, but in no sense justify her. It is not only that, in asserting her right, or at least determination, to act as freely as a man, she has taken to her bed the "womanish" Aegisthus. The whole house has been wrong since the quarrel of Atreus and Thyestes. Atreus was hideous in murder, but this does not justify Aegisthus in murdering Agamemnon, any more than the sins of Agamemnon justified his murder by Clytaemestra, or the sins of Paris and Helen justified the obliteration of Troy. All the executioners plead that they act for just retribution, but the chain of murder has got out of hand and is perpetuating itself, until it seems no longer to come from personal purpose but has grown into a Curse, a Thing. Every correction is a blood-bath which calls for a new correction.

> The truth stands ever beside God's throne
> eternal: he who has wrought shall pay; that is law.
> Then who shall tear the curse from their blood?
> The seed is stiffened to ruin.

Clytaemestra answers, over the corpse of Agamemnon, that she has been bloody but the house is clean. No more evil need be done. Orestes is to make the same claim over the corpse of Clytaemestra herself. Both are mistaken.

The tragedy is no simple matter of right and wrong, of pride and fall, though these enter in. It is a matter of love and hate working simultaneously to force distorted action, and the situation is given depth by cross-characterization. Clytaemestra imagines before the chorus the scene in captured Troy, opening with savage satisfaction in the thought of what is going on and closing with a prayer for peace, that her husband and his men may use their victory temperately, so that no fresh wrong may follow. As she speaks these words, she is herself plotting the fresh wrong she deprecates. There is surface contradiction, but under it lies not only the fact that Clytaemestra is intensely proud of the husband she is about to murder but also the lyric imagination, akin to the diviner's gift, by which the character's mind can transcend time and distance and penetrate to a sphere of objective truth which is beyond the character's own desire and prejudice. When she tells Agamemnon and the public of the torments she went through in his absence at Troy, she is flattering him and misleading all, but by means of truth, not fiction. This is the past, and this is real.

> It is evil and a thing of terror when a wife
> sits in the house forlorn with no man by.

Flattery, confession, reproach combine (through how much longing
for the memory-ghost, as with Menelaus for Helen, might Clytaemestra
have gone before she took Aegisthus as a lover; or even after?). Agamemnon, on the point of being entangled by flattery and dragged to
his death, soberly describes himself as proof against flatterers. In a
sense this is irony; it corresponds to his entrance full of the pride of
capture on the heels of a warning by the chorus against pride; to
the gloomy speculations of the chorus on sackers of cities that presages
the return of the herald to tell of Troy's obliteration. But that is
mainly a matter of timing; here the point is that Agamemnon's intelligence is partly engaged with the course he does not mean to take. He
is proof against illusions except at the one point where they will be
fatal to him. When Aegisthus, in the height of his dispute with the
challenging chorus (1668), says of Orestes,

> Exiles feed on empty dreams of hope. I know it. I was one,

the jibe turns into a flash of instantly forgotten sympathy. The actors,
in particular Clytaemestra and the chorus, do not collide with purely
external forces but act always against a part of their own will or
sympathy which is committed to the other side, and what they kill
is what they love.

The action of the play in itself, of the trilogy as a whole, is thus
bound inward upon itself. Its course is not logical, not even strictly
dramatic sequence. After the fashion of choral lyric, it is both united
to itself and given inward dimension through persistent ideas and a
complex of symbols.

Idea and Symbol

By "idea" I mean motive, theme of subject, or type of situation
which is dominant in the dramatic action. By "symbol" I mean a
particular thing, usually material, which may be taken to represent
the idea. And by a "complex of symbols" I mean a group of such
objects which are related to one another in their nature or use.

A central motive in the *Oresteia* is the idea of entanglement: the
taming of wild things, the subjugation of the powerful, the involvement of innocent creatures as well. It is expressed in the *curb* forged
to subdue Troy (132) or Cassandra (1066); the *bit* that gags Iphigeneia
(234); the *yoke* of circumstance that forces Agamemnon to his crime;
the *yoke* of slavery forced on Troy (529), on Cassandra (933, 1071,
1226), on the defiant citizens (1635), even the yoke of teammates (842);
the *snare* of the huntsman, in which Agamemnon captures Troy (358,

821) and Cassandra (1048) and in which he is presently captured (1115, 1375, 1611).[2] Curb, yoke, snare—different objects for related purposes—might have been no more than persistent and thematic metaphors, but they have one embodiment which is not metaphorical, and this is the robe or shawl in which Clytaemestra actually entangles Agamemnon in order to strike him down and which is to be displayed on stage as a murder exhibit by Orestes in *The Libation Bearers* (980–84, 997–1004). Clytaemestra anticipates herself when she tells of her dreams and imaginations of terror in Agamemnon's long absence (866–68):

> Had Agamemnon taken all
> the wounds the tale whereof was carried home to me,
> he had been cut full of gashes like a fishing net,

and returns to her imagery in her challenging confession of murder (1382–83):

> as fishermen cast their huge circling nets, I spread
> deadly abundance of rich robes and caught him fast.

This is the idea seen in the thing and the thing embodying the idea, both in metaphor and in action. There are numerous other symbols and other ideas. Symbols are the snake (specially the viper) and the poison of the snake; the archer; the house; the ship; gold. Ideas are (in addition to entanglement) persuasion (flattery); recurrent sickness; hate-in-love; blood and sex; light in the dark; sound (of terror) in the night; dream and memory. The bare lists are not complete, and, in particular, neither symbols nor ideas are exclusive, nor does a given symbol stand toward a given idea in a one-to-one relation. The viper, who turns against his own family, whose mating is murder, stands principally for the idea of hate-in-love and, as such, might be called the prime symbol of the *Oresteia,* but its poison is involved also in the idea of recurrent sickness, and its coils in the idea of entanglement (elsewhere signified by yoke, net, etc., as we have seen). So *The Libation Bearers,* 246–49:

> Behold
> the orphaned children of the eagle-father, now
> that he has died entangled in the binding coils
> of the deadly viper.

The spider web in which Agamemnon was trapped (1492) is one more variation of entanglement, spun by another creature who murders in

---

[2] The idea of the manhunt appears in the retributive expedition against Troy (127, 695), and in *The Eumenides* it characterizes the Furies' pursuit of Orestes.

marriage. Entanglement may come by outright force or by seduction and surprise. Clytaemestra lures Agamemnon into it by flattery, persuasion, by her sex (1116):

> Or is the trap the woman there, the murderess?

Cross-binding and coherence of idea in symbol is seen where Agamemnon recoils (he is soon to surrender) from stepping on the gorgeous robe Clytaemestra has spread at his feet (922–27)

> Such state becomes the gods, and none beside.
> I am a mortal, a man; I cannot trample down
> these tinted splendors without fear thrown in my path.
> I tell you, as a man, not god, to reverence me.
> Discordant is the murmur at such treading down
> of lovely things.

On the level of discourse, the speech is moral. The male rationalism is fighting against the irrational persuasion of the woman, the Greek defends his code ("as if I were some Asiatic"), the king deprecates the subjects' disapproval; this is colored also by lyric memory. The "treading down of lovely things" recalls Paris, who "trampled down the delicacy of things inviolable" (371) and on whom Persuasion also worked (385). Agamemnon, who punished the barbarians, is being turned barbarian in order to be punished. He is a victim of his wife's flattery and the magnificence of his own possessions. Lastly, the robe itself on which he walks prefigures the robe in which he is to be entangled and killed.

Cut anywhere into the play, and you will find such a nexus of intercrossing motives and properties. The system gives the play its inner dimension and strength. An analogous but separable principle dominates the larger structure.

Dramatic Structure and Lyric Dimension

As theater, *Agamemnon* and its companion pieces are simple. The scene of *Agamemnon* is the familiar fixed position before the doors of a house, which is, as most often in subsequent drama and in the nature of things, a palace. The same setting serves for *The Libation Bearers*; *The Eumenides* has one of those shifts of scene which are relatively rare in extant Greek tragedy, for we begin before the doors of Phoebus at Delphi and end before the doors of Athene in Athens, but this shift can easily be signified by addition or subtraction of a very few properties.

Characters are used sparingly. Aeschylus has at his disposal the three actors who were by now allotted to each poet or producer; but, far from reveling in this sober allowance, he is most reluctant to use all three at once in speaking action. Cassandra is on stage with Agamemnon and Clytaemestra, but does not speak until the other actors (not counting the chorus or chorus leader) have gone out.[3] Dialogue is, for the most part, just that, a passage between two persons, one of whom may be the chorus leader, at a time, not as in modern drama a complex in which three, four, or a dozen speaking persons participate. There are supernumeraries to be sure, handmaidens attending Clytaemestra and soldiers returning with Agamemnon, the significant bodyguard of Aegisthus; and at the close of *The Eumenides* the stage is quite full of people, and the exodus takes on the dignity of a processional. Agamemnon clearly must enter with Cassandra beside him in a horse-drawn chariot. The unrolling of the robe for Agamemnon's feet is an effective use of showy gesture. Yet, on the whole, the trilogy is physically unpretentious, relying less on staging and properties than *Prometheus* appears to do. Also, it is physically static; not much physical activity or motion is called for. The use made of materials, of what might appeal to the eye, is measured and temperate.

There is a corresponding simplicity in plot. Considering the length of *Agamemnon,* there are few events that take place, nor are the major events displayed against any variety of subplot. It therefore takes dramatic time for these events to happen. The return of Agamemnon, assured from the watchman's opening speech (25), does not take place until line 782. The only other *event* of the play is his murder, which does not take place until line 1344. Audience and actors occupy the times preceding these events in a growing strain of suspense, which gives the events redoubled impact when at last they do take place. The means by which the anomaly of many lines-little action is solved are the same as the means by which action and motive are deepened. The simplicity is on the surface. As, on its major plane, the action of the tragedy moves deliberately forward, in another dimension lyric memory and forecast take us, by association of ideas

[3] Clytaemestra, apparently on stage at 83, does not respond to the chorus at that point and remains silent through their stasimon (ode); she speaks only when, 258–63, they address her again. In *The Libation Bearers* Pylades, present almost through the entire play, speaks only three lines (900–902); these have critical force in the action. In *Prometheus,* the titan is silent all through the first scene, where he is being fastened to the rock. We know also that Aeschylus exploited the silent character in many of his lost plays. On the silent characters of Aeschylus, see the scene in the *Frogs* of Aristophanes, where the ghost of Euripides challenges that of Aeschylus in the presence of Dionysus and Hades (911–22).

rather than in obedience to order in time, deep away into the past, the future, and the elsewhere.

Memory and forecast are a part of imagination, that divining spirit which takes men beyond the limits of what their senses can perceive. He who habitually, and under patronage of a god, so divines is the *mantis* or prophet. The prophet knew "all things that were, the things to come, and the things past" (*Iliad* i. 70); that is, he knew not only past and future, but *present,* what is occurring right now beyond that fragmentary point of space where he stands. Calchas the prophet of the Achaeans is remembered in the first ode, Cassandra the prophetess of Troy appears in person. But, apart from these formal prophets, the chorus assumes divining powers ("still by God's grace there surges within me singing magic"; "why this strain unwanted, unrepaid, thus prophetic?"), and the imaginations of Clytaemestra, the herald, Agamemnon, and Aegisthus range far away. Calchas, in the memory of the chorus, goes deep into the past in order to make predictions which will be fulfilled, years away, in the subsequent action of the tragedy. Cassandra, who knows of a past she never witnessed, sees in its light the invisible network of treachery that waits for Agamemnon and her. The swan, who sings in the face of death and is helplessly dedicated to Apollo, is her symbol.

The choristers remember in their entrance chant the departure of the armament ten years ago (40–59), and it makes them see the struggle going on in Troy (60–68). They remember the portents that attended the gathering of the ships, the predictions of Calchas, and the sacrifice of Iphigeneia that was their sequel (104–257). Clytaemestra's living imagination follows the course of her beacon system, itself a device to defeat space and diminish time, as it breaks out from peak to peak on its way to her (281–316), and she sees the Achaeans in captured Troy, now, though far away (320–37). The chorus broods on the moral that Troy fallen conveys, but they think in pictures; of a man secure in wealth kicking over an altar (the audience will remember the golden Persians, their pride, sacrilege, and defeat); of Persuasion as a siren; of false fires and spurious metal gilded; of a greedy innocent child trying to catch a bird—the images, not the propositions, of delusion (367–95). This is Paris, and they fall at once to re-creating in imagination the flight of Helen (403–8). And there were *prophets* there, to be sure, who imagined the loneliness to follow for Menelaus with an empty bed and empty-eyed images of his wife, whose loveliness eluded him in dreams (408–26). But dream image is memory image, and there are others who remember too. The families of the common soldiers see brought back to them the ashes of their dead, transubstantiated by the money-changer, who is the god of war.

They murmur against the king; their muttering is inarticulate and not clearly heard in high places but may be the symptom of a storm that waits for the returning king (427–74). *Te deum laudamus* has been transformed into foreboding, not through logical succession of ground and consequent but through a lyric succession of images whose forms melt into one another. Agamemnon's herald remembers the campaigning before Troy (551–81). At first, it is the dirty and brutal details of war-business that come out of the mist, but the sense of achievement infects him with Agamemnon's fatal pride, so that at the end the wings of his imagination take him out of the past across the present and far into the future and the days when the capture of Troy will be an antique glory of Argos. He is shaken out of this mood, however, by the questioning of the chorus leader, who wants to know what happened to the rest of the army and to Menelaus. He tells of the storm (650–70) in terms that make living things out of fire, wind, water, and rocks, and shows the wide seascape on which at dawn lay the wreckage of the Achaean fleet, torn flowers on the water.

The chorus, far now from the momentary exaltation they felt at news of the victory, now chant in terms of disaster: the sinister name of Helen, with the imagination once again of her flight to Troy (681–98); the lion's cub, the pet turned murderous (716–36), who is fatal Helen beguiling the Trojans (737–49). We remember Iphigeneia when Helen's eyes, like Iphigeneia's, sweep the beholder with soft arrows, and the victorious and guileful charmer recalls the innocent charmer who failed. The moralities which follow to prelude Agamemnon's entrance, the terms in which he is greeted, work again through images: houses gilded to hide dust, false coin, the smile of the charmer. Action follows in the public encounter of Clytaemestra and Agamemnon, but the wife's welcome brings back out of the past the fears that attended her during the years of separation (858–94). When he has gone into the house, the chorus turn uneasily from memory to forecast, and their gloom is abetted by Cassandra, who has vision on vision of the past, of the present (the intention behind Clytaemestra's face and words, the scene preparing behind closed doors), and the far future on the day when the avengers shall punish for the crime not yet committed (1069–1330). The death cry tells the chorus only what they already know. We do not see the murder take place, but we are told what happened (1381–92). In the scene that follows, where Clytaemestra faces the people, neither side can escape the memory of the hideous past which has forced these things to happen. Aegisthus' defense is a recounting of the crime of Atreus (1583–1611). At the end, Clytaemestra speaks as if all were over, but we know it is not, that the future holds more violence and it is the past which has made this so.

Lyric Tragedy

The brief dramatic time of the play is a point of convergence for actions that come from deep in the past and project far into the future. The limited stage is a pivotal point from which we can be transported far away. The tragedy of Agamemnon, Cassandra, and Clytaemestra is involved with and opens into the tragedy of the children of Thyestes, of Iphigeneia, of Troy and all the Achaean army; and its action, in return, is partly dictated by the figures never enacted, remote but always present in memory, of Atreus, Iphigeneia, Paris, and Helen.[4]

This is the form of lyric tragedy, perfected here and never since so completely realized. Its manner is due partly to the historical accident in which two forms of fiction were combined: drama, still relatively primitive and naïve, with choral lyric, now, after generations of mature practice, brought to its highest point of development by Simonides and Pindar. But the direction taken by this form is due also to deliberate choice. The desire is to transcend the limitations of dramatic presentation, even before these limitations have been firmly established. . . .

The direction in which [Aeschylus] steered tragedy was not generally followed. Sophoclean drama prevailed, since Euripides, under protest, framed tragedy in accordance with Sophocles, not Aeschylus. Sophocles turned tragedy inward upon the principal actors, and drama becomes drama of character. His plays may open with public scenes, but, as they progress, the interest focuses hard on the hero. *Oedipus Tyrannus* begins with the plague in Thebes, but its ending is all Oedipus, and Thebes is as good as forgotten. It is true that the dead hand reaches out of the past to strike down Oedipus, Antigone, Aias, Heracles. But this is their tragedy, and theirs alone. *Agamemnon* is a play about the Trojan War, but *Antigone* is not a play about the Theban War, though that lies in the background. In Sophocles, the choruses are commentaries on the action, not part of the larger action, and their imagery is functional to the choruses themselves but not to

---

[4] We may compare *The Persians*. The cast of actors consists only of Darius, his queen, Xerxes, messenger, and chorus. The visible scene in Persia is static. But the scene of the action which the play is *about* is Salamis, and then all the water and land between; the persons of this action are all the vast army of the Persians, and all the Greeks. *The Persians* is the great messenger-play.

the tragedy as a whole. Trilogy gives way to single drama. The enormous background becomes mainly irrelevant and is screened out. Lyric tragedy gives way to actor's tragedy.

Agamemnon is, in fact, the culmination of lyric tragedy, because the action narrows in *The Libation Bearers,* and when in *The Eumenides* it opens out again, it is with a new kind of meaning and composition.

The Libation Bearers

The second play of the trilogy takes place some years after the close of *Agamemnon.* The usurpers have grown secure in power. Orestes, sequestered in Phocis, is now a young man, and his sister Electra, resentful and bitter, awaits his return. The opening event is simple recognition, the identification of Orestes and the confirmation of the fact that, as Electra and the chorus hope, he means to avenge his father and regain his throne. Recognition is thus at once transformed into conspiracy. The children, with their faithful chorus, gather at Agamemnon's tomb, where Electra has gone on her mother's behalf, but without sympathy for her, to propitiate the dead king by reason of terrifying dreams which had shaken Clytaemestra in the night. The dead king is now a hero; his arrogance and his mistakes have been annulled by death, and his grave is a center of power. Therefore, the children with the chorus turn to him, invoke his ghost to anger against his murderers, with twofold driving intention: to enchant actual power out of the spirit and the grave and to incite themselves and arm themselves with the anger that will make them do what they must do. They then plot the means for assassination. Orestes poses as a traveling merchant who brings news of the death of Orestes; Clytaemestra, with archaic and stately courtesy, invites him in and sends for Aegisthus. As the messenger who is sent to summon him (she happens to be the slave who nursed Orestes when he was little) goes out on her errand, she encounters the chorus, who tell her not to suggest that Aegisthus should bring his bodyguard. Orestes and Pylades kill the king, and Clytaemestra stands at their mercy. She dares Orestes to kill her, and he stands irresolute until a word from Pylades solidifies his will. The bodies are brought out and displayed, with the robe in which Agamemnon had been entrapped, and Orestes declares publicly, as Clytaemestra had done, that this act is his own and that it is justice. But his wits are going, he sees the Furies, the avenging spirits of his mother (no one else can see them), and leaves in flight. This time, even before the play is over, the assassin knows that his act was not final but has created more suffering yet to come.

Once again the plot is simple, and the dramatic actions are few. Once again, despite these facts, the texture is saved from thinness, but the factors are different from those that give *Agamemnon* its coherence. First, this is a far shorter play. Second, the emphasis and direction have changed. We have, in a sense, more plot; there is intrigue, a practical problem. In *Agamemnon* the king's murder is felt by the witnessing chorus in their bones; it happens, is mourned, and defended. The problems of Clytaemestra, *whether* she can kill the husband she has loved and *how* she will do it, are implicit, but we are not present while she is solving them. But in *The Libation Bearers,* we are present at the deliberations of Orestes as he decides whether he can kill his mother, and how the assassination is to be effected. In recognition, decision, conspiracy, and climactic action we have, in fact, the mechanism, in naïve or even crude form, of that drama of revenge or play of successful action which we found in the Homeric story.

But *The Libation Bearers* is only superficially a drama of intrigue, and, in so far as it is one, it is hardly a significant specimen of its kind. The mechanism of the assassin's plot is simple, as the mechanism of recognition and identification is primitive. The emphasis lies on the mood in which the characters act.

For this is not a simple revenge play in which the young hero, long lost, returns to his sister and his kingdom to strike down the murderous and usurping villains. Orestes hardly gets a sight of his kingship before he must leave, haunted, driven, and alone. It is not until much later, near the close of *The Eumenides,* that he can speak as a king with subjects. Also, here the emotions of Orestes and Electra are, like those of Clytaemestra, half-committed to the side against which they act; and Clytaemestra, in turn, loves the son whom she fears, who kills her, and whom she would kill if she could. It is the *philos-aphilos* still, or love-in-hate, the murder committed not against an external enemy but against a part of the self.[5] The hate gains intensity from the strength of the original love when that love has been stopped or rejected. Electra ("the unmarried") has love to lavish, but her mother has turned it aside. The chorus, like the captive women they are, cling to the memory of Agamemnon, who enslaved them. Orestes, together with the sense of outrage over the loss of his rightful inheritance (the dynastic motive), nurses a deep sense of jealousy against his mother for having sacrificed not only Agamemnon but *Orestes* to her love for Aegisthus. The children were the price for which she bought herself this man (132–34). It is the venom of

---

[5] So *Hamlet* is transformed from the vigorous revenge-intrigue drama it might have been into the tragedy it is, because Hamlet is emotionally involved with the queen and Ophelia, who are on the side of the enemy. Even the arch-enemy is close in blood and perhaps once admired.

such jealousy that spills out in the bitterly salacious mockery of the dead lovers, and jealousy on his father's behalf and his own is the theme of his last sharp dispute with his mother. Clytaemestra, when she hears the false news of her son's death, is in a temper where relief and sorrow cross, though relief wins. Her very dream of bearing and nursing the snake (symbol of ingratitude), who fixes his poisonous fangs in her breast, enacts terror through a gesture of love. Aegisthus, at the word that Orestes is dead, goes soberly back to the image of the poison and the snake:

> For our house, already bitten
> and poisoned, to take this new load upon itself
> would be a thing of dripping fear and blood.

The chorus consider that both the tyrants are hypocrites, but even such hypocrites know what they are doing, and to whom.

This mood of tangled motivation means that the conspirators must work strongly upon themselves before they can act. Between the recognition and the resolve to act comes a scene of incantation. Sister, brother, and chorus turn to invoke dead Agamemnon. They implore his blessings and aid, they set forth their grievances and his, they challenge and taunt him to action. . . . But, while they are invoking a power and a tradition whose force is felt but only dimly believed, they are also lashing themselves into the fury of self-pity that will make them do what they have to do. So the theme of lyric prophecy which was at work in *Agamemnon* is altered here. There is dealing in both cases with what lies beyond the powers of perception, but there it was lyric memory and vision on the part of those who were to witness, and to suffer from, the ugly act; here those who are themselves about to commit the ugly act manipulate the unseen, in a mood more of witchcraft than of prophecy.

For this reason and because the drama focuses on the will to act, *The Libation Bearers* ties back to *Agamemnon,* but *Agamemnon* ties back to the whole world of action latent behind the beginning of the tragedy. The symbols of the earlier play are caught up and intensified, particularly viper and net. But the emphasis is changed, because we see things from the point of view of the murderers. In *Agamemnon,* vice was alluring, wearing all the captivating graces of Helen and her attendant symbols; in *The Libation Bearers,* duty becomes repulsive. Both tragedies are carried on a strong underdrift of sex, but in the second play the sex impulse, though it works, has lost its charm. Orestes at the end has done a brutal, necessary job.

Like Clytaemestra at the close of *Agamemnon,* Orestes defends his position in terms of: "I have cleared my house. It was bloody, but necessary. Now we can have peace." As for Clytaemestra, his claim is no better than a desperate challenge flung at circumstances. The blood-bath was no cleaning-out, and it means more blood. Clytaemestra had to reckon with resentment in the state and the younger generation to come. The enlightenment of Orestes, the defeat of his hollow optimism, comes without delay. "The house has been rid of snakes": and at once, on the heads of his mother's Furies, more snakes appear.

The Eumenides (*The Furies*)

The last act of the trilogy finds Orestes cleared by Apollo but still pursued by the Furies. Is he clear, or not? Plainly, one divine decision has clashed with another decision which is also unquestionably divine. The fate of Orestes is referred to Athens and to a third divinity, Athene, who, reserving for herself the casting ballot, refers it to a jury of mortal men. When their vote is even and Athene has cast her deciding vote in his favor, the Furies must be propitiated by a new cult, as a new kind of goddess, in Athens. It is this episode that closes the play and the trilogy of the House of Atreus. The chorus has returned to its archaic part as chief character in the drama.

Who are the Furies, and what do they mean? And, since they stand up and identify themselves and protest their rights in the face of Apollo and Athene, we must also ask, What do these better-known Olympians represent for the purposes of Aeschylus?

As seen in the grand perspective, Agamemnon was only an unwilling agent in a chain of action far bigger than the fortunes of a single man. From the seduction of Atreus' wife, the murder of the children of Atreus, the sacrifice of Iphigeneia and the youth of Hellas, claim and counterclaim have been fiercely sustained, each act of blood has been avenged in a new act of blood. The problems of public good have been solved through private murder, which is no solution, until the situation has become intolerable to the forces that rule the world, and these must intervene to see that the contestants and the impulses in nature which drive the contestants become reconciled and find their places in a scheme that will be harmonious and progressive, not purely destructive.

Behind the personal motivations in the two first dramas of the trilogy, we can, if we choose, discern a conflict of related forces: of the younger against the elder generation; of male against female; of Greek against barbarian. As the gods step out of the darkness, where, before, they could be reached only in fitful visions of the prophetic mind, and take their place on the stage, they personify these general forces, and, because they are divine and somewhat abstract, they can carry still further dimensions of meaning. The

Furies are older than Apollo and Athene, and, being older, they are childish and barbarous; attached to Clytaemestra as mother, they are themselves female and represent the woman's claim to act which Clytaemestra has sustained from the beginning; in a Greek world they stand for the childhood of the race before it won Hellenic culture, the barbarian phase of pre-Hellenism, the dark of the race and of the world; they have archaic uprightness and strictness in action, with its attendant cruelty; they insist on the fact against the idea; they ignore the justifications of Orestes, for the blood on his hands means far more than the reasons why the blood is there. Apollo stands for everything which the Furies are not: Hellenism, civilization, intellect, and enlightenment. He is male and young. He despises cruelty for the fun of cruelty, and the thirst for blood, but he is as ruthless as the Furies. The commonwealth of the gods—therefore the universe—is in a convulsion of growth; the young Olympians are fighting down their own barbaric past.

But they must not fight it out of existence. In the impasse, Apollo uses every threat of arrogant force, but Athene, whose nature reconciles female with male, has a wisdom deeper than the intelligence of Apollo. She clears Orestes but concedes to the detested Furies what they had not known they wanted, a place in the affections of a civilized community of men, as well as in the divine hierarchy. There, gracious and transformed though they are, their place in the world is still made potent by the unchanged base of their character. The new city cannot progress by exterminating its old order of life; it must absorb and use it. Man cannot obliterate, and should not repress, the unintelligible emotions. Or again, in different terms, man's nature being what it is and Fury being a part of it, Justice must go armed with Terror before it can work.

Thus, through the dilemma of Orestes and its solution, the drama of the House of Atreus has been transformed into a grand parable of progress. Persuasion (flattery), the deadly magic of the earlier plays, has been turned to good by Athene as she wins the Furies to accept of their own free will a new and better place in the world. By the time Orestes leaves the stage, he has become an issue, a Dred Scott or Dreyfus, more important for what he means than for what he is; and, when he goes, the last human personality is gone, and with it vanish the bloody entanglements of the House of Atreus, as the anonymous citizens of Athens escort their protecting divinities into the beginning of a new world.

It is appropriate, and characteristic of Aeschylus, that this final parable, with its tremendous burden of thought, should be enacted on the frame of a naïve dramatic structure, where the basis of decision on matricide is as crude as the base of Portia's decision against Shylock.

The magnificence of *The Eumenides* is different from that of *Agamemnon*. The imagery—the lyric imagination in memory and magic—is gone, because we are not now merely to see but to understand. The final act comes down into the present day and seals within itself the wisdom, neither reactionary nor revolutionary, of a great man. But in its own terms *The Eumenides* is the necessary conclusion of a trilogy whose special greatness lies in the fact that it transcends the limitations of dramatic enactment on a scale never achieved before or since.

Personal Freedom and Its Limitations
in the *Oresteia*

by N. G. L. Hammond

There has been a tendency in recent studies of Aeschylus to exalt
Zeus or Fate into a position of supremacy from which they dictate
and determine the actions and the conditions of men. The argument
of this paper is that Aeschylus believed men to be free in taking some
actions and at the same time recognised the limitations which circum-
scribe the conditions of men. This argument is developed through a
study of the issues which Aeschylus set forth in the *Oresteia,* and it
leads on to an analysis of the meaning of Moira and of the extent
of human responsibility.

I take as a starting point Professor H. Lloyd–Jones' interpretation
of the guilt of Agamemnon.[1] It expresses the exaltation of Zeus and
the powerlessness of man in a precise and striking manner. In his
view Agamemnon had no choice when he was faced with the demand
for the sacrifice of his daughter at Aulis; and even if he had had a
choice he could not have excercised it, because his power of judgement
was taken away by Zeus. As Lloyd–Jones puts it, "Zeus is indeed determined that the fleet must sail; Agamemnon has indeed no choice.
But how has Zeus chosen to enforce his will? . . . by sending Ate to
take away his judgement so that he cannot do otherwise." Lloyd–Jones
sees the same thing happen when Agamemnon is asked by Clytemnestra
to walk on the purple carpet. "Zeus has taken away his wits. But why
has Zeus done so? For the same reason as at Aulis; because of the
curse." Agamemnon is seen as a puppet, of which the strings are pulled
by Zeus. But Agamemnon is only one figure in what Lloyd–Jones
describes as "the grand design of Zeus." This design is traced back
by Lloyd–Jones to the *prōtarchos atē* (primal act of doom) of Thyestes.

"Personal Freedom and its Limitations in the *Oresteia*" by N. G. L. Hammond.
From *The Journal of Hellenic Studies,* LXXXV (1965), 42–55. Copyright © 1965
by The Society for the Promotion of Hellenic Studies. Reprinted by permission of
The Society for the Promotion of Hellenic Studies.

[1] In *CQ* xii (1926) 187f., which should be read together with his important
article "Zeus in Aeschylus" in *JHS* lxxvi (1956).

As he puts it in his concluding sentences, "the curse comes first and determines everything that follows."

At this point we must draw a distinction between a drama written for production and a text studied in isolation. If the curse is to come first and to be the *fons et origo* of the ensuing actions in a living drama, then it must be presented early in the drama by the playwright. Yet Aeschylus does not mention anything like "the curse" until the *Agamemnon* is two-thirds done! We the audience, if we can imagine ourselves at the dramatic competition, have already had our opinions formed by the creative art of the poet on the subject of the guilt of Paris, Helen, the Trojans, the Greeks, Agamemnon, and Menelaus before any mention whatsoever is made of the *prōtarchos atē* or generally of the curse. In a play the dramatic evolution is of sovereign importance. One cannot reverse the sequence on the stage as readily as one can read back a motive in a written text. In terms of drama I do not think that "the curse" can possibly be the *fons et origo* of the actions which bring us to the moment before the murder of Agamemnon. What in fact is "the curse" *in the play*? Cassandra does not use the word. When she mentions the *kōmos syngonōn Erinyōn* (the rout of kindred Erinyes) and the *prōtarchos atē* (1189f.), she immediately explains the context as being the adultery committed by Thyestes with the wife of Atreus. It is this adultery which aroused the kindred Erinyes and involved Thyestes and his descendants, just as it later involved Atreus and his descendants when Atreus retaliated. Cassandra mentions no curse arising from this affair; if the audience is expected to fill the lacuna, it should imagine a curse affecting the house of Thyestes as much certainly as the house of Atreus. We come at last to "the curse" at line 1601. Aegisthus tells the audience that Thyestes kicks over the table and curses; his curse being aimed at the utter destruction of his brother's family, the so-called Pleisthenid branch of the Pelopid line. We are nearly at the end of the play. I do not find the mention of this curse so vivid that it illumines the whole motivation of all that has preceded with a new light. Moreover, it is a curse which is concerned only with Atreus–Agamemnon–Orestes. The much more dramatic words of Cassandra were concerned with the adultery and the *kōmos syngonōn Erinyōn* which involved Thyestes–Aegisthus as well as Atreus–Agamemnon–Orestes, and it is these Erinyes who are active in the trilogy after her speech has introduced them.

Returning to the theory of Lloyd–Jones we note that, as the curse is held to determine everything, "such guilt as the king contracts from the sacrifice of his daughter and from the annihilation of Troy with its people and its temples is only a consequence of the original guilt inherited from Atreus." This is not stated or suggested by any char-

acter or by the Chorus in the passages which describe the sacrifice of
Iphigeneia or the annihilation of Troy. Even when Agamemnon is
persuaded to walk on the purple carpet, there is no word in the play
to suggest that Zeus or "the curse" has taken away his wits and determined that he should act as he does.

But more important than the question whether and when the cur
begins to be prominent in the play is the other facet of such an interpretation, namely the belief that, because "the curse comes first and
determines everything that follows," Agamemnon and Clytemnestra
have no freedom of choice or of action, but each is merely "an instrument of Zeus' destructive purpose." We are presented with a picture
of Kismet, anthropomorphised indeed in the person of Zeus but less
familiar in the days of triumphant Athenian democracy than in the
atmosphere of oriental despotism or of disillusion at Athens: "God's
job it is; hold no man responsible" (Euripides *Cyclops* 285).

There is one passage in the *Agamemnon* where the theory of Lloyd–
Jones is more or less stated. Clytemnestra, wishing to deny her personal responsibility for the murder of Agamemnon, says "it is the
fierce Avenger of earlier time who took the form of this dead man's
wife and made him pay for the cruel preparing of the banquet"
(1500f.). The playwright's means of supporting or refuting this statement lie in the reply of the Chorus. If he intends us the audience
to suppose that Zeus took away her wits and so achieved his destructive purpose, then he can make the Chorus say as much. But no; the
Chorus expresses a less simple view of the matter. "No one will testify
that you are guiltless of this murder; how could anyone? Yet the
Avenger may be a collaborator from the time of his father. Black
Ares forces his way through floods of kindred blood, advancing to
the point where he will exact justice for the clotted gore of the children's flesh." The Chorus places the responsibility fairly and squarely
on the shoulders of Clytemnestra. She chose to murder Agamemnon
and Cassandra. Indeed one of the objects of the long scene which
Aeschylus placed after the murders is to show the true motives of
Clytemnestra, who has now no need to dissemble: her motives are
hatred of Agamemnon (1374f., 1391, 1407f.), lust for blood (1384f.
and 1427f.), and adulterous love for the despicable wolf Aegisthus
(1224f., 1258f., 1435f., and 1625f.). These motives figure more prom-
inently in the play than any grief for Iphigeneia; indeed Clytemnestra's picture of Iphigeneia greeting her father with a kiss in the
underworld (1555f.) is inspired not by love for Iphigeneia but by
hatred for Agamemnon. These motives are important precisely because Clytemnestra acted of her own choice; they and the thoughts
she expresses determine the quality of her action, and Aeschylus

leaves us in no doubt that her motives and so her acts were criminal. Aristotle, who is (not surprisingly) the best interpreter of Greek tragedy, throws special emphasis on the importance of such *proairesis* (deliberate choice) and its motivation.

The collaboration of God and man, whether or not man is aware of does not deprive man of his ability to choose. This is common enough in fifth-century literature, in poetry and in prose. When Thucydides, for example, records the response of Apollo that he will collaborate with the Spartans whether bidden or unbidden (i 118.3), he does not imply that the Spartans have lost the ability to choose for themselves. Aeschylus had made his own position clear in an earlier play. For the ghost of Darius saw in Xerxes' fall the fulfilment of oracles but explained that "when a man is eager himself, the god takes part as well" (*Persae* 742). This idea of coincidence between human choice and divine will is found in many religions. The gospels portray Jesus as fulfilling the purpose of God in his death but as being free to choose in the Garden of Gethsemane. Judas Iscariot is the instrument of betrayal; his treachery is foretold by the prophets and by Jesus (St. Luke 18.31f. and St. Matthew 26.2) and Satan enters into him (St. Luke 22.3); but Judas is represented as choosing of his own will and for motives of monetary gain to betray the Christ. The ideas which are expressed in Darius' comment on Xerxes are very much the same as those in the gospel account of Judas.

A related problem in religious thinking is the relationship between foreknowledge (whether it is shown in oracles, dreams, or prophecy) and fatalism. Aeschylus gives one insight into the problem in the *Prometheus Bound*. Prometheus, having prevision, knows that if Zeus acts in a certain way, a certain result will ensue; and in the event Zeus does not act in that way. Here foreknowledge does not determine the future. He gives another insight when he portrays Cassandra. She knows what will shortly happen inside the palace and what will happen eventually to Aegisthus and Clytemnestra; and the irony of the situation for her (as for other human beings with prevision) is that she cannot change what will happen. Here prevision is, as it were, an extension of normal vision. Just as my vision of what I did this morning does not preclude my having had free choice to act as I did, so a prevision of what will have happened by noon tomorrow does not preclude my having free choice to act until noon tomorrow. The *revolubilis hora* has moved ahead, exposing to those who have prevision what will have happened by noon tomorrow. The idea is not unfamiliar to us. Jesus prophesied that Peter would deny him thrice; but there is no suggestion that Peter was not a free agent each time he made the denial (St. Luke 22.34 and 55f.).

In Clytemnestra's murder of Agamemnon there are three forces at work. The first is Clytemnestra's eagerness, inspired by personal hatred, to kill Agamemnon. The second is the will of Zeus which punishes the moral crimes of Agamemnon in accordance with the laws of Justice. The third is the call of blood for blood, personified in the Avenger, Black Ares and later the Erinyes. At one point in the play these three powers coincide in the killing of Agamemnon. Those who discuss the *Agamemnon* in isolation are apt to think that Zeus and "the call of blood for blood" or "the curse" are interchangeable, as Lloyd–Jones implies in his final summary. But this is not so in the *Eumenides,* which revolves on the point that the Olympian Gods and the Erinyes are fundamentally different in outlook. Aeschylus had already stressed the difference in the *Seven Against Thebes* 720f., where the Chorus sang of the triumph of the Erinys "a goddess not like the gods." The difference between Zeus and the Erinyes is so well known that a brief summary will suffice.[2] The Erinyes are primaeval goddesses, daughters of Night, who carry out the laws of the natural world mercilessly and automatically. They require, for instance, the persecution of Orestes to the death (e.g. *Eum.* 225), because he has killed one of his own blood and "blood calls for blood." They are not concerned at all with the motives which determine the quality of his action in terms of morality; for the natural world was in the beginning, its laws are immutable, and the Erinyes implement them without regard to personal motives. The gods of Olympus, on the other hand, came into existence later than the Erinyes. Zeus was born later still, being the grandson of the first ruler of the sky. He would not always rule the Olympian gods, if he relied on force alone, as Aeschylus indicated in the *Prometheus Bound*; and he certainly had no power over the primaeval gods and goddesses. Zeus never had been and never was omnipotent. At the end of the *Oresteia* he wins the Erinyes to his way of thinking not by force but by the persuasive powers of his daughter Athena (*Eum.* 885f.).

The opening scenes of the *Agamemnon* are dominated by Zeus. The complication of the religious issues is delayed until Agamemnon and Clytemnestra have entered the palace (1068). Aeschylus has written thus in order to drive home the first stage of his beliefs about Zeus. In the opening ode (170f.) the chorus expresses its faith in Zeus not as one who is omnipotent but as one who gives a purpose to human experience:

> If I am to expel the fruitless burden of anguish from my heart in very truth, I cannot find anything comparable to Zeus, even though I measure all things. . . .

[2] See for instance F. Solmsen, *Hesiod and Aeschylus* 196f.

For it is Zeus who leads man along the path to understanding, Zeus who lays down the sovereign law that suffering leads to learning, Zeus who brings understanding to man even against man's will.

The Chorus sees the justice of Zeus at work in the Trojan War. They feel that the sin of Paris is about to be punished through the agency of the Atreidae; for Zeus is sending the Atreidae against Paris (40–63). The beacon signal confirms their expectation; they acclaim the justice of Zeus in the sack of Troy (362–7 and 704f.). But the Chorus is not so simple as to suppose that, if Paris and Troy are in the wrong, the Atreidae and the Greeks are in the right. In this war, as in many wars, both sides are in the wrong: Troy in accepting and defending Paris and Helen, and Greece in going to war for the sake of a woman who knew many lovers (62f.). Paris, of course, was in the wrong. So was Agamemnon, as the Chorus says to his face (799–804):

> So surely, I will not deny it, when thou
> Didst marshal the host to recover
> Helen, willing wanton, with thousands of lives,
> I accounted thee like to a picture deformed
> Or a helm ill-turned by the pilot.[3]

Paris and Agamemnon now have the blood of many men and women on their hands. The gods do not fail to mark those who are responsible for much blood, and the Erinyes bring them to darkness in the course of time (461–67). The punishment of Paris and Troy has been carried out through the Erinys which took the form of Helen herself (749); and the punishment of Agamemnon will be carried out by an Erinys which takes the form of Clytemnestra (1119). But this does not mean that Helen and Clytemnestra were right to do what they did, or that they had lost their freedom of choice. Clytemnestra has committed murder for criminal motives and Justice, the daughter of Zeus, overtakes her in due course (*Ch.* 948f.), as Cassandra had forseen (*A.* 1284–85).

Agamemnon's case is very similar. Agamemnon's purpose in promoting a war against Troy happened to coincide with the will of Zeus to punish Paris and Troy. This coincidence is no credit to Agamemnon. It does not relieve him of responsibility for his motives in going to war. The point is clearly made by the Chorus. For while the Chorus says that Zeus sends the Atreidae against Paris (6of.) it censures Agamemnon for marshalling the army in order to recover a willing wanton (799f.). When Agamemnon had taken this first step, the adverse wind was sent by Artemis, because "she loathes the feast of the eagles" (135f.), that is because she loathes the bloodshed of

---

[3] The translations in verse are from G. Thomson's translation of the *Oresteia.*

the war which Agamemnon and Menelaus are starting. This is an independent action by Artemis, such an action as we may expect in a polytheistic world, where Zeus is not omnipotent. For Artemis is no servant of Zeus; she is the goddess of the weak and helpless, and she abominates the brutality of the impending war (140f.). Calchas, having second sight, had already foreseen the reaction of Artemis to the prospect of war (135f.); and when the wind came, he declared it was the doing of Artemis (202), and he indicated to the sons of Atreus that the wind would cease to be adverse, if Agamemnon sacrificed his daughter Iphigeneia.

Aeschylus puts the following words into the mouth of Agamemnon:

> A bitter thing surely not to hearken
> And bitter too
> To slay my own child, my royal jewel.

Agamemnon sees two courses open to him—either to reject the course recommended by Calchas, or to accept it and kill his own daughter. Those who say that Agamemnon has no choice between these two courses can only mean that the choice is difficult; for Agamemnon mentions two courses of action and chooses one course deliberately. It is, as E. Fraenkel expresses it, "Agamemnon's own voluntary decision." The choice is, of course, a difficult one. It is very familiar to those who are engaged in a war and exercise command, as so many Athenians were doing in 458 BC; for the question is this—is one to stop or is one to take an action which will involve the death of innocent persons? It is immaterial whether the instrument of death in war is the sword, the bullet, or the bomb.

The choice is bitter. But it is very much a choice, and a choice for which one bears a heavy personal responsibility. The words which Aeschylus makes Agamemnon say show a deep understanding not only of war (as so often in this play) but also of the type of general who takes such a decision as Agamemnon took. They form a soliloquy of deep psychological insight.

> A bitter thing surely not to hearken,
> And bitter too
> To slay my own child, my royal jewel,
> Myself her father, to spill a girl's pure blood.
> Whate'er the choice, 'tis ill.
> How shall I fail my thousand ships and desert my comrades?
> So shall the storm cease, and the host eager
>   for war crieth for that virginal blood righteously! So
>   pray for a happy issue.

The order in which Agamemnon puts the alternatives shows his own preference. The rhetorical question marks his choice. He prefers the pomp and the ceremony of the ships and the confederation, just as later in the play he prefers the ceremony of the purple carpet. In the next sentence he tries to shrug off his own responsibility by saying that the passionate desire for the virgin's blood to stop the wind is—right and proper (*themis*). These words are almost blasphemous. They show that passion for war and fear of public opinion are turning Agamemnon into a hypocrite. He and Menelaus are described next as "lovers of war," when they disregard the supplications of Iphigeneia (230). We know that passion for war has many crimes to its credit. Agamemnon himself is uneasy. He knows he is committing a wrong but he hopes for the best, as he does later when he walks on the purple carpet (944–7). Therefore he ends his words with the phrase "may all be well."

The speech of Agamemnon has revealed his decision. His inner mind is made up. It is this decision, as much as the action to which it leads, that now alters the personality of Agamemnon (218f.): "From the moment when his spirit veered to an impious, unclean, unholy quarter and he put on the strap of the yoke of necessity, from that moment he changed his mind [4] to adopt a course of utter recklessness. For what emboldens men is a dreadful delusion, which counsels dishonour and is the beginning of sorrow. So then he dared to sacrifice his daughter, in furtherance of war for a woman and in initiation of the fleet" (218–227). What we may call the psychological consequences of the decision are here expressed in typically Aeschylean terms. Agamemnon takes the decision with utter impiety of spirit. This decision subjects him to inevitable consequences; he has put on the yoke, he has passed under the bar and there is no turning back. From then on he is utterly reckless in carrying out the sacrifice of his own daughter. In generalising terms the source of this recklessness is a delusion of mind, through which a man takes a dishonourable course and pays for it with pain.

An utterly reckless decision such as that of Agamemnon sets up a series of inevitable consequences, spreading like ripples on a pool. "The impious deed begets other deeds like to their parent" (758f.). The war into which Agamemnon now leads the Greeks will bring sufferings to the Greeks as well as to the Trojans (66f.), and the curses of those who lose their dearest ones will rest upon the leaders, responsible as they are for shedding much blood. The gods will not fail to mark the leaders, and "the Black Furies" wait (429–467). The full significance of this passage was felt by the audience in 458 BC; for it was probably in this year that the Erechtheid tribe suffered the loss of 177 men "in Cyprus, Egypt, Phoenicia, Halieis, Aegina, and the Megarid."

The first part of the play is concerned not only with Agamemnon but

---

[4] The metaphor of the changing wind and the changing course is graphic to anyone trained in sailing; it is particularly apposite here because the wind at Aulis is about to veer likewise.

with the fulfilment of the Justice of Zeus in the context of Troy and the Greeks. Paris has sinned against Zeus Xenios, and Troy has sinned in defending Paris and Helen. Once the high altar of Zeus has been kicked aside, there is no protection (whether at Troy or at Argos), but the man who sins in his satiety (*Koros*) "is driven on by fell Persuasion (*Peitho*), dread child of fore-scheming Delusion (*Ate*)" (381–6). The sinner sets a dread brand upon his city (395). Such a one is Paris (399). The sequence is the same with Paris as with Agamemnon: a choice made in impious satiety or over-confidence, a reckless delusion, an impious act begetting further impious acts, and the branding of the group or state which supports the sinner. Helen is another example. She made her choice in recklessness (408), and she brought destruction upon her associates (689f.). Now Zeus has punished Paris, Helen, and Troy in accordance with his own laws of Justice (355f.). The Chorus has a sense of foreboding; Agamemnon too has sinned and has blood on his hands, and many of the Greeks have already been destroyed in the storm which was "sent by the gods' anger" (649). There is a dreadful irony in the words on his homecoming, that "the gods who sent him forth have brought him back" (*A.* 853). The final test of Agamemnon comes when Clytemnestra asks him to walk on the purple carpet. He knows it is wrong to do so, but in his arrogance, his recklessness, and his weakness he does; and he passes into the palace, while Clytemnestra prays to "Zeus the Accomplisher." We know that the blow of Zeus is about to fall upon the guilty man, as it has already fallen on Paris, Troy, and many Greeks as well as Trojans for their acts of impiety. The first part of the religious movement is now complete.

Cassandra and also those who speak after the murders introduce new themes, which will continue to be important until the final resolution of the harmonies and discords in the reconciliation of Zeus and Moira. We learn from Cassandra, for the first time as far as the play is concerned,[5] that a long history of crime lies upon the house of the Pelopidae and involves Agamemnon and Aegisthus in its consequences. Cassandra speaks clearly of the *prōtarchos atē*, the act of delusion which marked the beginning of suffering, namely the seduction by Thyestes of the wife of his brother Atreus (1192–3). In revenge Atreus killed Thyestes' two older children and served them up to their father (1217f.). Now Aegisthus, the surviving son of Thyestes, has seduced the wife of Agamemnon, a son of Atreus (1258f.); and, as Cassandra sees, the wife of Agamemnon is about to murder Agamemnon at the instigation of Aegisthus (1224). The sacrifice of Iphigeneia by Agamemnon is not mentioned by Cassandra. It is not included in the series of crimes which have arisen between the brothers and their descendants, and it

[5] It is important to keep to the dramatic sequence, because the play was written for performance.

is not this which prompts Clytemnestra to murder Agamemnon. This feud within the family has roused the revel of Erinyes, who sit upon the palace-roof, the *syngonoi Erinyes*. Their desire to exact vengeance from Atreus coincides with the plot of Clytemnestra and Aegisthus to kill the son of Atreus, Agamemenon. There seems to be no suggestion here that, because Aegisthus is involved in the desire of the Erinyes to exact vengeance, he is "not responsible"; and in the *Choephoroe* reference is made to him as "the responsible one." He is portrayed in the speech of Cassandra as a cowardly lion and as a wolf (1224 and 1259) and in the interchanges with the Chorus as a crafty, cowardly, and bullying adulterer (cf. *Ch.* 990). When Aegisthus hails the murder as the work of the Erinyes (1580) and claims that he is "a just designer" of the murder (1604) the Chorus censures him for hybris (1612) and says he planned the murder *hekōn* (deliberately)—that is, not under compulsion from the Erinyes. His suggestion is as absurd as the plea of Clytemnestra (1498f.). He has made his own choices, and they have coincided with the purpose of the Erinyes. The play ends with the guilt of Clytemnestra and Aegisthus made clear. Cassandra has foretold that they too will pay (1280f.). The Chorus hopes for the return of Orestes to repay murder with murder (1646f.).

In the latter part then of the play the Erinyes dominate the divine stage, and they continue to be prominent for the next two plays of the trilogy. The *Erinyes syngonoi* and the daimon have their place on the palace-roof or swoop down upon the house (1191 and 1467); but their wishes coincide with the purpose of Zeus, in whom the Chorus has already put its faith in measuring the universe. The daimon and Zeus are both the accomplishers of what has come to pass.

Thus the *Agamemnon* ends with the triumph of Justice, daughter of Zeus, in the punishment of Paris, Troy, Agamemnon, and the Greeks for the unjust war, in which they all engaged; of Paris especially for the breach of hospitality which offended Zeus Xenios; of Agamemnon especially for his lawless sacrifice of his own daughter (cf. *Ch.* 935f.). At the same time the punishment of Agamemnon coincides with the desire of the Erinyes to avenge the killing of Thyestes' children by Atreus through the killing of Agamemnon, the son of Atreus, by the agency of Aegisthus. This is all overseen by Zeus, but it has come about without any infringement of the free will of the agents—Agamemnon, Clytemnestra, and Aegisthus. They acted as they did for their own personal reasons, which were in each case sinful. Punishment has already come or will in future come upon them.

Another religious theme appears in the *Agamemnon,* namely that of Moira. The word means "apportionment." Its significance is made clear by the Chorus at 1017f., "When the blood of a man is shed dark upon the ground, no magic can recall it. Otherwise when he (Asclepius) raised the dead by his skill, Zeus would not have stopped him (as he did) to avert damage. For ordained Apportionment prevents (our human) portion from gaining more than its due in accordance with the will of the gods; if this were not so, (my) heart would outstrip (my) tongue and pour out its thoughts." Here "the ordained Apportionment" is the primaeval allocation of powers and spheres to gods, men, and all physical things. The wardens of this allocation are the Moirai and the Erinyes, whom I have described above as carrying out the laws of the natural world mercilessly and automatically. "The ordained Apportionment" makes things what they are: it makes bloodshed final (*Ch.* 48, *Eum.* 261f.), the loss of virginity irretrievable (*Ch.* 71f.), marriage a strong bond between man and woman (*Eum.* 216f.), and death unavoidable for man (*Eum.* 648f.). The order of the natural world, the kosmos, depends upon the maintenance of this apportionment, and any disruption of the order produces damage and disorder. Prometheus upset this order by giving fire to man; he and man suffered from the consequent disorder, and Zeus put an end to the activity of Prometheus. So here Asclepius upset the order of the universe in resurrecting the dead; Zeus therefore stopped him in order to avert further damage and disruption. So too in the *Eumenides* 171f. the Furies accuse Apollo of overvaluing the cause of man and of damaging the ancient apportionments (as Prometheus had done) in trying to liberate Orestes.

Each of us has his or her personal apportionment. So have Orestes and Cassandra. Through no choice of hers Cassandra is a daughter of Priam. She has been captured at the sack of Troy and brought to the palace of the Atreidae. The Chorus says that she has been caught in the net of Moira (*A.* 1048). She is free to decide her own attitude to this situation, and the Chorus urges her to yield to the necessity of her situation (1071). The chorus of Trojan slave women suffers from the same *aisa*, "lot," and *anankē*, "necessity" (*Ch.* 75f.), and they have come to terms with it. The free as well as the enslaved are involved in the chain of events which form the history of the palace (*Ch.* 103). Moira has cast the lot of Clytemnestra and that of Orestes in this environment. But Moira is not even partly responsible for Clytemnestra's decisions as she claimed (*Ch.* 910f.).

In a wider sense Moira is the "apportionment" of all that has happened, not only of past events[6] but also of the whole structure of the universe. The original separation of the elements into their parts, into Sea and Earth, Day and Night, was itself Moira. The goddesses "the

---

[6] Events which lie in the future but on one day will have happened can be viewed in the same way as due to or in accordance with Moira, but not for that reason as preordained and as overriding the power of choice in men. Calchas, for instance, has a glimpse into the future and tells of what will happen and the Chorus looks forward to the appointed day of the future.

Moirai" were, like the Erinyes, born from the womb of Night (*Eum.* 321 and 962). They are guardians of the way things are, that is of the Dike of the universe which is unalterable, impersonal, and implacable; and the Erinyes punish offenders against the rules of Moira and Dike, the two goddesses which give them their authority (*Eum.* 333f. and 931). Aisa is evidently synonymous with Moira (*Ch.* 911 and 927). Moira or Aisa and their agents apportion good and evil to men as it were in a lottery (*Eum.* 310).

As a man cannot alter his individuality and his environment so heredity is a part of anyone's moira or apportionment. In some cases heredity may restrict the choice open to an individual, because he inherits a particular dilemma. Orestes is in such a position. He is drawn onwards by a variety of powers: the fortune of his father (the "aisa" of Agamemnon), the dead man's desire for revenge, the demands of Justice, daughter of Zeus, who speaks through the oracular response of Apollo (*Eum.* 618f.), and the Erinys as the agent of the family apportionment with its cry of "blood for blood." These powers are all vividly portrayed in the *Choephoroe* in prayer and in narration (18, 148, 244, 283, 382, 394f., 400f., 640f.). The family apportionment has a further personification in the form of the Curses, the Arai, sent up from the wrathful dead (*Ch.* 405f.), and the Erinyes identify themselves with the Arai (*Eum.* 417). The family apportionment appears itself as a Curse on the house (*Ch.* 692), and the Chorus speak of the "family anguish" (*Ch.* 466). In the latter part of the *Oresteia,* where the "family anguish" is so powerful, the feeling may be uppermost in us that Orestes has little choice. But we should remember that his own wishes coincide with the wishes of the gods as he says himself (*Ch.* 299–304). Here too we are shown a case where the choice of a man and the desire of the gods coincide and make the sequel almost inevitable. The day when murder will avenge murder is approaching in accordance with the will of Orestes, the decrees of Justice and the wishes of all the powers which have been invoked—it is "the day of apportionment which has been long in coming" (*Ch.* 464).

The involvement of a whole family in a series of crimes which all offend against the right order, that is against the relationship laid down by Moira, and also against the moral sense of Justice for which Zeus stands, raises in the most acute form the problem of individual freedom. We have seen that Agamemnon, Clytemnestra, and Aegisthus are portrayed as individuals who choose of their own volition to commit a *dyssebes ergon* (impious deed). Their acts coincide with the purposes of Zeus, and those of the last two coincide with the wishes of the Erinyes. Orestes, however, is portrayed as a man who is not brought by his own hybris and thrasos to commit a *dyssebes ergon.* Indeed he is *eusebēs* (pious) so far as Apollo, the mouthpiece of Zeus, is concerned.

But his act, though it may be represented as morally justifiable, offends against the relationship laid down by Moira and arouses the anger of the Erinyes, the ministrants of Moira's rights. Is he to be saved by Apollo or is he to be punished by the Erinyes? The climax of the *Oresteia* comes when Zeus persuades the Erinyes to accept his wish, namely the release of Orestes from their punishment; and to become the Eumenides, the well-wishers of mankind. It is only in the final chorus, when "Zeus, who beholdeth all, is at last reconciled with Moira" (*Eum.* 1045) that we see that Zeus is indeed the centre of man's hopes in the universe (*A.* 163f.). Zeus works within the framework of Moira, but he does so intelligently and benevolently for the betterment of man; and he has persuaded the Erinyes to accept his benevolent purpose. Man will continue to suffer (for suffering is part of his "moira"); but Zeus will use man's suffering to teach man the wisdom which lies in that quality of moderation known as *sōphrosynē*.

The chief obstacle to our understanding of Aeschylus' ideas is our concept of "fate." We tend to think of "fate" and "free-will" as incompatible opposites, mutually exclusive and never co-existent; and there is therefore a tendency to read our ideas of "fate" and "determinism" into the vocabulary of Aeschylus. Thus to translate Moira not as "apportionment" but as "fate" is the beginning of error. "Fate" with its Latin derivation has a finality which implies fatalism and despair; we see the idea becoming established in the civil wars of the Roman Republic and in the disillusionment which set in when the Principate became an autocracy. But Moira has an entirely different milieu and meaning. It derives from *meiromai,* "to be divided" or "to be part of a whole." This "being a part of a whole" cannot be cancelled out. The elements are parts of the cosmos; men and women are parts of humanity, of nations, of families, and of married pairs; body, mind, and soul are parts of a human being. Moreover, the parts bear a certain relationship to one another and to the whole, which makes for unity and order. This relationship is the orderly way, *dikē.* A breach of it causes *adikia.* These are not moral but factual relationships which are "necessary," products of *anankē* (necesssity). The consequences of abusing these relationships are also "necessary." Moira also apportions to us our individual endowments, which cannot be rejected by us. Cassandra affords a good example of the interrelationship of these words. She is caught in the net of apportionment (*A.* 1048), must bow to its necessity (1071), accept her lot (1136), and have the same portion as Agamemnon (*A.* 1313).

The general conclusion to which we have come is that Aeschylus believed men to be free in making some decisions and that at the same time he recognised the limitations imposed upon men by their "moira" or portion, in terms both of identity and of circumstance. The language of the plays shows his deep interest in degrees of personal responsibility or, if we prefer to put it so, causation both in god and man. At one point Zeus is described as *panaitios* (*A.* 1486); the meaning is "fully responsible" as is apparent from the case of Apollo (*Eum.* 199–200). Apollo is not "jointly responsible" (*metaitios*), in the sense in which Agamemnon addresses the gods as "jointly responsible" for his homecoming (*A.* 811). Moira is alleged by Clytemnestra to be "partly responsible" (*Ch.* 910 *paraitia*). Apollo is "liable to responsibility" (*Eum.* 465 *epaitios*). The net is "co-responsible" (*A.* 1116 *xynaitia*). Aegisthus is "responsible" (*Ch.* 69 *aitios*), Clytemnestra is not "un-responsible" (*A.* 1505 *anaitios*); and the chorus wishes to be "un-responsible" for the killing of Aegisthus (*Ch.* 873). Similarly Aeschylus stresses deliberate, willing action by the use of *hekōn* and action under compulsion by the use of *anankē*, e.g. in the matter of slavery (*A.* 953 and 1071). This is clearly defined in *Eum.* 550 and in *Prometheus Bound* 266. The Chorus applies the word *hekōn* to Aegisthus when he claims that the Erinyes and Justice took part in the killing of Agamemnon (*A.* 1613). The characters whom Aeschylus depicts in the *Oresteia* are the final proof of his belief in the freedom of man in making some crucial decisions. For they are bold, confident, and decisive persons—even the wolf-like Aegisthus, whose "wide-eyed mind will never be deceived" (*Ch.* 854), and it is part of their heroic stature that they act on their own responsibility.[7] They are making the "deliberate choices" which illustrate personality in the Aristotelian sense.

The limitations which are imposed upon man by the nature of circumstance are sometimes cosmic and sometimes personal. The condition of human life is a part of this cosmic condition which is due to Moira, "apportionment." The gods too, if they are wise, work within the limitations of the cosmic condition. Prometheus did not do so when he gave fire to man in his self-will; therefore his gift was "a thankless favour" (*Prometheus Bound* 545). Asclepius made a similar mistake in raising a man from the dead (*A.* 1022f.), and Apollo used deceit to secure the salvation of Admetus from death and upset "the ancient dispensations" (*Eum.* 723f.). Zeus, however, works within the limitations of the cosmic condition. In the same choral ode in the *Prometheus*

---

[7] Orestes does not just shelter behind the oracles of Apollo, powerful though they are (*Ch.* 297 and *Eum.* 594). He faces the fact that he would have to act, even if he disbelieved the oracles (*Ch.* 298f.). He accepts responsibility for the killing of Clytemnestra (*Eum.* 463f.). In the same way Orestes and Electra take the initiative in calling upon the spirit of Agamemnon; and the ghost of Clytemnestra appears not to urge on men (as the ghost of the king does in *Hamlet*) but to urge on the Erinyes.

Bound "the plans of man," particularly those inspired by the gift from Prometheus, will not transgress (successfully) "the harmony of Zeus" (*Prometheus Bound* 551). I take this phrase to be the cosmic condition within which Zeus works. The word *harmonia* is well defined by W. K. C. Guthrie: for "to be a harmony meant that all its parts were organised in the correct order and proportion for the best performance of its function." In the *Oresteia* too Zeus is represented as working with Moira. He ended the activities of Asclepius in order to avert damage to the system of *moirai*, that is to the apportionment of the world-order (*A.* 1024f.). Zeus coincided with Moira and Dike in the first two plays, as the opening words of the litany in the *Choephoroe* show (306f.), "O great Apportioners, in accordance with the desire of Zeus bring this matter to the conclusion in which Justice has her place." The discord which develops between the children of Zeus (Apollo and Athena) and the Furies is resolved by the inspiration of a common purpose, which will guide the collaboration of Zeus and Moira in the future. The last words of the *Eumenides* answer the opening words of the litany in the *Choephoroe*.

When a god or man flouts the limitations of the cosmic condition, he is involved in necessary consequences, *anankai*. Prometheus sees that his act in giving fire to man has made him subject to the invincible power of *anankē* (*Prometheus Bound* 105). He has thereby become yoked to *anankai* which take the form of torture (*Prometheus Bound* 108). The freedom of action which he exercised in giving fire to man has involved him in the necessary consequences. Cassandra and the Trojan women are involved in the necessary consequences of the acts of other people which brought Troy to ruin and them to slavery. Cassandra is yoked to this necessity (*A.* 1071), and the Trojan women have received from the gods "a necessity which encompasses the state" (*Ch.* 75f.). Any generation which has experience of war knows the nature of these necessities. Agamemnon too by his decision to kill his daughter, like Prometheus by his gift of fire to man, "put on the yoke of necessity" (*A.* 218); for he flouted the limitations of personal life, the proper relations between father and child. So too Clytemnestra flouted, by her actions of adultery and murder, the proper relations between husband and wife (*Eum.* 217f.). Their acts involve not only themselves but also innocent persons in the necessary consequences. The image of the pregnant hare (*A.* 135f.), the comparison of Orestes to the hare (*Eum.* 252 and 326), and the pathos of Cassandra bear poignant testimony to this truth. The involvement of the innocent is the tragedy of the human situation. It is the core of many plays, from the *Oresteia* to *Hamlet*. The full impact of it is conveyed not by any literary analysis but by the experience of seeing the *Oresteia* played. For, if we are to learn anything from Plato and Aristotle who saw Attic tragedy on the contemporary stage, it moved men with pity and fear. It was above all an emotional form of drama. It also contained religious and intellectual ideas. The *Oresteia*—"the masterpiece of masterpieces" as Goethe called it—excels in emotional force and in profundity of religious ideas. Its effect on us today is due to the fact that the picture of human freedom and of its limitations is true to life.

Aspects of Dramatic Symbolism:
Three Studies in the *Oresteia*

by Robert F. Goheen

Opsis or spectacle and *lexis* or diction Aristotle assessed as secondary elements of Greek tragedy to focus attention on the well-knit plot motivated out of character. By and large subsequent scholarship has followed these lines set down in the *Poetics,* though several recent studies have struck out for wider perspectives and made it somewhat less exceptional to see that in Greek Tragedy, as in Shakespearean drama and in much modern literature, additional principles of organization may be at work than simply those which Aristotle conceived within his order of "probability and necessity." [1]

Generally speaking it is now possible, I believe, to distinguish in the extant dramas of the Greek tragic theater three main types of symbolic imagery which can be observed to operate toward the development and organization of given works. That is to say, we have imagery which is symbolic when concretes of perception, "things," are employed to represent ideas, attitudes, or qualities of thought. In poetic drama such developments are invited either in the order of language, or in the embodied action of agents, or as a matter of the setting accorded to the action. These will often interpenetrate, but at least approximately they relate to distinguishable parts of the medium and form the three types—namely, verbal imagery, the imagery of action, and imagery of scene (including setting and "props").[2] Theoretically it is also possible to mark off a fourth type, and perhaps term

"Aspects of Dramatic Symbolism: Three Studies in the *Oresteia*" by Robert F. Goheen. From *American Journal of Philology*, LXXVI, 2 (1955), 113–37. Copyright © 1955 by The Johns Hopkins Press. Reprinted by permission of The Johns Hopkins Press.

[1] Notably H. D. F. Kitto, *Greek Tragedy* (2nd ed., London, 1950); R. P. Winnington–Ingram, *Euripides and Dionysus* (Cambridge, 1948); W. B. Stanford, *Ambiguity in Greek Literature* (Oxford, 1939); E. T. Owen, *The Harmony of Aeschylus* (Toronto, 1952); R. Lattimore, *Aeschylus: Oresteia* (Chicago, 1953), pp. 15–25.

[2] See Alan Downer, "The Life of Our Design," *Hudson Review*, II (1949), pp. 242–63. I have somewhat expanded the range of each of his categories while also joining "the language of props" and the "language of setting."

it imagery of figure, to designate the symbolic character. Type characters (as Aegisthus largely is in Sophocles' *Electra*) and most divinities bear "given" values when they appear in the theater, but we come to perceive the symbolic cast of major characters, like Prometheus, Oedipus, and the Dionysus of the *Bacchae,* from how they act and react in dramatic situations. Therefore I suggest we include such developments in the imagery of action and let that be an extensive term.

The range of manner and degree is immense in the ways the several Attic tragedians exploit the symbolic potentialities of their medium. It varies with the particular intent in the given play so as to preclude adequate comparative illustration in the space at my disposal. Probably of the three playwrights Euripides has suffered the worst in a cross-fire where Aristotelian canons and those of "slice-of-life" dramatic realism have been ranged in to fire for effect. His sometimes unfortunate situation asks for fresh appraisal and is worth mention, even though I cannot develop the matter here. Instead, for the body of this study, I propose to stay within the *Oresteia* whose symbolic aura is frequently more patent and to examine in some detail there three instances where, it seems to me, a precise understanding of the drama must rest upon an adequate understanding of symbolic developments. While verbal imagery will be seen to be of considerable importance in helping to establish and sustain and inter-relate the insights enfigured in each of these three cases, they themselves involve the exploitation of visual resources which belong to the trilogy as an action of agents on a stage and in a setting. It is on this that I wish to focus attention by considering in turn the carpet of the *Agamemnon* (imagery of scene), the persuading of Agamemnon to walk the carpet (collateral imagery of action), and the rôle of the Nurse in the *Choephori* (imagery of action and type character). Singly and together these are instances where the modes of communication employed and the levels of perception involved are something more than that interest and agony which works out of plot and character and situation: i.e., the Aristotelian "action" and "soul" and "end" of tragedy.

1. The "color" of the carpet in Agamemnon, *908–74.*

The costly carpet which is spread on the stage and on which Agamemnon is persuaded to make his fateful entry into the palace on the occasion of his home-coming is described as a *porphyrostrōtos poros* (910) and thing of *porphyra* (957, 959). Color terms are often rather vague in Greek poetry,[3] but so far as I know there has been little

---

[3] Cf. A. E. Kober, *The Use of Color Terms in the Greek Poets* (Geneva, N.Y., 1932).

close investigation of the actual or the metaphorical color here. Some
have asserted it was crimson and hence connoted blood. I shall be
arguing for this *connotation,* but for reasons which will emerge I
doubt if the color words here *denote* crimson. More generally now the
color is taken to be purple ("a purple-strewn path"), and the two most
recent major editions of the play allow no alternative in their treatment of this episode.[4] As such, we may remind ourselves, the carpet
signifies "barbaric, and more particularly, Persian acts of homage." To
accept these is presumptuous and invites divine retribution (*phthonos,*
921). This is patent and the metaphorical coloration of the scene into
an occasion for pride is valid whether the rich, orientalizing carpet be
purple or crimson or some color in between. But I suggest we can go
further, and, if we do, we shall see that the carpet was not what we
usually regard as purple or crimson. Instead it was almost certainly
an ambiguous blood-color, probably the dark purplish red or deep
reddish brown which blood takes on after it is exposed to the air—or
when it forms stains in the dust. As a darksome thing of blood, the
carpet in its magnificence still bears the hybris-value, but it has been
imbued both with Clytemnestra's lethal intent and by the blood which
is to flow and flow again before the resolution of the trilogy is
reached.[5] Moreover, so seen, the carpet bears the closest sort of relationship to other elements of the tragedy. Its latent values are developed in terms of verbal imagery, action, characterization, and further
elements of setting as the trilogy moves on.

It is in the final analysis of these internal elements of the drama
that we must rest this view of the carpet as a thing darkly pooling
blood and death while overtly sheening pomp and pride. And rightly
so, for it is by the organized context which he has established that
alone we may know which areas of signification Aeschylus intends to
call up and bring to bear in the image of the carpet from out of the
broad and sometimes opaque range of meanings embraced by the
Greek color word *porphyreos* and its related forms.[6] The relevant

[4] I.e., E. Fraenkel, *Agamemnon* (Oxford, 1950) and George Thomson, *The Oresteia
of Aeschylus* (Cambridge, 1938).

[5] For the performance of the *Agamemnon* at Syracuse shortly after World War I,
Ettore Romagnoli as director sought the effect by having the carpet represent
blood almost as literally as possible. The color was attained by dyeing material
in the blood of an ox, producing a dark reddish brown. Instead of running the
carpet straight back to the palace door, it was unrolled to form a sinuous track
"like a vein running down a muscular arm." I have the information from discussions with Count M. T. Gargallo who prior to the Fascist regime was a leading
force in the revival of the Greek theater at Syracuse.

[6] For the broad and indefinite potentialities of the term see L. M. Wilson,
The Clothing of the Ancient Romans (Baltimore, 1938), pp. 6–13. The tests with
murex and ancient recipes for dyes which Miss Wilson reports indicate that "the
term 'purple' as used by the Greeks and Romans is a most flexible one and that it

evidence is not, however, entirely internal, and before proceeding into matters of structure and thence into the aspects of thought which this symbolism concretes for the play, it will be well to observe how in terms of Greek poetic usage the questioned term is equipped to bear the sanguinary implications I have assigned to it.

Three instances suffice to show that there are in Greek poetry uses of the term where it cannot signify the color we commonly denote by purple and that in significant cases the term is applied to blood, especially to blood shed fatally. Thus in the *Persians,* 314–17, Aeschylus describes the death of Matallus as follows:

> and Matallus, satrap of Chrysa,
> Dying, leader of a thousand horse,
> Changed to richest red his thickset flowing
> Beard, and dipped his skin in crimson dyes (*porphyra baphē*).
>   (translation by S. Benardete)

Exact translation for the final phrase is difficult, but the sense is clearly one of blood and of color, and the piling up of color words is suggestive. Its original fiery color, its dense texture, the suggestion that Matallus was dark-skinned, all seem to indicate a dark coloration of the beard in the final event. So also in the *Iliad,* XVII, 361, as the Trojans fall before Ajax, *haimati de chthōn/ deueto porphyreō.* A. T. Murray renders this, "The ground grew wet with dark blood," and "dark" is probably the best English translation: for as anyone who has seen blood in the dust of the battlefield knows, it is hardly any specific color: only its dark, indeterminate self. Moreover a reference of Pliny the Elder confirms this interpretation, and further testifies to the value of *porphyreos* as an accurate designation of darkened blood. The passage is *Natural History,* IX, 135:

> For Tyrian purple the wool is initially soaked with sea-purple for a preliminary pale dressing and then it is completely transformed with whelk dye. Its highest glory consists in *the color of congealed blood,* dark to a direct view, but with a latent sheen. It is for this reason that "purple" blood is spoken of by Homer.

So far as external evidence can go, Pliny's comment seems fairly conclusive and so it is that in the *Iliad* one finds the beginnings of the literary association by which *porphyreos* comes to be linked with blood and then may itself sometimes signify things sanguinary. The

---

applied to distinctively different shades," including some thirty shades of green, crimson, various purples, and reddish brown. Amidst all this variety there is perhaps some specific guidance for our interest in the fact that recipes for "Tyrian purple" and "Phoenician purple," the two most famed and prized oriental *porphyrai,* were found to produce a dark reddish brown.

latter occurs in the lines quoted from the *Persians* and the usage passes also into the Latin word *purpureus* (e.g. *Aeneid,* IX, 349). For our interest in the *Agamemnon,* we should also observe that in the Homeric phrase the reference is to blood on the ground. We find that to be its characteristic and telling location in the *Oresteia.*

Indeed this last fact constitutes one of three developed aspects of the internal, verbal-dramatic structure of the *Agamemnon* and of the trilogy which join with the obvious fact of Agamemnon's murder to indicate that the colors of blood and death lurk in the carpet and have significance there. Verbal imagery of *blood on the ground* forms a recurring motif, carefully articulated and impressively sustained. Significantly it gets its first explicit statement in the choral ode which immediately follows the carpet-scene, and from here it is carried through the trilogy to form one of the more patent lines which bind the three plays into a single whole. In the ode following the carpet-scene, the figure of a man's dark, death-marking blood on the ground is part of the agitation and fear that weigh hard upon the Chorus. Blood once shed, they see, is beyond all recall:

> But when the black and mortal blood of man
> has fallen to the ground before his feet, who then
> can sing spells to call it back again?
> (*Ag.,* 1018–21; translation by R. Lattimore)

Fraenkel insists that we are to feel no specific implication in these lines; I would agree only that the Chorus, as actor, is not making a specific application. For the particular image is closely in line with the carpet as a blood-symbol, and, coming where they do, the lines bear a close potential relevance to it, while also serving more generally to express uncertain fear. The Chorus is not consciously predicting Agamemnon's death.[7] The imagery permits wider associations, and the form of expression encourages them, building up a pervasive, general feeling of fear for the blood already spilled and for the possibility of blood to come. But within the expression of general disquiet there remain specific ominous undertones if we bear in our minds, as I think we must, the preceding carpet-scene. Probably we should say that these undertones are the poet's work rather than the Chorus', though one could perhaps say that the Chorus' collective mind has been unconsciously colored by the carpet and for this reason it finds

---

[7] The Cassandra episode indicates that the Chorus does not yet fully grasp Clytemnestra's intent or realize that death is immediately in store for Agamemnon, though they have feared he must pay for Iphigenia (150ff., 248ff.), felt foreboding also about the other deaths he has caused (461ff.), tried to warn him against subversion (795ff.). Cf. section 2 below on the choral prediction of the pattern of his end in 381ff., where also the Chorus is more than "actor."

here this particular expression of its fear in the image of dark blood on the ground.

In either case, the image of blood on the ground, reiterated and modulated like a motif in music, leads from this point on through the entire *Oresteia*.[8] In the *Choephori* it appears three times: 48, 400–2, 520–1; and in the most fully delineated of these the figure is adapted to crystallize the vengeful ethos of that play:

> It is but law that when the red drops have been spilled
> upon the ground they cry aloud for fresh
> blood.
>
> (*Cho.*, 400–2; translation by R. Lattimore)

Blood-vengeance in this play lays claim to being a "Law" set in the ultimate nature of things; here it is part of the vitalism of blood itself and is inexorable. In the *Eumenides,* however, the earlier and countering sensitivity reemerges in terms of blood on the ground. That is to say, both of the previous general applications of the image are caught up and repeated in the third play: the irremediable finality of death and blood's demand for blood. The latter is marked early in the play through the Furies' gruesome tracking of Orestes (e.g. 246–9); the former sounds near the turning point of the plot, at 647–51. This time it serves, as George Thomson has observed, "to show that the case of Orestes cannot be decided by a simple appeal to the *lex talionis.*" It sounds just once more, in 980–6, and there, as we shall be able to observe more fully later, it figures only to be withdrawn in the promise of a new mode of life. We may say, then, that the imagery of dark blood on the ground, which I believe gets its first, visual statement in the carpet of the *Agamemnon,* helps to develop within the trilogy one of its thematic ideas—namely, since blood shed is irredeemable, bloodshed is not an adequate solution; legal process and a willingness to reach understanding offer more hope. Furthermore, the care with which Aeschylus seems to have developed this verbal imagery at critical points seems indicative of how we should take the carpet-scene. At least we know that Aeschylus had the image of blood on the ground very much in his mind during the making of the trilogy, and thus it might well have colored the carpet for its prominent rôle in the critical scene of Agamemnon's home-coming.

A second indication for so regarding the carpet may be found in the episode itself. It lies in the ambiguous quality which marks Clytem-

---

[8] In addition to the instances cited in the text, observe the strikingly distorted variation of the image in *Ag.*, 1389–92 where Clytemnestra (all but?) imagines herself as mother earth receiving the rain of Agamemnon's blood. The crossing of the fecundity and the blood imagery here is a master-stroke. I treat it in section 3 below.

nestra's words at several points. Here I refer not so much to the magnificent, brazen irony with which she extols her own and Agamemnon's virtue, though that is also relevant.[9] More indicative are her
words at 866–73:

> Had Agamemnon taken all
> the wounds the tale whereof was carried home to me,
> he had been cut full of gashes like a fishing net.
> If he had died each time that rumor told his death,
> he must have been some triple-bodied Geryon
> back from the dead with threefold cloak of earth upon
> his body, and killed once for every shape assumed.
>   (translation by R. Lattimore)

Death *netted* in a *cloak,* his body *holed* at least *thrice* (and *pouring*
blood) is of course precisely the fate we find that Clytemnestra has
prepared and awaiting Agamemnon, and here with a masterful touch
Aeschylus shows us her mind. Even as she protests her loyalty and
sympathy for Agamemnon, she cannot but toy and exult in what she
has awaiting him inside the palace. Unquestionably the sharply visual
quality of Clytemnestra's mind, its imaginative range, and the sense of
relentless inner drive which emerges in this and other passages combine to form one of the great accomplishments of this play, an accom-
plishment which is at once poetic and dramatic.[10] The immediate
point for us here, however, is that it is entirely consonant for this
daring and deep-working mind to imbue the carpet with a fatal color,
even as she imbues her words. In the order of spectacle the carpet is
the potential analogue of the ambivalent images which function so
effectively in the order of language. Moreover, taken together with the
fact that fatal blood is designated as *melan* (dark) in 1020, the manner
in which Clytemnestra's lethal intent is cast verbally may be taken as
internal evidence that the blood-symbolism of the carpet was not
vested in glaring crimson. By implication the carpet poses a powerful
latent threat whose full significance only emerges in time—in the pro-
gressing course of the drama.[11]

---

[9] Cf. 855ff., 895ff.

[10] Salient steps in this portrayal are the beacon-speech, as a vividly externalized
expression of her imagination—281ff.; her description of conquered Troy, as an
expression of remarkable empathy or imaginative human insight—320ff.; her reply
to the Herald, as an expression of her self-assurance in purpose, more or less
regardless of immediate cause for excitement—587ff.

[11] The words with which the Watchman closes his, the first, speech of the play
have in part prepared us for attention to undercurrents expressed in word and
symbol: "I speak out to those who understand; for those who do not, I pass them
by" (38–9).

The third and final of the arguments from structure which I wish to apply to the color of the carpet takes us to the final scene of the trilogy. Schematically stated the argument is this: The *Eumenides* catches up many specific elements that were initiated in the *Agamemnon;*[12] it is a major function of the concluding portion of the third play to convert the forces and images of blood, blight, and destruction into forces and images of physical and moral fecundity in the life of the city;[13] a striking development at the very close is a red-robed, torch procession, the color *(phoinix)* of whose robes relates closely to the color *porphyreos* and, metaphorically, transmutes the earlier threat of serried bloodshed into a recognized and respected prophylactic symbol.

The "red" robes bear also a sign of civic good will [14] and this in company with the reversal of the earlier imagery of blood on the ground is signalled verbally by the Furies (now, Eumenides) a mere twenty or twenty-three lines before the procession is introduced. To replace dark blood in the dust, shed in internal strife, they evoke for the city shared joys and understanding:

> Let
> not the dry dust that drinks
> the black blood of citizens
> through passion for revenge
> and bloodshed for bloodshed
> be given our state to prey upon.
> Let them render grace for grace.
> Let love be their common will;
> let them hate with single heart.
> *(Eum.,* 980–6; translation by R. Lattimore)

---

[12] E.g., the ideas of learning through suffering *(Ag.,* 176–8, etc.; *Eum.,* 521), of a long-range philanthropy in Zeus' rule *(Ag.,* 160–83; *Eum.,* 850ff., etc.), of the mean *(Ag.,* 1000ff.; *Eum.,* 530), of the punishment of the sinner through overwhelming blindness *(Ag.,* 385–7, 469–70; *Eum.,* 372–80); the verbal motif of blood on the ground we have noted, the *peithô*-motif *(Ag.,* 385–9, 1049; *Eum.,* 829ff., 885); the near-relationship of Clytemnestra and the Furies *(Ag.,* 1468–1512; *Eum.,* 94ff.); the imagery of the fecundity of sin *(Ag.,* 750ff., 1565; *Eum.,* 534 and, reversed, 910–13), of trampling the altar of Justice *(Ag.,* 383–4; *Eum.,* 539–41), etc.

[13] Verbally this conversion is most obviously marked in the verbal imagery of fecundity and growth. I treat it in part in section 3 below.

[14] Robes were a local, civic element of ritual. Red robes were worn by the resident foreigners *(metoikoi)* of Athens in the Panathenaic procession. The color of these festal robes is regularly termed *phoinix,* and Aeschylus no doubt used the term to match local custom, though so far as the color is concerned he could apparently have as accurately again used *porphyreos,* since the terms overlap and neither is exact in itself.

The recurrent verbal imagery of blood on the ground does much to bridge the distance between the two terminal images of scene or props: the carpet and the robes. But there follow other indications that their relation is not fortuitous. As suggested, it is part of a general movement. The movement includes parallel rephrasings of other elements of spectacle drawn from the *Agamemnon*. Thus the final spectacle of the *Eumenides* offers us, in company with the red robes, a chanting, torch-bearing, ritual procession. The procession moves off in an aura of solemn but expansive benevolence, raising as its refrain the *ololugmos* cry of victory. In the *Agamemnon* the light bearing and ritual chant of this procession have had specific proto-types whose promise has been blasted, their effect turned to the negative. For the ending of the long destructive war torches were carried around to altars and the *ololugmos* was raised. (It is not certain if any of that celebration was represented on stage, as back-ground action during the Parodos, as at 83ff. Possibly it constituted imagined rather than seen spectacle, but our attention is called to the celebration three times; so it made its effect.) Moreover, the light in word and torch which helps close the *Eumenides* had its spectacular first blaze in the beacon of the *Agamemnon,* 22–5, 281–316. The imagery of light, with its traditional connotations of liberation and of hope, is forcefully initiated there, carried verbally through the *Choephori*,[15] and brought to its final positive turn at the close of the *Eumenides*. In the first play these elements (the beacon, the lighting of the altars with torch procession, the *ololugmos*) have expressed a joy in victory and prospect of liberation from long sorrow only to have that joy turn to fresh sorrow and to have us discover that the expression has been engineered as a masking prelude for an act of planned destructiveness. In the last play these same elements are rein-troduced to culminate the reverse movement from destructiveness to safety, from anguish to hope. The connections and development are clear, and the guidance they afford seems surely to indicate a planned connection from strikingly colored carpet to strikingly colored robes. If the carpet was, as we have been led to feel, an ominous blood color, then the "red" of the robes is its inverted restatement. It represents the conversion of the (darkly) lethal carpet into a (perhaps more brightly

[15] I.e., beside its literal function as a bearer of news, the beacon affords a brilliant example of the use of light as a more or less stock figure for liberation and renewed hope—here in respect to the long anxiety at home and the war abroad. This same value of light versus dark is applied in *Ag.*, 508, 522 and repeatedly in *Cho.*, particularly for the hope vested in Orestes (e.g., 50ff., 863–9, 961, and, probably, 131, 809–11). At the same time the presentation of the beacon through Clytemnestra affords, of course, an enfiguration of her imaginative power, while, as things turn out, her enthusiasm for the racing beacons is part of her exultation in coming revenge.

tinted) symbol of blessing. Blood has been taken up off the ground and made an element in the sacramental life of the city.[16]

To consider, as we have, just some of the facets of technique and meaning rendered active in the carpet-scene inevitably makes one more than ever aware of the intricate connections of thought and image which exist from part to part of the *Oresteia*. Aeschylus seems often to think in concrete images, and as his thought unfolds, faces obstacles, works to a resolution, so do many of the images in which it has found its expression. Thus the movement of the whole impresses us as a mass movement on several inter-relating levels. Character, situation, ideas, images are all operative and all with power, but perhaps especially the last two. And as in his striking verbal imagery, so also in his imagery of scene Aeschylus forges a telling instrument. Where we can observe it still, we can see that he made it also an element of structure, working for the whole. The carpet-scene and the close of the *Eumenides* both illustrate this; so, more obviously, does the whole spectacle Aeschylus contrives by bringing the Furies into its orchestra in the *Eumenides,* for it is a realization on stage of a daemonic movement which has been begun in the *Agamemnon* and which there brings the sinner to his justice.[17]

2. *The persuading of Agamemnon.*

If one undertakes to explain why Agamemnon ever is led to walk the fateful carpet when he knows that to do so is an act of self-incriminating presumption, one is involved by necessity in a series of levels: the characterization of the two principals within the scene; the marked preparation which has been made for our moral assessment of this "hero"; the pattern of ideas about Providence in which we have been caught up, lyrically and recurrently, in the odes prior to the home-coming scene. It is in this last, I am convinced, that the essential answer lies, namely, that the power Clytemnestra exerts over Agamemnon to lead him onto the carpet is a dramatic representation of what the Chorus has sung as the way retribution overtakes the sinner. *Peithô* (Persuasion) the agent of *Atê* (Ruin) conducts him to his doom,

---

[16] As a final minor sign of the relevance of details of the home-coming scene to details of the close, note *Eum.,* 996 on the fitting use of wealth (*ploutos*) as against the tempting of Agamemnon to insolence in wealth (*ploutos*) in *Ag.,* 948–9, 958–62. Cf. also *Ag.,* 381ff. and my section 2 which follows.

[17] There has been also of course the snake imagery of the *Choephori* (starting actually with Cassandra's words in *Ag.,* 1232–6) helping to build and carry this movement (cf. *Cho.,* 246ff., 527ff., 549, 928, 993–5, 1047–50). The verbal snake imagery transmutes of course into a stage image, an image of scene, when the snaky-locked Furies appear in the *Eumenides.*

unable longer himself to control his destiny. Consequences of his past
lie in wait in his future to reduce him perforce.

The initial, choral statement occurs in the second ode (Stasimon I),
381–9:

> There is not any armor
> in gold against perdition
> for him who spurns the high altar
> of Justice down to the darkness.
> Persuasion (*Peithō*) the persistent overwhelms him,
> she, strong daughter of designing Ruin (*Atās*).
> And every medicine is vain; the sin
> smolders not, but burns to evil beauty.[18]
>
> (translation by R. Lattimore)

The specific application of this idea within the ode is, to be sure, to
Paris (399ff.), but the idea is introduced first and in emphatic terms
as a general rule for understanding the meaning of human life (367–
73), and about the fact that Agamemnon bears the rôle of sinner and
that this part of the ode is relevant to him there can be no doubt. The
preceding ode has devoted a long section to his sacrifice of Iphigenia as an act impious, desecrating, unholy (*dyssebê . . . anagnon,
anieron*, 219–20; cf. 151). Then later in the same second ode the
notion of supernaturally imposed delusion and destruction is applied
specifically to Agamemnon. It is the fate which the Chorus fears for
him as one of the *polyktonoi:* i.e., in his responsibility for the Argive
dead in the war (459–70). This whole later passage of the ode also
serves to associate Agamemnon the more closely in our memory with
the first strophe, for it is the thought of makers of war (373–8) which
leads directly into the telling lines about the sinner succumbing to
Persuasion for his ruin.

If we consider the characterization within the home-coming scene
and the way it is handled, they can be seen to lead into the symbolic.
Thus Agamemnon reveals few signs of personal depth and no indication of inward search or struggle such as might make his action significant as an issue of character. We may, and indeed should, recognize
that Agamemnon prior to this appearance has been depicted as a
person of unsteady judgment, prone to give way to external pressures
in cases of moral issue. Such was his way in the telling case of

---

[18] *Atê* includes both the notion of an infatuating power and of ruin. She is
the power who leads men to their ruin through mental or moral blindness, but
here part of the infatuating power is vested in her "child," Persuasion (Tempta-
tion), and the ruin which results seems carried on into the medical imagery of
the last two lines.

Iphigenia (184–91, 218–23).[19] Knowing his more recent past we may further choose to regard him, with Fraenkel, as a thorough *pukka sahib* in whom "decorum" and war-weariness combine to forestall a "scene" with Clytemnestra. This is less certain, but despite Agamemnon's pomp and sense of proven prestige which helps to make him vulnerable to Clytemnestra (935–9), despite also his parading of Cassandra before his wife, the text offers no real grounds for denigrating his motives. He says all the right things. The striking fact is that even so and having correctly recognized the general moral issue posed by the carpet, he gives way on it in the particular event and lets himself be led more or less blindly by Clytemnestra. As a person, it is not wrong motives which Agamemnon exhibits but lack of insight and an abeyance of will.

Two things, then, are manifest in the treatment of Agamemnon on the occasion of his home-coming. First, he is depicted in broad outline, without personal depth, so that we are invited to concern ourselves with what he stands for, with the load of responsibility which he bears with him, more than with what he himself now is. Secondly, while there are some indications that he is self-infatuated, the dramatic emphasis is not cast upon these. Instead their respective speeches work to set a telling breach between his perception and Clytemnestra's intent, and the action then works to show Agamemnon subdued. More than agent he becomes a patient. Infatuation works on him forcibly and from the outside in: i.e., from Clytemnestra who is so much verbally and emotionally his superior that she can direct his mind.

In contrast to the characterization of Agamemnon, Clytemnestra's striking audacity and the driving power of her personality are all the more marked. She is in herself an imaginative creation of the highest order, but, again, her depiction serves a telling dramatic economy in which there are two major strands. As person, Clytemnestra is the more fully worked than Agamemnon because through her we are being intimately involved in a fresh burgeoning of evil and moved forward in the plot of successive acts of violence. Agamemnon's determinative acts have been in the past. Wronged (indirectly) by Paris, he has put himself in the wrong (directly) with the sacrifice of Iphigenia. Thereby he propagated a chain reaction of violence in his own house which, as the immediate subject of the drama, we are to follow to its end in the *Eumenides*. Hence the title of the play. The governing issue is sin and retribution. Agamemnon now pays for *past*

[19] Agamemnon, of course, carries with him from the *Iliad* a record of unsteady judgment even in the field of war: most markedly in his nearly catastrophic misappraisal of the morale of his own troops in *Il.* II.

hybris, exactly as Paris and Troy have paid for theirs. His wife in taking vengeance for Iphigenia breeds fresh human hybris, out of deep-set emotions and strength of will and abundant power of imagination to implement her hate, but the forces at work are not only personal ones. Such it seems to me is a second clear implication of the kind of supremacy which Clytemnestra takes over the "hero." As she wins control over Agamemnon and moves him onto the fatal carpet she is, incarnate, "terrible *Peithō,* the irresistible child (i.e., agent) of Ruin."

Rhetoric is persuasion's means, and in this scene Clytemnestra's rhetoric is of the boldest sort, successful even in voicing patent untruths. When Agamemnon hesitates, she plays on his pride (935–9) and leads him easily, almost passively, into the final symbolic act of treading the carpet. The infatuation works from without in, taking him by force (*biatai*). Moreover her persuasive power over Agamemnon is underscored by the contrast of the scene which follows. There Clytemnestra's *peithô* fails completely on Cassandra and that failure is marked out for our attention by recurrences of the word (1049—three times; 1052). Cassandra is a guiltless sufferer and toward her Clytemnestra is no longer an *agency* of retribution; she is simply vengeful.[20]

The daemonic agency within Clytemnestra should not be emphasized to the exclusion of her character, for through the latter, as her motivation is revealed, we are led to glimpses of a personal tragedy largely withheld from Agamemnon, and in the trilogy the full daemonization of Clytemnestra is a gradual process. In the scene of Agamemnon's home-coming the daemonic is interior to her, and only by stages of representation as well as of act does she reach the form of daemonghost driving on the Furies to vengeance.[21] In the *Agamemnon,* one is led to feel, the eloquent driving power of her hate rises from deep within her, while with it she is the agent of "Zeus." Or, more accurately, she is an agent both of Zeus and of darker powers. Later we are to see these distinguished before they are brought once more together.

For Aeschylus fully to have internalized the treatment of Agamemnon or made Clytemnestra more exclusively human might have made for more interesting character study in some respects, but it would almost certainly have meant a great alteration in the scope and quality

[20] If we look again at the *Eum.*, it should now be apparent that the stress there on saving *peithô,* as an instrument of reasonable agreement, has as one of its functions the replacement or conversion of the direful *peithô* of the *Ag.* Cf. *Eum.*, 794ff., 824ff., 881ff., 968ff. There, too, *Peithô* is personified (885 and 970; cf. *Ag.*, 385) and she is in the stage-form of Athena again rendered incarnate.

[21] E.g., *Ag.*, 151–5, 1228–38, 1385–92, 1432–3, 1468–1536. In *Cho.* the running serpent imagery applied to her includes, besides obvious implications of inhumanity, chthonic associations and a link with the Gorgon magic. All the implications come together in 1046–50.

of the world he has envisioned for us in the *Oresteia*. In this world
there is notable interplay between outer forces and inner conditions.
Action and thought take place in a continuum extending from the inwardly human to the far-ranging cosmic, and the sense of the interplay
is carried out in many ways besides the kind of action we have been
observing. It penetrates indeed even into mannerisms of the verbal
imagery where exterior and personal juxtapositions of the same image
are a noticeable trait. (Thus in *Agamemnon,* 182ff., the god's piloting
of life's voyage shifts into the storm-born veering of Agamemnon's
mind [187, 219]. Pastoral imagery used to describe a storm at sea [654ff.]
crosses over as a figure for worried thought [669]. Conversely the singing of the Furies as an expression of inward fear [991–4] becomes externalized in Cassandra's vision [1188–90], while inward whirlpools of
anxiety [995–8] transmute into a generalized appraisal of the sea of life
[1005ff.]. Examples could be multiplied. Here because of its particular
relevance to the way Agamemnon is led to act upon his home-coming, I
would only point again to the way in which, in the *Eumenides,* the
darkness of the Furies and their habitation, externalized in costume
and often commented on, takes its internal form in the darkening of
the sinner's mind [*Eum.,* 377–80]. There, too, it overwhelms the sinner
from without.) In the *Oresteia* the resolution of individual problems
and the achievement of personal and civic justice depend on a humility
before cosmic forces which are not remote from life. It is in terms of
them that the good life must be gradually worked out. Not only in its
broad lines of movement but in its detail the tragedy is built to keep
that fact always before us.

3. *Extensive relevance in the Nurse-scene of the* Choephori

The vividly natural portrayal of the old Nurse and the kind of immediate human complication which she introduces in her few moments on
the stage are so striking that they seem to carry us into a very different
dramatic world from that with which we have been concerned. Obviously here again as in the home-coming scene of the *Agamemnon* we
have a striking piece of stagecraft marking a turning point of the plot;
yet, the texture of the episode is radically different, and it may be that
the kind of emphasis which is gained through the sudden injection of
this thoroughly "down to earth" character is inordinately disruptive of
the general movement and tone previously established. If so, I feel, the
impression comes largely from an incomplete view of the episode, for
here once more the dramatic economy is woven of several strands, and
the part of the homely, affectionate Nurse is closely bound into issues
of sustained import and tension for the trilogy.

With her close memories of Orestes' babyhood, the Nurse poses against Clytemnestra's claims of motherhood other claims of a more typical and acceptable kind. In this respect she is a vehicle, a sharply delineated, particularized symbol, of general human traits. Her appearance and her intimate memories serve to withdraw from Clytemnestra more or less forcibly much of her status as mother, and they do so in the moments just prior to Orestes' act of matricide; but, as it turns out, the elemental fact of Clytemnestra's maternity is not so simply dissolved, and Aeschylus means us to be aware of that also in the longer run. There are elements of a radical conflict here which has yet to be worked out.

Since attention to this episode has largely concentrated on the "Shakespearian" realism with which we are here met for almost the first time in the history of Greek tragedy, it will, I think, not be amiss to focus our attention exclusively upon this other side which I have just outlined. In so doing we shall not need to consider so much the local details of the episode, but the context within which the Nurse has her rôle—particularly, the issue of the relation of mother and child. When we have done so, we should see that the Nurse-scene, if a *tour de force,* yet has intimate bearing for the whole and, even, that the forced disruption of dramatic tone which it exhibits is representative of a clash of attitudes, at this point held still in conflict but finally to be resolved.

One scarcely need resurvey the trilogy to get the sense that the deeply irrational ties in the relation of mother and child concern Aeschylus deeply, and in the choice of this story he has faced almost inevitably into the problem of the natural horror which matricide invokes. When first we meet Clytemnestra in the *Agamemnon,* long before the germ of her hate is shown explicitly, the inward nature and seed of her purpose is suggested by the reiteration of the womb image, applied to the dawn, in her first ten lines (265, 279). After the murder of her husband we get that driving motive fully exhibited: it is the loss of the fruit of her womb, Iphigenia (1415–20), and Aeschylus does not, as do Sophocles and Euripides, undermine the force of this motive by emphasis upon her possible lust for Aegisthus. Because Agamemnon has destroyed her child, Clytemnestra's fertility is now in lethal bloodshed; nor is this terrible wrenching of love into hate allowed to be written off by any simple moralism. Indeed it is depicted with fascinating insight and impressive vividness as Clytemnestra is made to stand before us and tell us how she felt as she stood over Agamemnon:

> Thus he went down, and the life struggled out of him;
> and as he died he spattered me with the dark red

and violent driven rain of bitter savored blood
to make me glad, as gardens stand among the showers
of God in glory at the birthtime of the buds.
            (*Ag.*, 1388–92; translation by R. Lattimore)

In this exultation and distortion of all that is life-giving, all the previous imagery of blood and of the womb, of fertility and of death, converge. From here on Clytemnestra's fecundity is only in hatefulness. Instead of fresh love for her other children to replace that lost with Iphigenia, that feeling has been replaced in the *Choephori* with indifference and dislike. More and more she is rendered as an "unnatural" mother. To her children she seems a snake or monster (248–9, 991–6); her proper rôle as nurturer and supporter is taken by mother earth (42–6, 66, 127–8); in and through the Nurse we have impressed upon us that Orestes has none of the conventional debts of affection to pay Clytemnestra even for his earliest years. Yet the attention given to the mother-son disrelation keeps their primal relationship before us. If Orestes is child of the eagle (246ff.), he is also child of the snake and it is out of her womb that he comes like a snake to kill her (549, 991–6). Aeschylus has chosen not to cut the relationship simply and all at once. Orestes' scruples remain before the murder (899), and, after the murder, I suspect Conington and Verrall are right in seeing him driven by horror into a partial inward break-up as he surveys the corpse and the "net" (991–1006). In any case there come next the outward form of horror, the Furies, to keep the primal, subrational claim of Clytemnestra upon Orestes' life and conscience sharply before our attention.

We may recognize, then, that Aeschylus has taken on the task of working in and through two not easily reconciled aspects of the mother-son relationship. He must bring it to a point where Orestes can be seen to kill his mother in some measure of good conscience and with some hope of being pardoned before a rational tribunal. The introduction of the Nurse to under-cut many of the mother's possible claims shortly prior to her murder works to this end, while the common-sense human normalcy the Nurse injects into the issue moves us on toward important developments in the *Eumenides*—particularly, the (partial) resolution of the chain of murders through the instrumentality of rational process and law. But alongside this movement toward the rational, Aeschylus, as we have noted, sustains a deeper, darker insight. He has us see the horror of matricide and feel with him the more elemental, irrational forces that link life to life. And so again in the final play of the trilogy, through the ghost of Clytemnestra and the Furies he represents that aspect with strik-

ing imaginative life, even as he undertakes to project, through the
formal trial, a rational resolution on grounds which deny to the mother
any significant bond with her child.

Almost inevitably the trial, though presented as a decisive process in
which divine and human wisdom agree, forms of itself an unsatisfying
resolution. Aeschylus makes clear, I think, that he himself so regards
it—or, that the argument from paternity is, because of all in which
we have been involved, rationalistic rather than fully rational: it is
not adequate for our conscious understanding. Despite the previous
divestment of Clytemnestra from normal civilized claims to filial
affection, through her and through the insistent imagery of fecundity
we have been too closely involved in contrary, subrational realities to
have them denied by the assertion that the mother is only a resting
place for male seed. Aeschylus' realization of this is clear from his staging of a more deep-reaching resolution in lyric and symbolic terms after the trial. However much he guides our thought to a conception of
a world directed with rational purpose and to a conception of society
founded on law, Aeschylus has vision enough not to deny the irrational
and its power. Instead of rejecting it, he encompasses it. Thus in the
concluding movement of the *Eumenides* it is made clear that the Furies are, as Clytemnestra too has been, agents both of fecundity and
destruction. When the verdict of the trial goes against them, this becomes a paramount issue. They will bring blight and fruitlessness to
the land of Attica, to her people and to their institutions—e.g., 784ff.,
801–2, 810ff., 830–1. It is a major part of Athena's task in this final
part of the play to convert, by persuasion, this fateful blighting power
into a productive fructifying power working for the good of Athens.
The resolution is signalled when she says, "Grant us the *fruit* of pious
men for our land, for I as one who *tends a garden* delight in this, the
growth of justly minded men; it brings no sorrow" (*Eum.*, 910–12). In
their reply the Furies accept the rôle of fecundative patrons (921–9),
and it is clear now, I hope, that the winning over of the Furies into
patronage of fecundity and the good life for Athens is a reverse
analogue and resolution to the course we have seen Clytemnestra
move in (and before) the *Agamemnon*. In lyric and symbolic terms
we are brought finally to where good-will grows in place of hate, a
hope of fecundity flourishes where there has been only one crime giving birth to another.[22] In place of violent inner drives within the
person (most notably in Clytemnestra) and within the family, setting it

---

[22] The story of self-perpetuating violence within the family has been paralleled
verbally with imagery of generative evil and violence: e.g., *Ag.*, 151–5, 750–71,
1388–92, 1565–6; *Cho.*, 66–7, (382–5), 466, (585 ff.), 806, 837; *Eum.*, 534. It is part
also of the final process to reverse this specific threat: supplant it with the generation of pious men.

at odds, pious men are now to bear justly minded offspring under the harmonious sovereignty of mysterious Moira and a rationally purposive Zeus.

The Nurse-scene of the *Choephori* occupies only an intermediate position in this large, slow movement of conflicting forces. Concretely and emphatically, as is necessary for the impending murders which the Nurse's testimony helps to engineer, it projects a whole range of normal human experience according to which Clytemnestra is not a mother and has no rational claims on Orestes. But this point of view is not complete and the emphasis the "realistic" characterization of the Nurse provides is part of a larger dramatic struggle. In another less rational but no less real way Clytemnestra is mother and is thereby representative of fundamental inner drives and demands. Aeschylus, for his own times, sees that these subliminal aspects of life must be met and dealt with, and not by a process of violent cautery; instead by a process of psychic integration: a process such as his own art entails.

Prometheia

by George Thomson

Prometheus, it was once said, is the patron saint of the proletariat. It was Prometheus who bestowed on man the gift of fire, which he had brought down from the sun stored in a fennel stalk. That is the primitive nucleus of the myth, which can be traced in this or similar forms all over the world. It is a genuine folk-memory of the earliest and one of the most revolutionary steps in the advancement of material technique. Its significance in this respect has been well described by Gordon Childe.

> In the comparatively short evolutionary history documented by fossil remains, man has not improved his inherited equipment by bodily changes detectable in his skeleton. Yet he has been able to adjust himself to a greater range of environments than almost any other creature, to multiply infinitely faster than any other near relative among the higher mammals, and to beat the polar bear, the hare, the hawk, and the tiger at their special tricks. Through his control of fire and the skill to make clothes and houses, man can, and does, live and thrive from the Arctic Circle to the Equator. In the trains and cars he builds, man can outstrip the fleetest hare or ostrich. In aeroplanes he can mount higher than the eagle, and with telescopes see farther than the hawk. With firearms he can lay low animals that a tiger dare not tackle. But fire, clothes, houses, trains, aeroplanes, telescopes, and guns are not, we must repeat, part of man's body. He can leave them and lay them aside at will. They are not inherited in the biological sense, but the skill needed for their production and use is part of our social heritage, the result of a tradition accumulated over many generations, and transmitted, not in the blood, but through speech and writing.

In the myth of Prometheus, the first of these technical advances became a symbol for the rest. Fire stands for the material basis of civilisation. That is the one constant element in the myth. The others vary, because this myth has a history of its own, being continuously reinterpreted and adapted to new developments in the process of which it is a symbol. The higher stages of that process were condi-

tional on the division of society into economically unequal classes—
into those that performed the actual labour of production and those
that enjoyed the wealth and leisure thus produced. This division
created, among the rulers, the need to justify their privileged position,
and, among the ruled, a sense of frustration springing from the
perception that their own wealth and leisure had not kept pace with
the increasing productivity of their work. The primitive form of the
myth, which simply registered the pride of the community in the
success of its collective struggle against its material environment, was
no longer adequate, because out of the struggle between man and
Nature had now emerged the struggle between man and man. Accordingly, it was complicated and elaborated.

The peasants of Hesiod were hungry and oppressed. Why were they
condemned to toil so hard and enjoy so little? Because man had
sinned against his masters. Once the human race had lived in happiness
without sickness or labour or the need to win their bread in the
sweat of their brows. That was the Reign of Kronos, when the un-
tilled earth had brought forth of itself abundance of good things,
which all men enjoyed in common; and in those days, of course, they
had possessed the gift of fire. This happy state of things was brought
to an end through the culpability of Prometheus, who, at a banquet
of the gods, tried to cheat Zeus of the special portion which was his
due. In punishment for this offence Zeus deprived man of fire.
Prometheus replied by stealing it from heaven and restoring it to
man. Zeus then impaled him on a rock, where he was tormented by an
eagle, which visited him daily to devour his liver, until he was released
by Herakles. Meanwhile, the human race remained in possession of
the gift of fire, but to it was added another gift—Pandora and her box,
which, when the lid was removed, let loose over the world labour,
sorrow, sickness, and a multitude of plagues. And so, Hesiod tells his
listeners, had it not been for Prometheus, who provoked the gods
into withholding from men their means of living, "you would have
been able to do easily in a day enough work to keep you for a year,
to hang up your rudder in the chimney corner, and let your fields
run to waste."

Thus, for the peasants of Hesiod, Prometheus, the pioneer in man's
conquest of nature, has been degraded to the level of a common male-
factor. Material progress has been complicated by the class struggle in
such a way that for them, instead of enlarging, it has diminished the
sum of human happiness. Such was the form which the myth had
assumed under the aristocracy. But that form was not final any more
than the aristocracy itself.

The story of Prometheus is not mentioned in the Homeric poems,
nor, so far as we know, was it treated in choral lyric. It was not the

sort of story to appeal to members of the aristocracy. In our records, its next exponent after Hesiod is Aeschylus himself; but, while his version was doubtless to a large extent his own creation, it contains certain structural features which clearly have their roots in the mystical teaching of the Orphics. At the beginning of the trilogy, Prometheus describes himself as banished from the company of the gods and as about to endure an agony that will last thousands of years; throughout the first play his torments are described with reference to the idea of Ananke or Necessity; at the end of it he is hurled down into Hades, whence, at the opening of the second, he has been brought up again to earth; and, finally, after his penance has lasted for a total period of 30,000 years, he is readmitted to Olympus. This is the Orphic Wheel of Necessity—the cycle that leads the soul from Divinity to birth and death and thence back to divinity. In the words of Empedokles:

> There is an oracle of Necessity, an ordinance of the gods, ancient, eternal, and sealed by broad oaths, that whenever one of the *daimones*, whose portion is length of days, has sinfully stained his hands with blood or followed strife or forsworn himself, he shall be banished from the abodes of the blessed for thrice ten thousand seasons, being born throughout the time in all manner of mortal shapes, exchanging one toilsome path for another. . . . One of these am I now, an exile and a wanderer from the gods, because I put my trust in insensate strife.
>
> Alas, unhappy race of men, bitterly unblest, such are the groans and struggles from which ye have been born!
>
> But at the last they appear among mankind as prophets, poets, physicians, and princes; and thence they arise as gods, exalted in honour, sharing with the other gods a common hearth and table, free from the miseries of mortality, without part therein, untroubled.

Set against this background, the sufferings of the Aeschylean Prometheus appear as the sufferings of man himself, cast down from heaven into misery and death but destined to rise again.

The cults of Prometheus were few and insignificant. At Athens, he was worshipped in the Academy together with Athena and Hephaistos, who were also closely associated with the handicrafts that man had learnt from his control of fire. All three were honoured with torch races, run by the *épheboi* from some point outside the city to one of the altars within it with the object of renewing the sacred fire. In origin, these races were probably ordeals of initiation, like the foot-races at Olympia.

Prometheus was delivered by Herakles, a figure far more prominent both in myth and cult, and far too complex to be discussed in detail here. He was a son of Zeus by Alkmene, a descendant of Io, and he was sent into the world to clear it of primeval monsters for the benefit of man. The last of his labours was a descent into Hades, for which he prepared himself by initiation at Eleusis, and after it he ascended into heaven and received in marriage Hera's daughter, Hebe. Here, too, we can discern traces of the mystical sequence of strife, death, and deification.

Turning to the *Prometheus Bound*, the first question that we ask ourselves is, where does the poet intend our sympathies to lie as between the two antagonists? It is a vital question, because the answer to it necessarily reveals so much both in the poet and his critics. If modern readers of the play have given sharply divergent answers to this question, it is not, as we shall see, because there is any ambiguity in the play itself, but because, on an issue so crucial as that of rebellion against the established order, they have been forced to disclose their own attitude to contemporary society. Thus, Mahaffy expressed himself as follows:

> Despotic sovereignty was the Greek's ideal for himself, and most nations have thought it not only reconcilable with, but conformable to, the dignity of the great Father who rules the world. No Athenian, however he sympathised with Prometheus, would think of blaming him for asserting his power and crushing all resistance to his will.

What Mahaffy has done is to shut his eyes to the democratic tradition and to present as the Greek's ideal for himself Mahaffy's ideal for himself—the ideal of the Anglo-Irish aristocracy, as formulated by another member of the same class, Edmund Burke:

> Good order is the foundation of all good things. To be enabled to acquire, the people, without being servile, must be tractable and obedient. The magistrate must have his reverence, the laws their authority. The body of the people must not find the principles of natural subordination by art rooted out of their minds. They must respect that property of which they cannot partake. They must labour to obtain what by labour can be obtained; and, when they find, as they commonly do, the success disproportioned to the endeavour, they must be taught their consolation in the final proportions of eternal justice.

I still remember my dismay, when, after reading the play for the first time at school, I was asked to accept Mahaffy's view, and the comfort I derived from Shelley's reassuring words: "But in truth I was averse from a catastrophe so feeble as that of reconciling the Champion with the Oppressor of mankind." Later we shall examine Shelley's treatment of the myth, and see where and why it differed from the Aeschylean; but, so far as the first play of the trilogy is concerned, Shelley's intuition was sound—there Zeus *is* the "oppressor of mankind" and their champion's "perfidious adversary." And the reason why Shelley came nearer to the truth than classical scholars, who have studied the evidence far more closely than he did, is that Shelley was, like Aeschylus himself, what they never were—a revolutionary poet.

Zeus is a tyrant and his rule is a tyranny. We learn this from his own ministers, who are proud of it (10); from Prometheus, who denounces it (238, 321, 373, 762, 782, 941, 974, 988–90, 1028);* from the Ocean Nymphs, who deplore it (201); and from the God of Ocean, who is resigned to it (326). The fact is incontestable, and the only question is how the dramatist intended his audience to interpret it.

In the history of the tyranny at Athens, we can see how the progressive character of its opening phase became obscured in retrospect by the reactionary tendencies which it subsequently developed. We can also see that, when the Athenians had to face a Persian landing at Marathon, the exiled Hippias was on the Persian side; and, even after the Persian menace had been removed, Athenian democrats found it necessary to remain constantly on their guard against the danger that some influential aristocrat, a Miltiades or an Alkibiades, might make a bid for the position which Hippias had lost. The result was that, in the fifth century at Athens, there grew up a traditional conception of the tyrant, endowed with all the qualities which the people had experienced in Hippias, and eventually, owing partly to similar experiences elsewhere and partly to the dominant influence exercised by Attic writers in the development of thought, this tradition became fixed. Thus, Herodotus describes the tyrant as irresponsible, with a dangerous tendency towards pride, suspicions of his best citizens, and, above all, violent, a ravisher of women. Similar arguments are repeated by Theseus in his dispute with the herald from Argos in the *Suppliants* of Euripides. The tyrant is a law to himself; he cuts off his leading citizens as he might the tallest ears of corn (in accordance with the advice which, so Herodotus tells us, was actually given by one tyrant to another); and, lastly, parents cannot safeguard their daughters from his violence.

The tragedians were naturally quick to turn this tradition to dramatic advantage. In the *Antigone,* for example, the heroine bitterly declares that one of the privileges of the tyranny is to do and say what it likes; and in the *Persians* Atossa raises her defeated son above the reach of popular reproach with the significant reminder that he is not responsible to his people. In the *Oedipus Tyrannus,* as Sheppard has shown, the character of the king is thrown into ominous relief by a number of such allusions, which, though for the most part implicit, were readily appreciated by an audience made familiar with such technique by Aeschylus.

* [Thomson's line numeration follows that of Wecklein's edition; the numeration in all other essays of this collection is the same as that of the Oxford Classical Text—ED.]

The ministers whom Zeus has appointed to escort Prometheus to his place of confinement are Might and Violence, the one signifying his power, the other the method by which he exercises it. He is described as harsh (202, 340), as irresponsible (340), as unconstitutional, acknowledging no laws but his own, a law to himself (159, 419, 202–3); he is suspicious of his friends—a feature described expressly as characteristic of the tyrant (240–1); implacable and impervious to persuasion (34, 199–201, 349); and, above all, in his treatment of Io, he reveals his violence (761–3). The brutality of this episode is not, as in the *Suppliants,* veiled in lyric poetry; on the contrary, the poet seems to be at pains to fill his audience, like his own Oceanids, with abhorrence. Zeus tried first persuasion and then threats to bend the unhappy girl to his will. This is the method Prometheus expected of him, and it is typical of the tyrant. Hence there can be no question where the sympathies of an Athenian audience must have lain—or, indeed, of any popular audience—when Prometheus breaks off his prediction of Io's future agonies with the impassioned cry (761):

> You see how he behaves
> To all the same, inhuman, brutal tyrant.

In view of this evidence, it is fairly clear that those critics who can pass judgment against the hero who has dared to rebel against this heartless despotism have been influenced by factors independent of the dramatist's intention.

The characterisation of Prometheus is more complex. In the opening scene, the sinister figure of Violence eyes the prisoner in silence. Might assails him with insults as he spurs Hephaistos to the task of binding him, but does not address him directly till he flings at him his parting taunt (82–7). Hephaistos alone is filled with compassion. He recognises his crime, by which indeed, as god of fire, he has been particularly affected; yet he forgets his own loss in sympathy for the sufferer. Prometheus is silent.

The compassion of Hephaistos is that of kin for kin (14, 39). The same feeling prompts the visit of the Ocean Nymphs (130–1) and is professed by their father Ocean (305–6), who counsels moderation, but with an underlying subservience to authority that marks him as a type of the trimmer or conformer; and Prometheus dismisses him with politely veiled contempt. The Ocean Nymphs have said nothing in the presence of their father, but after his departure they are forced to confess that with them, too, sympathy is tempered with disapproval. So far the indignation of Prometheus has been controlled; but during his discourse with Io we feel the anger rising in him, and, when his enemy's victim is carried away in a sudden agony of pain, the reaction is immediate. The Nymphs, horrified and terrified, bow down in helpless submission. Prometheus, on the other hand, hurls at his antagonist a speech of reckless denunciation and defiance. Yet he does not forfeit our sympathy, because this change of attitude corresponds to our own reaction to the brutality of Zeus manifested in the spectacle of Io. The Nymphs remonstrate, but he is deaf to their appeals. Hermes arrives with a peremptory demand that he shall reveal the secret with which he threatens his master's supremacy; yet even Hermes, when he perceives the prisoner's state of mind, joins with the Nymphs in a sincere attempt to reason with him. But Prometheus, who received the insults of Might in silence, himself assails Hermes with insults; and in dramatic fulfilment of his own prayer (161–8, 1083–6) he is cast into the pit of Tartarus. The ambivalent effect of the last scene on the audience is faithfully reflected in the attitude of the Chorus, who, while disapproving as strongly as Hermes of the prisoner's lack of restraint, nevertheless refuse to desert him.

Thus, the play ends in a deadlock. The ruler of the gods is a tyrant, the champion of mankind has been reproved by his own friends for exceeding the bounds of moderation. The wrath of Zeus is a disease, and the unrestraint of Prometheus is a disease. This metaphor, which is of course intended to suggest the hope of a cure to come, recurs again and again throughout the play. The world is out of joint, and only a change in both antagonists can set it right.

While insisting on the tyrannical nature of the rule of Zeus, Aeschylus is careful to impress on us at the outset, and to remind us repeatedly, that his power is new. He is displaying the world not as it is now but as it was in the beginning. In the course of 30,000 years, taught by experience, the adversaries will be reconciled. So we are told, early in the play, by Prometheus himself, whose vision is as yet unclouded by passion (206–8). Later, forgetting his own prophecy, he can foresee nothing in store for his enemy but destruction (939–59); but the truth re-emerges in his final altercation with Hermes (1011–14). Reminded of his lost bliss, Prometheus inadvertently utters a cry of grief—"Ah me!"—of which Hermes is quick to take advantage:

> "Ah me!"—that is a cry unknown to Zeus.

At the mention of his enemy, Prometheus recovers himself:

> Time, as he grows old, will teach everything.

But again Hermes is ready with his retort:

> Yes, *you* have yet to learn where wisdom lies.

With this allusion to the doctrine of wisdom through suffering, the scattered hints of an impending change in both antagonists are significantly brought together at the end of the play.

It is clear, therefore, that in the sequel both antagonists will learn by experience; but of course that is very far from saying that Prometheus ought not to have done what he has done. It is true that, when they hear of his theft of fire, the Oceanids exclaim, shocked by his audacity, that he has sinned; but, if so, it is a sin which has saved humanity for annihilation, and, if any further doubt remain as to the dramatist's attitude on this point, it is dispelled by the hero's narration of the consequences of his sin for the destiny of man (458–522):

> Now listen to the sufferings of mankind,
> In whom, once speechless, senseless, like an infant,
> I have implanted the faculty of reason . . .
> At first, with eyes to see, they saw in vain,
> With ears to hear, heard nothing, groping through
> Their lives in a dreamlike stupor, with no skill
> In carpentry or brickmaking, like ants
> Burrowing in holes, unpractised in the signs
> Of blossom, fruit, and frost, from hand to mouth
> Struggling improvidently, until I
> Chartered the intricate orbits of the stars;
> Invented number, that most exquisite
> Instrument, and the alphabet, the tool
> Of history and chronicle of their progress;
> Tamed the wild beasts to toil in pack and harness
> And yoked the prancing mounts of opulence,
> Obedient to the rein, in chariots;
> Constructed wheelless vehicles with linen
> Wings to carry them over the trackless ocean . . .
> And yet more matter is there to admire
> In the resource of my imagination,
> And this above all. When sickness struck them down,
> Having no herbal therapy to dispense
> In salves and potions, their strength neglected ran
> To waste in moping ignorance, till I
> Compounded for them gentle medicines
> To arm them in the war against disease . . .
> And last, who else can boast to have unlocked
> The earth's rich subterranean treasure-houses
> Of iron, copper, bronze, silver, and gold?
> That is my record. You have it in a word:
> Prometheus founded all the arts of man.

All this, as the details of the passage show, belongs to the tradition of the Pythagoreans—the same tradition which can be illustrated from

Hippokrates' account of the origin of medicine; and the striking thing about it is its bold materialism. This combination of materialism with mysticism, noticeable elsewhere in the work of Aeschylus, was evidently characteristic of the early Pythagoreans. We find it again in Empedokles, whose preoccupation with the revival of magical practices and beliefs did not prevent him from making solid contributions to science. How the Pythagoreans reconciled these two sides to their teaching, we do not know; but it seems clear that, while the first was derived from the Orphic movement, of which their own was an offshoot, they owed the second to their political activity in the initial stage of the democratic revolution; and from them it was transmitted through Hippokrates and the sophists to Demokritos and Epicurus.

The mystical form in which Aeschylus has clothed this tradition does not disguise its essential significance—on the contrary, the myth itself has been reinterpreted so as to throw into relief the underlying doctrine that progress is the outcome of conflict. If Prometheus has erred, it is because *es irrt der Mensch solang' er strebt*. The champions of a new order offend inevitably against the old. If Prometheus has to suffer, it is because man himself has suffered in the course of his advancement. Without suffering he would have lacked the stimulus to invention. The truth which both Aeschylus and Hippokrates, in different ways, were seeking to express was one that had been grasped in practice by primitive man from the earliest stages of his history and was eventually formulated by Epicurus in the words:

> Human nature was taught much by the sheer force of circumstances, and these lessons were taken over by human reason, refined and supplemented.

The view of human progress expressed by Aeschylus is therefore not far removed from the position of modern dialectical materialism:

> Until we acquire knowledge of the laws of nature, which exist and act independently of our mind, we are slaves of "blind necessity." When we acquire knowledge of them, we acquire mastery of nature.

Intelligence, the gift of Prometheus, had made man free, because it had enabled him to comprehend, and so to control, the laws of nature. Freedom consists in the understanding or necessity.

The *Prometheus* contains very little action; yet it is intensely dramatic. Technically, it is the most accomplished of the extant plays, and shows that by the end of his life Aeschylus had become an absolute master of his craft. It is therefore worth examining in some detail from this point of view.

The play contains three marked pauses. The first is at the end of the *párodos* (208) after Prometheus' first prediction of the future, which carries us, without revealing the intermediate steps, to the ultimate reconciliation, and at the same time lets fall the first allusion to his secret. The second comes at the end of the second episode (541), where he declines to reveal this secret, which, we are now told, is to be the means of his deliverance. And the third comes at the end of the next episode (912), after he has predicted the actual coming of his deliverer. These pauses divide the play into four movements. In the first, Prometheus is nailed to the rock; in the second he relates the past history of gods and men; in the third he predicts the future; in the fourth he is cast into Tartarus.

Each of these movements has an internal structure of its own. Each falls into three parts, except the third, which falls into two such sets of three. Further, in each set of three, there is an organic relation between the first and third parts, the second being in the nature of a digression or development. Thus, in the first movement, Prometheus is punished by his enemies; he delivers his soliloquy; and he is visited by his friends, the Ocean Nymphs. In the second, he relates the story of the war among the gods and his own services to Zeus; he is interrupted by the visit of the God of Ocean; and he proceeds to relate his services to man. In the first part of the third movement, Io appears and entreats him to reveal her future; at the request of the Oceanids she tells the story of her past; and then, after predicting her wanderings as far as the borders of Asia, Prometheus hints at the fall of Zeus and his own deliverance. In the second part, he continues his prophecy as far as her destination in Egypt; then, in proof of his veracity, he reverts to her past (thus completing her own account); and, finally, he predicts her ultimate fate and the coming of his deliverer. In the fourth movement, he alludes once again, more openly, to his secret, which, he now declares, will effect his enemy's downfall; the emissary of Zeus seeks in vain to extort his secret from him; and Prometheus is cast into Tartarus.

Now turn to the choral odes, which are integral links in this development. In the *párodos,* the Oceanids offer the sympathy of the gods (169–70): Prometheus goes on to relate his services to the gods. In the first *stásimon* (413–51) they sing of the compassion of mankind: Prometheus relates his services to humanity. In the second *stásimon* (542–80) they sing of the helplessness of man and contrast his present state with the happiness of his wedding day: Io appears, helpless mortal persecuted by a brutal suitor (765–6). The theme of the third *stásimon* (913–38) is wisdom; and this prepares us for the final scene, in which they join with Hermes in an appeal to the sufferer to follow the course of wisdom.

Thus, the subject of the first movement is the binding of Prometheus—the present; of the second, the history of the past; of the

third, the destiny of Io and the birth of Herakles—the future; and
the fourth movement, with its increase of the penalty, balances the
first. Yet, throughout the play, these threads of present, past, and
future are interwoven with such skill that at each turning-point our
attention is thrown with increasing emphasis on the future. The opening speech of Might ends with a declaration that Prometheus must be
taught by suffering to accept the tyranny of Zeus (10–11) while the
speech of Hephaistos which follows ends with a suggestion that the
tyrant himself, in course of time, will change his ways (35); and both
these themes will be developed in the *párodos* (180–201). In the middle
of his task Hephaistos utters the impassioned cry, "Alas, Prometheus!
it is for you I weep" (66). The retort of Might comes at the close
of the scene, where our attention is redirected to the future (85–7):

> We called you God of Foresight. It's a lie.
> Now you need all your foresight for yourself
> To shuffle off *this* masterly work of art.

And again this parting insult will be answered at the end of the first
movement, where we are permitted a glimpse of the final reconciliation, welcomed by both antagonists (202–8).

We are brought back abruptly to the past (209). At the request of
the Nymphs, who entreat him to "reveal all things," Prometheus
reluctantly begins his exposition. Later, shocked by his audacity, the
Nymphs are anxious to change the subject (277–8); but now it is
Prometheus who insists on continuing, urging them to listen to his
revelation of the future (288–9). Then comes the interlude—the visit
of the God of Ocean. After his departure the exposition is resumed,
leading to the end of the second movement, where, eagerly questioned
about the secret to which he alluded at the end of the first, Prometheus
draws back, refusing to disclose it (538–41):

> No, think of other things. The time to speak
> Of that is still far distant. It must be hidden.
> That is my secret, which if closely kept
> Contains my sure hope of deliverance.

To resume, we have seen that the opening speeches of the play
ended by directing our attention to the future, thus anticipating the
close of the binding scene and the climax at the end of the first
movement, the last speech of the *párodos*. The second movement began by taking us back into the past; but at the end of the first of its
three parts and still more intently at the end of the third we looked
once again to the future. Then comes the Io scene, so divided as to
throw the future into still greater prominence: future, past, future;
future, past, future. Hence the tremendous effect, like a goal to which

the whole exposition has been straining, of the prophecy of the coming of Herakles (897–9), which, again, is abruptly broken off, and then crowned at the opening of the last movement (939–59) by the completion of that other motive, the fatal secret, which marked the culmination of the first movement and again of the second. The narrations and predictions of Prometheus have been handled with such artistic mastery of the material as to concentrate at the end of the play our whole attention on the sequel.

That sequel has been lost, but some important fragments of the second play, the *Prometheus Unbound,* have survived.

The play began with the entry of the Chorus of Titans. Many thousands of years have elapsed, giving time for many changes, on earth and in heaven. Prometheus is still chained to his rock, but he has been restored from Tartarus to the light of day. The Titans describe their voyage from the banks of Ocean, where the Sun waters his horses after their day's labour, to the borders of Europe and Asia. They are brothers of Prometheus—bound to him therefore by ties closer than those which wrung compassion from Hephaistos and brought the God of Ocean and his daughters to his solitary rock. In the war against Kronos they had sided with the old order, and for this offence Zeus cast them, with Kronos, into Tartarus. They have now been released; and Kronos, too, we may presume, in accordance with the tradition, has been removed to his new home in the Islands of the Blest. Zeus has learnt to temper his power with mercy. No doubt the Titans recount these events to their brother. They can hardly fail to make a deep impression on him; but, as at the beginning of the first play, Prometheus is silent.

His opening words have survived in a Latin translation by Cicero. He appeals to them to bear witness to his agony. Pierced by cruel bonds and tormented by the eagle whose coming Hermes had predicted, he longs for the death which is denied to him. The speech is as notable for the speaker's absorption in physical pain as his speeches in the first play are notable for his indifference to it. There is not a word of his deliverer, not a word of his secret. And he longs to die. In the first play, which represented a time when the will of Zeus had been weaker than the Moirai (531–4), he had dared Zeus to do his worst, defiantly declaring that he was fated not to die (1086). Now he laments that he is being kept alive by the will of Zeus himself. The implication is that during the interval Zeus and the Moirai have come together. The old and the new are being reconciled.

The ensuing scenes must have acquainted the audience with the changes that have taken place in the interval between the two plays; but it is likely that on this occasion the narrator is not Prometheus himself, who is hardly in a position to know what has happened, but the Titans, who, we may suppose, relate for their brother's benefit both the advances which Zeus has made in the consolidation of his power and the mercy he has begun to extend to his former enemies. In the first play we learnt that, but for the intervention of Prometheus, Zeus would have destroyed the human race; but we may be certain that any such intention has been abandoned, because, as we shall see, the greatest of his sons is shortly to be sent down to earth for the improvement of their lot. Thus, if Prometheus remains obdurate, his motive can no longer be fear for the future of mankind: it can only be resentment for past wrongs. And if the Titans proceed to advise their brother to prepare the way for his own release by surrendering the secret which Zeus demands of him, appealing, like the God of Ocean, for wisdom and restraint (325–6), their advice, unlike his, will not be ignoble: they will urge him to submit to his old enemy, not merely because he rules the world, but because he now rules it well. Nor can Prometheus reply, as he did to the Oceanids, that advice comes ill from those who are not themselves in trouble (279–81), because his brothers' sufferings have been hardly less terrible than his own. Yet, in view of further evidence, we must, I think, assume that Prometheus rejects their appeal. He cannot yet bring himself, by revealing his secret before his release, to "unsay his high language."

In the Medicean manuscript of Aeschylus, the list of *dramatis personae* prefixed to the *Prometheus Bound* includes the names of Ge, the Goddess of Earth, and Herakles. As it is known that Herakles appeared in the *Prometheus Unbound,* it is generally agreed that both names have been inserted by mistake from another list, which gave the characters of the second play or of the two plays together.

The Goddess of Earth was traditionally regarded as the most ancient and in some ways the most august of the divinities of Greece—the origin of all things into which all things return, and the fountain of all wisdom, from whom all prophets, divine and human, drew their inspiration. And she was the mother of Prometheus. It was to her that he appealed in his opening soliloquy and again at the end of the first play to bear witness to his wrongs. From her he learnt the destined course of the war in heaven, and at her advice he took the part of Zeus. It was she who foretold to him the coming of his deliverer, and it was she who imparted to him his secret.

It has already been noted how in the first play both Hephaistos and the God of Ocean stressed their kinship with the prisoner, and how at the beginning of the second he is visited by still closer kinsmen, the sons of Earth. Their visit is followed by a visit from the Goddess of Earth herself, which will thus mark the culmination of a motive introduced at the beginning of the trilogy. And we may infer that her purpose is similar to theirs—to offer him her sympathy, and at the same time to urge upon him the wisdom of submission. The voice of his mother is now added to the entreaties of the rest of his kin, beseeching him to soften his obduracy and remove the bar to his deliverance.

His secret is this. If Zeus unites with Thetis, she will bear him a son who will overthrow him. Now, in the tradition recorded by later writers, Zeus was actually in pursuit of Thetis when the revelation of the secret deterred him. Thus, the situation is highly dramatic. Prometheus has only to hold out a little longer, and the downfall of his enemy is assured. On the other hand, his mother pleads with him to submit, before it is too late, not merely in order to effect his own release, but to prevent the fall of Zeus, who, no longer the vindictive tyrant who sought the extinction of the human race, has already, in the birth of Herakles, taken them under his care. Prometheus is asked, not to quail before his adversary, but to sacrifice his pride for the sake of that very race for which he has already sacrificed far more.

With regard to the actual manner of the revelation, it should be observed that, since the Goddess of Earth is as well acquainted with the secret as Prometheus himself, all she requires is his permission to divulge it. There is no need for it to pass his lips. And, further, if she is intent on such a mission, she will take advantage of the occasion to urge Zeus to deliver Prometheus in return for his own deliverance. And what more influential mediator could be found than the goddess who is the author of the being of Zeus himself, as of all created beings, who helped him to his supremacy, who is, moreover, the personification of Right?

It is at this point, I believe, that Prometheus yields: but one further agony awaits him. After his mother's departure, he hears a rush of wings. We remember the alarm in which he awaited the coming of the Ocean Nymphs, and how they hastened to reassure him. This time his fears are well-founded. The eagle is returning to its feast. Prometheus bends his gaze in the direction from which it is approaching. From the opposite direction appears a warrior, armed with bow and spear and clad in the famous lion skin. He draws his bow and, with a prayer to Apollo, whose gift it is, he shoots the eagle down. Recognising his deliverer, Prometheus greets him as "a hated father's son beloved," and we may suppose that he followed up this greeting with an appeal to Herakles to release him from bondage in accordance with his destiny. Herakles, however, who has now learnt who the sufferer is, may well be reluctant to assist his father's inveterate enemy. Prometheus will then explain that he has already removed the main obstacle to their reconciliation, and will doubtless recall the services which he rendered many centuries before to his ancestress on that very spot. Moreover, he can direct him on his travels and foretell what the future holds in store for him when his labours are at an end. He is now eager to let flow the fount of prophecy, which he unsealed so reluctantly to Io, if only his own request is granted in return. Herakles "pities the suppliant." Prometheus is to predict his future, and in return Herakles will release him. An arrangement of this kind, parallel to the bargain struck by Prometheus with Io and the Oceanids (804–11), would enable the dramatist to reserve the climax of the actual release for the end of the scene.

The surviving fragments suffice to show that, just as the wanderings of Io covered the eastern and southern limits of the world, so those of Herakles will extend to the north and west. The two prophecies are complementary, embracing the whole surface of the earth. In particular, we know from other sources that it was Prometheus who directed Herakles to the Garden of the Hesperides and instructed him how to get the Golden Apples with the help of Atlas, to whom we were introduced in the first play. We also know that in the second the dramatist explained the origin of the constellation called the Kneeling Herakles. During his fight with the Ligurians on his way to the Hesperides, the hero's weapons gave out and he was forced to his knees. This means that Prometheus predicted that, in memory of his encounter, the image of Herakles, like that of other departed heroes, would be set after his death among the stars. That being so, the prophecy can hardly have ended with the quest of the Golden Apples, or even with the last of the hero's labours, the descent into Hades, without some allusion to his final destiny—his ascent into Heaven. It must have been carried to its proper conclusion in the deification of the hero, in harmony with the prediction to Io, which concluded with his birth.

Prometheus has now fulfilled his part of the agreement; it remains for Herakles to fulfil his. The hero mounts the rock and shatters the handiwork of Hephaistos.

We still await the result of Earth's mission to Zeus, and we also remember that at the close of the first play Zeus declared through the medium of his emissary that the sufferings of Prometheus could not end until he found another god to surrender his immortality in his stead (1058–61). It is possible, therefore, that Hermes reappears. He announces first of all that the mediation of Earth has been successful. With the revelation of the secret the cause of offence has been removed, although, for reasons which will appear immediately, it is probable that the formal reconciliation has still to be effected. Further, it is possible that Zeus transfers part of his displeasure to his son, who, as predicted of him, has delivered the prisoner without the Father's consent (797). Herakles is said to have bound himself with olive—

probably in allusion to the olive planted by Athena in the Academy at Athens; and the motive for this act appears to have been his desire to avert his father's anger by binding himself vicariously on the prisoner's behalf. This point is dramatically important, because it provides a starting-point for the third play. In the regular manner of the trilogy, one difficulty is solved by the creation of another. Finally, the prisoner must find a substitute. At this point Herakles comes forward and explains that he has accidentally wounded the Centaur, Cheiron, who, suffering incurable pain, longs to die, but cannot: let him, therefore, relinquish his immortality in place of Prometheus. His offer accepted, Herakles departs, with the blessings of all present, to fulfil the remainder of his historic destiny.

If we consider the situation in which the dramatist has left us, we see that, just as in the first play the prophecy to Io raised an expectation which has only been satisfied by its fulfilment in the second— namely, the coming of Herakles—the prophecy to Herakles has now raised an expectation no less far-reaching, his deification; and our minds will not be at rest until we are assured that this, too, has been realised. It is therefore difficult to resist the conclusion that the plot of the third play was concerned, not merely with the readmission of Prometheus to Olympus, but with the future of Herakles. The destinies of the two heroes have become interlocked, and at the close of the second play our interest has been transferred in some measure to the latter.

Before leaving the *Prometheus Unbound,* let us compare its structure, so far as it can be recovered, with that of the *Prometheus Bound.* The silence of Prometheus at the opening of the first play is balanced by his silence at the opening of the second; the visit of the God of Ocean in the first by the visit of the Goddess of Earth in the second; the Daughters of Ocean, the chorus of the first play, by the Sons of Earth, the chorus of the second; the wanderings of Io in the east and south by the wanderings of her descendant in the north and west; the prophecy of the birth of the great benefactor of mankind by the prophecy of his deification. Thus, it appears that the two plays were constructed with that organic symmetry which the study of his other work leads us to expect.

The third play was entitled *Prometheus the Fire-bearer.* This epithet probably refers to the torch which Pausanias saw (mistaking it for a sceptre) in the right hand of the archaic image of Prometheus in the Academy, where, as already noted, the god was worshipped as one of the three divinities who had taught man the use of fire and were honoured with annual torch races.

We have already made some progress with the conclusion of the trilogy. In the first place, Prometheus is a suppliant, seeking readmission to Olympus. In the *Oresteia,* the suppliant was saved by the intervention of Athena, the goddess of wisdom and patroness of the city which claimed to uphold that virtue among men. The same goddess had an ancient connection with Prometheus. We are told that Prometheus assisted at her birth, when she sprang fully armed from the head of Zeus, and that the two collaborated in the creation of mankind. But above all Prometheus was granted a place in the Academy—an honour which he could not have won without the goddess's consent. Of the three fire gods, we made the acquaintance of the two elder at the opening of the trilogy, and I believe, therefore, that in the conclusion we were introduced to the youngest and greatest of the three. It is she who reconciles Prometheus with her father and invests him with the human honours that are his due.

Before his descent into Hades, Herakles visited Eleusis with the intention of becoming an initiate, but he was unable to behold the mysteries until he had been cleansed of the blood of the Centaurs: accordingly, he was purified at Agra and then initiated. We are also told that the Lesser Mysteries of Agra were founded by Demeter for the express purpose of purifying Herakles after the slaughter of the Centaurs. These traditions, preserved by Apollodoros and Diodoros, relate to Aeschylus's birthplace. They must have been known to him, and it is extremely probable that they were derived by the later writers from him. It appears, therefore, that here again the poet was working with an ulterior purpose—namely, the inception at the end of the trilogy of another and far more important feature of Athenian ritual, the Lesser Mysteries of Demeter.

The agony of Io was due in part to the jealousy of Hera, and her descendant suffered much from the same cause. Ultimately, however, when Herakles was admitted to Olympus, he was reconciled with Hera and received in marriage her own daughter, Hebe, the goddess of eternal youth. Furthermore, if the marriage of Herakles and Hebe signifies the reconciliation of Hera with the House of Io, it signifies just as clearly her reconciliation with her lord. Her hostility to Io and Herakles was prompted by conjugal jealousy, of which Zeus was the guilty cause. In the first play we saw Zeus heartlessly pursuing a mortal girl; in the second we saw him in pursuit of Thetis; but in the third, when he joins with Hera in blessing the union of their son and daughter, the two stand together as guardians of the sanctity of marriage, thus marking a further step in the advancement of humanity.

In the beginning, Zeus crucified Prometheus for the salvation of mankind. In the course of time, which taught wisdom to them both, Prometheus saved Zeus from destruction and was himself saved by the son of Zeus, who, under his father's guidance, carried on the work of Prometheus, clearing the path of human progress; and the divine feud was eventually resolved by Athena, who completed her father's purpose by her patronage of the city which stands at the summit of human civilisation. Hence, at the close of the trilogy, these three—Prometheus, Herakles, Athena—appear together as representatives of the inception, development, and consummation of the idea of God, and as the founder, promoter, and perfecter of the destiny of man.

If this view of the trilogy is essentially correct, it means that, for all the profound differences in their interpretation of the myth, Aeschylus was continuing the work which Hesiod had begun. The story of Prometheus has now been infused with an intellectual content far beyond the compass of the tale told by the rude peasants of Boiotia; but the advance which the new interpretation marks over Hesiod, no less than his advance on the primitive nucleus of the myth, has only been rendered possible by the underlying advancement of society itself. As the material basis of human life is extended and enriched, there emanates from it an ever-growing profundity and fertility of thought; but, since the material process is continuous, the new being at first secreted within the old, intellectual progress takes the form of incessant adaptations of traditional ideas. Of this truth the legend of Prometheus is a clear example. The work of Aeschylus on this subject was so widely known and admired that it might well have fixed the tradition, if anything could have fixed it; but this tradition was no more capable of rest than the world it so vividly reflected. It is therefore interesting to see how the story of Prometheus was subsequently interpreted.

The following passage is from a lost play by Moschion, a writer otherwise unknown:

> And first I shall unfold from the beginning
> The early origin of the life of man.
> There was an age long since when mortals dwelt
> Like beasts in mountain caverns and ravines
> That seldom saw the sunshine, for as yet
> They had no vaulted houses and no towns
> With walls of stone securely fortified,
> No ploughshares to cut deep into the sod
> And make it mother corn, no blade of iron
> To tend row upon row the blossoming vine.
> The earth was still a virgin without child,
> And men fed on each other's flesh, for then
> The place of Law was lowly and Violence
> Was throned on high at the right hand of Zeus.
> But when at last Time, who brings all to birth,
> Transformed the manner of our mortal life,

> Whether through the contrivance of Prometheus,
> Or through Necessity, or whether long
> Practice had learned from Nature's own instruction,
> Then men discovered how to bring to fruit
> Demeter's gift, discovered too the draught
> Of Dionysus, then, furrowing the soil
> With teams of oxen, raising roofs above
> Their heads, and founding cities, they
> Forsook the beasts and became civilised.

This passage provides just the link in the development of the tradition that our argument has led us to expect. On the one hand, the mythical integument has been shed, the surviving vestiges being no more than poetical embellishments; and one of them, the allusion to Violence, is clearly a conscious reminiscence of the *Prometheus Bound,* showing that the writer has correctly interpreted the intention of Aeschylus in introducing Might and Violence as ministers of the god who was in the beginning "a law to himself." On the other hand, the mention of Necessity points just as clearly to the fourth-century materialists. The tradition has been stated in a form which would have been equally acceptable to Aeschylus and to Epicurus.

Our next evidence is another dramatic fragment—from a play by Plato's uncle, Kritias:

> There was a time when human life was ruled
> By force, being brutal and disorderly,
> When there was no reward for righteousness
> And wickedness went unpunished. Then, I think,
> Men laid down laws as penalties to make
> Justice supreme and insolence her slave;
> But even then, although the laws restrained
> Mankind from deeds of open violence,
> They still did wrong in secret, until some
> Shrewd and far-sighted thinker had the wit
> To invent gods, that all who did or said
> Or even imagined evil might be afraid;
> And so he introduced the Deity,
> Teaching men faith in an eternal spirit
> Who sees and hears with his intelligence
> And pays close heed to all men say and do.

Here we find ourselves in a different atmosphere. Kritias was one of the Thirty Tyrants who instituted a reign of terror at Athens in the closing years of the Peloponnesian War (404 BC). As an active and class-conscious counter-revolutionary, he openly avows the repressive function of "law and order" and recognises with cynical frankness the value of religion as a means of keeping the masses in ignorance and subjection. This analysis of the idea of God, which, if we look to the essence rather than the manner in which it is expressed, is sound, would perhaps have shocked Aeschylus; yet his own master Pythagoras is reported to have declared that, realising the need for justice, men had assigned the same function to Themis in Heaven, Dike in Hell, and Nomos on earth, in order that those who committed the sin of disobedience might appear as offenders against the whole structure of the universe; and Aeschylus himself had taught that God, as well as man, was a product of evolution, the two processes being closely parallel. Further, when we hear that the function of the law is to intimidate, we are reminded of the words which Aeschylus put into the mouth of Athena when she instituted the reign of law in the *Oresteia*—"What man shall be upright without fear?" The later work of Aeschylus has brought us to a point in the history of Athens at which the *isonomia* of the middle-class supporters of Kleisthenes is being revealed with increasing clarity as an instrument to be used by that class for the enforced maintenance of its own privileged position.

Returning to Prometheus, the story of his services to man is told again by Plato in a new version which he puts into the mouth of Protagoras in the dialogue of that name. It may be summarised as follows.

Living creatures were made by the gods out of earth and fire. After they had been created, Prometheus and his brother Epimetheus (a foil to the god of Foresight, ignored by Aeschylus but going back to Hesiod) bestowed on them their appropriate faculties, giving them hoofs or wings or underground dwellings, so that each species might have the means of self-defence; wrapping them in furs and skins for shelter against the cold; ordaining that some should be the natural prey of others and at the same time ensuring their survival by making them exceptionally prolific. All this was done by Epimetheus under his brother's direction, but at the end of his task he found that he had inadvertently bestowed all the available faculties on the animals, leaving none for man. Faced with this difficulty, Prometheus gave men fire, which he stole from its owners, Hephaistos and Athena, and he was subsequently prosecuted for theft. Being akin to the divine, men were distinguished from the other animals by their innate belief in God and by their faculty of speech. They began to make clothes and shoes, to build houses and till the soil, and eventually, for protection against the animals, they founded cities. Unfortunately, however, after gathering together in cities, citizen began to prey on citizen; and so, fearing that the race might perish, Zeus commanded Hermes to confer on them the gifts of shame and justice. Asked whether these were to be bestowed indiscriminately or assigned to selected individuals like the specialists in the handicrafts, Zeus replied, "Let them be given to all in common, and give them too a law from me that any man who cannot partake of shame and justice shall be put to death as an infection in the body politic."

The author of this interpretation is at one with Kritias in his attitude to justice and the law, but shows superior insight in acknowledging that strife between man and man—the class struggle—only began with the inauguration of city life; and he discreetly places man's belief in God far back in the very origins of his existence. In contrast to Aeschylus, the divine government of the world is fixed and stable, and the credit for human progress is transferred from Prometheus, whose part is subordinate, to an all-wise, omnipotent, and unchanging Zeus.

Let us now see how these things appeared to the lower orders. Philemon was a comic dramatist of the fourth century, and, like the majority of comic dramatists at that time, he was a resident alien, not an Athenian citizen. It was Philemon who said:

> The slave has human flesh the same as ours.
> Indeed, in Nature all men were born free.

And this is what he said of the gifts of Prometheus which had raised man above the level of the beasts:

> Thrice blest and happy are the beasts that have
> No reason in these things, no questioning,
> Nor other harmful superfluities—
> Their law is their own nature; but the life
> Of man is more than he can bear—he is
> The slave of fancies, he has invented laws.

A similar view was expounded at length by Diogenes the Cynic, a popular philosopher whose social outlook is indicated by his condemnation of the lectures given by Plato to rich young men in the Academy as "a waste of time," and by a remark he is said to have made in Megara, where he saw sheep protected from the weather by leather jackets, while the backs of the children were bare—"It is better," he said, "to be a Megarian's ram than his son."

Diogenes declared that it was luxury that had made human life more miserable than that of the animals. The animals drink water, eat grass, go about naked for the most part all the year round, never enter a house or make use of fire, and so, unless they are slaughtered, they live out the term of years that Nature has appointed for them in health and strength without any need for medicines or physicians. Men,

on the other hand, are so attached to life and so ingenious in pro-
longing it that most of them never reach old age and live burdened
with diseases too numerous to mention. It is not enough for them that
the earth furnishes them with natural medicines—they must have sur-
gery and cautery as well. . . . As soon as they came together in cities,
they began to commit the most terrible crimes against one another, as
though that were what they had come together for. Accordingly, he
understood the story of how Prometheus was punished by Zeus for the
discovery of fire to mean that this was the origin and starting-point of
human luxury and fastidiousness; for Zeus, he declared, did not hate
mankind nor would he have grudged them anything that was for their
good.

Prometheus has now become an upstart justly punished for the gift
of what is regarded, not as a blessing, but as a curse. Diogenes's view
of the corrupting effects of civilised life brings us back to Hesiod—
it is the fable of the successive ages of man, each more degenerate than
the last, in a new form; and it shows that in his day the struggle
between rich and poor in the decaying city-state had bitten into human
consciousness as deeply as the old struggle between the landowner
and the serf.

It would be an interesting and profitable task to pursue the history
of this myth in its successive reinterpretations through the Middle Ages
down to our own day; but for the present it must suffice to conclude
the subject with some remarks on what Shelley made of it.

Gilbert Murray, who believed that "the strong tradition in the
higher kind of Greek poetry, as in good poetry almost everywhere,
was to avoid all the disturbing irrelevances of contemporary life," and
could see "no evidence of any political allusions" in the *Oresteia,*
remarked that "it is surprising that out of material so undramatic as
a mere contest between pure evil and pure good Shelley has made
such a magnificent poem." It would indeed be surprising, if it were
true, but, unlike Aeschylus, Shelley was in the habit of writing prefaces
to his poems with the object of explaining what they were about, and
in his preface to the *Prometheus Unbound* he wrote as follows:

> We owe the great writers of the golden age of our literature to that
> fervid awakening of the public mind which shook to dust the oldest
> and most oppressive form of the Christian religion. We owe Milton to
> the progress and development of the same spirit; the sacred Milton
> was, let it ever be remembered, a republican, and a bold enquirer
> into morals and religion. The great writers of our own age are, we have
> reason to suppose, the companions and forerunners of some unimagined
> change in our social condition or the opinions which cement it. The
> cloud of mind is discharging its collective lightning, and the equilibrium
> between institutions and opinions is now restoring, or about to be re-
> stored.

If we are curious to know what these institutions were that Shelley found in conflict with his opinions, we have only to read his *Mask of Anarchy Written on the Occasion of the Massacre at Manchester*:

> 'Tis to work and have such pay
> As just keeps life from day to day
> In your limbs, as in a cell
> For the tyrants' use to dwell
>
> So that ye for them are made
> Loom and plough and sword and spade
> With or without your own will bent
> To their defence and nourishment.

This conflict was something more substantial, as well as more disturbing, than "a mere contest between pure good and pure evil," and it was also inherently dramatic, because it sprang straight out of contemporary strife. Only those who have studied the brutality, duplicity and hypocrisy of the ruling class of that date as revealed in their Enclosure Acts and Game Laws, their Speenhamland system and their truck system, and who stand where Shelley would have stood in relation to the sufferings no less great that are the common lot of the majority of mankind to-day, are in a position to appreciate the indignation which burns in the challenge of Prometheus:

> Fiend, I defy thee! with a calm, fixed mind,
> All that thou canst inflict I bid thee do;
> Foul Tyrant both of Gods and Human-kind,
> One only being shalt thou not subdue.

During Shelley's lifetime, the last of the English peasants had been turned out of their common fields on to the roads, and from there herded into the work-houses, prisons, cotton-mills, and coal-mines, where they worked, men, women, and children, in conditions still paralleled in such places as Jamaica, Johannesburg, and Bombay. It was the period of the Industrial Revolution, which enriched the the rich and impoverished the poor—the period in which the new manufacturing class was engaged in overthrowing the privileges of a corrupt landowning oligarchy, while the new proletariat, notwithstanding hunger and squalor and police persecution, was slowly and painfully learning how to organise for action.

Aeschylus was a moderate democrat, who had seen the long struggle between the landowners and the merchants culminate in a *concordia ordinum,* marked by the abolition of aristocratic privilege and the extension of the franchise to the whole of the citizen body. It is essential, however, to remember that this *concordia* owed its completeness to the fact that there was another class which was not free. The slaves were the proletariat of ancient democracy, and if they had not been slaves, incapable of organisation and therefore politically powerless, the overthrow of the landed aristocracy would have been followed by a struggle between them and their masters. It was only by excluding this class from his very conception of democracy that Aeschylus was able to regard the democratic revolution as a fusion of opposites symbolised in the reconciliation of Zeus and Prometheus.

Shelley was a member of the upper middle class who had transferred his allegiance to the proletariat. But this was not a slave proletariat; it was free, and already clamouring for the suffrage. Between this class and the capitalists there was no room for compromise, because their interests were contradictory, and that is what made it impossible for Shelley to accept the Aeschylean conclusion. He was bound to revolt against the idea of reconciling the champion with the oppressor of mankind. As for his alternative, even in those early days there were a few who saw more or less clearly that the only possible solution of the conflict was the expropriation of the ruling class by the class which it had expropriated; but, owing partly to the immaturity of the proletariat, which at this time was hardly conscious of its future, and partly to his own middle-class outlook, which he had not entirely outgrown, Shelley shrank from the idea of revolutionary action. Accordingly, his Jupiter is overthrown, but only by the mystical power of passive resistance.

In fairness to Shelley, it must be added that, whereas Aeschylus was celebrating a revolution which he had already seen accomplished, Shelley's revolution was at this time no more than a hope of the future; and so, for a century, it remained.

References

Childe, V. G. *Man Makes Himself.* London, 1936.

Mahaffy, J. P. *History of Classical Greek Literature.* London, 1880.

Burke, E. *Reflections on the Revolution in France.* 4 ed. London, 1790.

Lenin, V. I. *Materialism and Empirio-criticism.* London, n.d.

Aeschylus: The Last Phase

by C. J. Herington

The starting-point of this article is a fact which now seems to me almost certain: that Aeschylus' *Suppliants*-tetralogy, *Oresteia*, and *Prometheia*—in that order—form a compact group of works at the very end of the poet's career. I accept (as I think most people now do) the implication of the papyrus-hypothesis that the *Suppliants*-tetralogy must date from 466 BC or later, perhaps 463.[1] It has always been known, beyond doubt, that the *Oresteia* was produced in Spring 458. And lastly I am convinced by a number of arguments of varying type, produced over the last fifty years, that the *Prometheia* must have been written after the *Oresteia* if it was written by Aeschylus at all (which I firmly believe). The *Prometheus* must in that case belong to the last two years of Aeschylus' life: between 458 and his death in Sicily, 456/5.

These datings mean that we still have, in whole or part, a very high proportion of the tetralogies that Aeschylus actually composed in his last ten years, or perhaps even in his last seven. It could be that they represent *all* the tetralogies which he composed in this time; but even if that is not so, there is hardly space for more than one other tetralogy in the period, or two at the outside. Now my belief is that they are not merely chronologically a compact group, but that they are so artistically as well. Even more: that in these last three surviving works Aeschylus created a new art-form, something that differs *in kind* from any work that was staged under the name of tragedy, either his own or anybody else's, before or after that final decade of his life. A consequence of this will be that the three surviving examples of what I think of as a unique art-form can be used, more than is generally recognized, to explain each other; and that, in particular, the *Prometheus* begins to make more sense than it did.

That, in outline, is the position whose meaning and consequences

"Aeschylus: The Last Phase" by C. J. Herington. From *Arion*, IV, No. 3 (Autumn 1965), 387–403. Copyright © 1965 by *Arion*. Reprinted by permission of *Arion*.

[1] A convenient publication, translation, and discussion of this papyrus is that by H. Lloyd–Jones in his Appendix to H. W. Smyth's *Aeschylus*, Volume II (second edition, 1957), 595f.

are to be discussed in this paper. But I feel it necessary, first, to step right back and ask a question of method. There seem to be some artists whose works gain little or nothing in meaning through being dated at a specific point in the maker's life, and grouped with the other works of the same period. This sort of artist engineers internally-consistent structures that are independent of himself: the façade is raised, is checked for symmetry and mechanical stress in all directions—and the little architect steps from behind it with a wave of the hand and wanders off anywhere, leaving behind him a thing made. With such work (I think, heretically perhaps, of the plays of Sophocles and the odes of Horace) dating and grouping seem to be largely antiquarian labor. But there exists another sort of artist, whose work, and whose relationship to the work, are altogether different. Not long ago a large exhibition of Picasso's works toured the northern parts of America, showing some of us (at least) for the first time a really representative selection of his paintings and drawings, in chronological order. The first impression of an innocent observer, after walking through the galleries from one end to the other, was: an exhibition by seven or eight different men, practising seven or eight different arts. What it actually was, of course, was an exhibition by an individual who many times, under the stress of a new technical idea or of something he had seen in the world, ruthlessly and abruptly threw overboard his previous achievement, and tried again. That drawing of a rampant Minotaur in Room VII really did not have a lot to do with that painting of a serene woman's face under a broad-brimmed hat in Room I. Each, in its own way, gave proof of a treasury of skill and experience. But the woman breathed the air and the style of Paris in the early nineteen-hundreds, the Minotaur had crept out of the labyrinth of the Spanish Civil War. Fully to come to grips with the monster, you had to realize that he was only a study, a fragment of a greater experience; you had to move to the canvases on the wall around him and even, in imagination, to Spain and to the war itself.

Now although the point is not mathematically provable, I believe that most people who have spent any reasonable time on Aeschylus will have felt that they are having to do with this second sort of artist. As a citizen and as a poet he lives in an age of crisis. Classical society—or, if you like, modern society—is being born out of archaism. Correspondingly, tragedy is being born out of song. We cannot at any stage of Aeschylus' life say that tragedy is; we can only say that it is becoming. Aeschylus' thought, and the technique to match his thought, are dynamic and evolutionary, receptive always to what is new. Such a poet as that might begin his career with a two-dimensional imagination like a Persian carpet, close-woven with archaic centaurs, hippocamps and horsecocks; he might end it with a mind fixed on the profound space that is opened by the coming of philosophy. If that was in fact so, then the grouping of the plays by date would be an unavoidable stage towards understanding.

On these assumptions I again turn to the main position: that the *Suppliants*-tetralogy, the *Oresteia*, and the *Prometheia* (to which I shall refer from now on as "the late group," for short) were composed in that order during Aeschylus' last ten or seven years, and that they represent most, if not all, of a phase in the tragic art which is sharply set off from anything discernible before or after.

The first step must be to survey the tragedies which lie on either side of the late group, chronologically speaking. Before 466 BC Aeschylus had already been composing for well over thirty years—a good working lifetime in itself. During that time the only two fixed dates and fixed points, so far as present knowledge goes, are the production of the *Persians* in 472, and that of the *Seven Against Thebes* in 467. Now, wildly different as these two tragedies are, thematically and musically, they yet imply the same cosmic background, and the same view of the human situation and human destiny. The cosmos here is—by comparison with what is to come in the late group— almost a comfortable one; in the sense that, however grim it is, however frightful the choices to be made within it, at least the roots of things remain the same. The archaic powers, both those in heaven and those below the earth, reign each unquestioned in their own spheres; in the *Seven,* infernal Furies and Olympian Apollo conspire towards the downfall of the house of Oedipus.[2] And in this universe the laws, though harsh, are not blind, nor purely deterministic. Catastrophe, when it comes, is doubly motivated: something said or done in the past (an oracle, a family curse) preordains it externally, but it is only triggered off by something internal, something in the man himself. The two types of motivation are not, indeed, equally stressed in each play. In the *Persians* the disaster due to Xerxes' pride is already known when the ghost of Darius suddenly produces an oracle (otherwise unrecorded, either in history or in the actual play) which has foretold the downfall of the Persian army (*Persians*, 739– 44, 801); conversely, in the *Seven,* it is the inner rage of Eteocles— long ago destined to destruction by the Curse—that is held back from the audience until comparatively late (653ff.). But in both plays the dual motivation of catastrophe is there for all to see. I would stress that it is not, of course, just a superficial matter of plot-mechanics; it involves, in itself, a subtle and not yet quite disproved view of human nature and destiny.

So much for the two tragedies that survive from the period before

---

[2] This point is well made by F. Solmsen in TAPhA 68 (1937) 204.

the Aeschylean late group. Paradoxically, but I believe truly, it must now be observed that their closest relatives, in some important respects, are to be found not in that late group, but in the earlier surviving plays of Sophocles: the *Ajax*, the *Antigone*, and the *Oedipus Tyrannus*, which were produced within the twenty years or so following Aeschylus' death. For those three Sophoclean plays fundamentally imply for dramatic purposes the same cosmos, and are constructed round the same double motivation, as the *Persians* and the *Seven*. In saying this, of course, I am not forgetting the great differences between the plays, and between the poets; each play has its individual soul, as it were, which at the moment I am not trying to approach. But behind all the differences I seem to see the same frame of reference, within which the drama is built. That is true, also, of yet another tragedy written down in the same period as the earlier Sophoclean plays, probably in the forties of the fifth century: the prose tragedy of Croesus, King of Lydia, which stands at the opening of Herodotus' *History*.[3] Here, in fact, the two motivations which converge towards the downfall of the hero are emphasized almost too clearly—the oracle which foredooms the end of Gyges' dynasty in the fifth generation (I. 13, 91), and the recklessness which springs from within Croesus himself.

So far as our evidence goes, then (and there seems just enough of it to exclude the possibility that we are being deluded by the accidents of preservation), tragic writing both before and in the generation after the Aeschylean late group, for all its variety in detail, moves against the background of the same universe. If there is any rift in that universe, it is between man and the unseen powers; whose laws he may challenge or misread, just as he may misread his own nature. In any of those events he, the individual, is due for destruction; but the universe itself remains as it was before, static, undivided. I repeat that the variety of movement against that cosmic background is immense, even to judge from the extant plays. And we should certainly have some shocks if the sands were to open up and yield some of the more eccentric lost tragedies of which the fragments now allow us only glimpses—Jason and the Argonauts rolling drunk on the stage in Aeschylus' *Kabeiroi*; the sword doubling back against the invulner-

---

[3] Herodotus I, chapters 6–91, *passim*. If Professor D. Page is right, this Herodotean story will have been based itself on an early fifth-century tragedy or group of tragedies by an older contemporary of Aeschylus; see *A New Chapter in the History of Greek Tragedy* (Cambridge 1951), with some startling evidence in support, *TCPhS* no. 186 (NS 8; 1962). In that case we should have the record of *three* tragic works, earlier than the Aeschylean late group, which presupposed the undivided cosmos discussed here. But it is right to add that Page's theory, excellently argued as it is, still faces certain difficulties, and does not yet seem to be generally accepted.

able flesh when the Aeschylean Ajax tries to commit suicide;[4] or the
Aeschylean Priam literally weighing Hector's body in the scales
against gold.[5] But there is nothing in the fragments to indicate that
such plays, too, did not move within the frame of this unified, archaic
universe.

It will at once be clear that the Aeschylean late group—*Suppliants*-
tetralogy, *Oresteia, Prometheia*—will not fit into that frame at all;
that from this point of view it forms a completely separate enclave
in the known history of Greek tragedy before *c.* 440 BC, or rather of
all Greek tragedy. But, although that is to my mind the most striking
of the features that link the three works together, I do not think
it is the only one, either in detail or on the grand scale. Of the many
others, there are four which seem to be of special significance: the
technique of trilogy-composition; the involvement of Gods in human
feuds; the comic (in the technical sense of *Old Comic*) element; and
the intrusion of contemporary philosophical speculation. I shall look
at these in turn.

Probably the most striking feature is the first: the technique of
putting together a tragic trilogy. The Aeschylean late group shows an
odd, unbalanced relationship between the three plays which constitute
the trilogy on the one hand, and the traditional myth which contributes its subject-matter on the other. The complete *Oresteia* is
the simplest example. Its trilogic form can be symbolized as *A, A, B*:
two responding plays to begin with and the third wild, non-respond-
ing. The *Agamemnon* and *Choephori* not only respond to each other
in movement—murder and counter-murder—but they are also
grouped together by the fact that the basic story in both, and even the
characters, are in conformity with the traditional myth already known
(in outline at least) a century before Aeschylus, and in part known
to Homer too. (Again I should emphasize that I am not trying to
touch the soul of these plays, nor forgetting that Aeschylus slants
the traditional story in ways all his own. Here I am trying to view
the grand overall movement, as if through the eyes of the designer
as he makes his first outline, sketch-block on knee.) But the *third*
member of the *Oresteia*, the *Eumenides,* has a totally different character and movement from the first two; and all the evidence which we
have so far, both internal and external, suggests that its plot was freely
invented by Aeschylus *ad hoc,* to resolve the issues raised, through
the medium of the traditional story, in the first two plays. The only
traditional legendary element visible in the *Eumenides* is, probably,
the purification of Orestes at Delphi—and my own reading of the
play suggests that even this element is not so much re-used by Aes-

[4] Aeschylus, *Threissai,* Fragment 292 in Mette's collection of the fragments.
[5] Aeschylus, *Phryges e Hektoros Lytra,* Fragment 254 in Mette.

chylus as perverted. Instead of a proof of Apollo's ultimate healing and reconciling power (as which it was surely intended by its inventors) it has become, in the context of this play, a proof of Apollo's inefficacy; instead of a pious and harmonious finale to Orestes' story it now serves merely as a horrific *proagon,* in which the two parties to the coming cosmic *agon* are first alternately paraded and then confronted.

The same curious principle of trilogic composition seems to have applied in the remaining two trilogies of the late group. Appallingly fragmentary as the *Suppliants*-trilogy and the *Prometheia* now are, there are still more solid reasons than one might think for this belief. To take the *Prometheia*: the basic story here, that Prometheus was bound by Zeus and later released by Herakles, is standard in Greek mythical accounts from Hesiod (*Theogony* 521ff.) until the end of the ancient world (and beyond the end). But there is no such universal agreement as to what happened *after* the release. Hesiod says nothing on the point, and if we look to the many later ancient versions of the Prometheus-story we find the wildest diversity. Now Aeschylus' *Prometheus Bound* and *Prometheus Unbound,* for all their deliberate rehandling and censoring of Hesiod's story, were fundamentally based on that story, and presupposed a knowledge of it in their audience. In fact, we know enough of the two of them to be sure that between them they covered approximately the same legendary area as the Hesiodic version, the boundary being drawn between the two antithetic parts: the binding and the releasing (compare the murder and counter-murder in the *Agamemnon* and *Choephori*). It is a necessary inference from these facts that the third play of the trilogy—which I believe, in common with the majority of those who have considered the problem, to have once existed, and to have been entitled the *Prometheus Pyrphoros*—abandoned Hesiod entirely. And it is a likely inference, since no important pre-Aeschylean source for the Prometheus story other than Hesiod is known, that it must have contained a freely invented synthesis of the antithesis set up in the first two plays.

Finally, the evidence about the earliest of the Aeschylean late group, the *Suppliants*-trilogy, strongly suggests the same pattern. All versions of the legend of the Danaid girls, at all dates, agree on the basic story: the escape of the girls and their father from Egypt to Argos, chased by their cousins; their eventual unwilling marriage; and those 49 murders on the wedding-night. But there is no fixed tradition at all as to what happened after that night; thenceforward there are as many versions as there are tellers.[6] What is known of

---

[6] The ancient versions of the Danaid story are surveyed, for example, by J. Vürtheim, in *Aeschylos' Schutzflehende* (Amsterdam 1928) 10ff. [See now A. F. Garvie, *Aeschylus' Supplices: Play and Trilogy* (Cambridge 1969), Chap. V—ED.]

Aeschylus' *Suppliants*-trilogy suggests, beyond reasonable doubt, that the first two of its plays, the *Suppliants* and the *Aigyptioi,* between them contained the two responding movements that are found in the universal tradition—the enforced flight, the enforced union. The third and last play of the trilogy, the *Danaides,* evidently opened [7] with the discovery of the massacre in the wedding-chamber, on the dawn after the wedding. But the most important fragment from this play (125 Mette; one of the most famous passages of Aeschylean poetry in its own right) indicates that it, too, subsequently ran wild, like the *Eumenides* and the *Prometheus Pyrphoros.* The speaker is the goddess Aphrodite herself, who has, it must be noticed, no business in any other recorded dénouement of the Danaid legend. And she is speaking, not about the *human* sexual relationship, with which the earlier two plays of the trilogy were concerned, but about the love which unites the Earth and Sky in the spring rains:

> Now the pure Heaven yearns to pierce the Earth;
> now Earth is taken with longing for her marriage.
> The rains showering from the mating Sky
> fill her with life, and she gives birth, for man,
> to flocks of sheep and to the lifegiving wheat.
> And from that liquid exultation springs,
> perfect, the time of trees. In this I share.

It seems certain from these lines that a deity has materialized in person on the stage in the Danaides, presumably to take one side or the other in the human feud. And it further seems likely from their mutilated context (preserved on a papyrus)[8] that Aphrodite's speech dealt *at length* with the question of the relationship between male and female right across the cosmos, including vegetable and animal fertility as well as the primal marriage between Earth and sky. This development, of course, would closely associate the ending of the *Suppliants*-trilogy with that of the *Oresteia;* where we can still observe in detail how one of the human motifs of the *Agamemnon* and *Choephori,* the relative roles of man and woman, is raised to cosmic importance in the *Eumenides.* In the latter play, as we all know, the male Olympian powers are ranged on one side, the female pre-

[7] Evidence: Fragment 124 in Mette (43 Nauck, Murray). Although the exact reading of this fragment is in dispute, its general drift and reference seem fairly certain.

[8] *Oxyrhynchus Papyri,* Volume 20 (1952), 21f.; reprinted by Mette as Fragment 125. The tiny fragments of the nineteen lines which preceded those translated in my text here contain one, possibly two, references to *cattle* (lines 2, 6); and perhaps references to *the mating of cattle* (line 2, as restored by Mette) and to *parturition* (line 7).

Olympians on the other; holding the balance is the sexually ambiguous figure, Athena (daughter who has no mother, earth-deity and Olympian deity, woman in hoplite-armor); and an issue that becomes of increasing importance as the play marches to its climax is the fertility of Athenian crops, cattle, and women.

To summarize: the principle of trilogic composition that appears to obtain in the Aeschylean late group means that the first two members of a trilogy follow the outline of the traditional legend and have responding movement, while the third is largely free invention, designed to synthesize the antitheses set up in the former two. It is useless to look for such a principle of composition in anything that was written after Aeschylus' death, because of course the practice of composing connected trilogies was then almost entirely abandoned (there are only three recorded instances later than 456 BC, and no details survive of these). But we do possess one example of a connected trilogy from immediately *before* Aeschylus' late group, the Theban trilogy of 467 BC, and the comparison is startling. Here there survives only the last of the three plays, the *Seven Against Thebes,* but the titles of the two plays that stood before in the trilogy, the *Laius* and the *Oedipus,* are known, and are revealing enough for the contents. The third member of *this* trilogy—which, as already mentioned, is played out against the background of a still undivided archaic cosmos—comes to its grim end in accordance with the universal legendary tradition, with the annihilation of the princely brothers, Eteocles and Polyneices, at each other's hands. In the *Seven* there seems to be very little rehandling of the basic legend, except to make it slightly more ghastly than the versions known to Pindar earlier and Herodotus later by causing the princes to die without issue. Here the Gods do not materialize on the stage; they do not take sides in the human feud, nor are their relationships in any way affected by it; far from being divided, they join hands to bring about the disaster on the mortal plane. In fact, in the Theban trilogy Aeschylus retains both the archaic cosmos and the archaic story, dramatizing the saga right to the end.

A word should be said here about the tetralogies of Aeschylus that are represented only by fragments, and by no surviving plays. Not one can be precisely dated, but the vast majority must certainly belong to the thirty-year period before the late group; as we have seen, there is simply not room for more than a minute fraction of them in the years from 466 onwards. What little can be seen of these lost works— and it must be admitted that it *is* little—implies the trilogic technique of the Theban trilogy rather than that of the late group; dramatization, that is, of the ancient saga to the end, not free invention and synthesis in the third play. This is almost certainly true of one of the most deplorable losses from ancient poetry as a whole, Aeschylus' trilogy on Achilles;[9] the final tragedy in that, the *Phrygians or Ransoming of Hector* followed the outlines, at least, of the twenty-fourth book of the *Iliad*. And the trilogies on Ajax and on Odysseus respectively, though no-one would dare to speak dogmatically about their contents, would seem to suit a straight treatment of the heroic saga, rather than the *A, A, B* movement of the late group.

Trilogy-technique, then, is one major feature which certainly links together the three works of the late group, and at the same time sets them sharply off from the immediately preceding Theban trilogy, if not perhaps also (though this is obviously far more speculative) from some other earlier trilogies. A second such feature has already entered this argument, and I need not add much to it here: this is the *involvement of the Gods* as partisans in the issues of the trilogy, and the concomitant split, not just on the human level, but in the cosmos itself. This happened very probably in the last play of the *Suppliants*-trilogy (we recall the speech of Aphrodite), and certainly at the end of the *Oresteia*. The *Prometheia* evidently contains this same feature, but gives an amazing twist to the pattern; for here the trilogy opens instantly with the involvement of the Gods and the cosmic split, and the humans, except the semi-human Io and (in the *Unbound*) Herakles, are kept off the stage altogether, at least in the first two plays. There is a distinct possibility, however, that the humans came back in the third play, the *Pyrphoros*; many enquirers have guessed, and with some sound reasons, that this play may have culminated in the founding of the Athenian torch-races in honor of Prometheus. If that is so, there will have been in the *Prometheia* a sort of inversion of the process seen in the *Suppliants*-trilogy and the *Oresteia* (where the problem climbed up through the human level to the divine), but the strong family resemblance is still there.

A third feature common to the late group must be stated at this time with dogmatic brevity;[10] it is the appearance in these trilogies of the forms and techniques of Old Comedy—an art which became a respectable form only in the last twenty years of Aeschylus' life. If I am right in my belief that the whole structure of the *Eumenides* is largely explainable in the light of the Old Comic convention, and that there are distinct traces of the same convention in the *Suppliants* and *Prometheus,* then this is at least further proof that Aeschylus' art was receptive, even in his comparatively advanced old age, to what was

---

[9] It probably consisted of the tragedies *Myrmidones, Nereides,* and *Phryges e Hektoros Lytra*; see Mette's collection of the fragments, pp. 70–92.

[10] For the detailed arguments (as I see them) I refer to my article on Aeschylus and Old Comedy in *TAPhA* 94 (1963) 113ff. Some new considerations are added here.

new: to what was new outside tragedy, as well as within it. But there is one likeness to Old Comedy (at least as we know it from Aristophanes' earlier plays thirty years later) that goes deeper than mere formal considerations. I think we are all agreed, unless we are theorists of the medieval school, that a play need not end in physical catastrophe in order to merit the name of "tragedy." And yet what other Athenian plays, outside the *Oresteia,* end in positive outbursts of *joy,* in a triumphal torch-procession, and with benedictions on the land for the fertility of its crops and its women? Practically the whole of the final song of the *Eumenides* consists in such benedictions, with the loud refrain "Rejoice!"

> Rejoice, rejoice in your just shares of wealth!
> People of the city, rejoice!   (*Eum.,* 996f.).

> Rejoice, again rejoice, our cry redoubles:
> all who in the city live!   (*Eum.,* 1014f.).

In fact, that sort of benediction is only heard once elsewhere in Aeschylus, in the *Suppliants* of all plays (625ff.); while for *dramatic finales* which contain such benedictions, and a torchlight procession, and the redoubled cry "Rejoice!", we have to turn to a comedian, Aristophanes. The end of the *Peace,* for instance, combines all three (1317ff.):

> We must carry torches . . . and pray the Gods to give wealth to the Greeks, and that we may all alike raise much barley and much wine, and eat figs, and that our women may bear us children. . . .

And then, in the final words of the *Peace* (1355ff.):

> Rejoice, rejoice, people, and if
> you follow me you'll have cakes to eat!

The *Oresteia,* I think beyond doubt, *ended* in what the spectators could at once see was the manner of Old Comedy—though of course transposed into a nobler key. In estimating what this means we must not forget that Comedy, down till near the end of the fifth century, was much closer to its origins in actual popular religious cult than Athenian tragedy was at any stage where we have knowledge of it. Paradoxically, to the conservative religious or pious spectator, an Old Comedy was probably a more serious act than tragedy itself; in that not only by its origins, but by its costumes and the very form of many of its jokes, it concerned the most ancient and urgent of human needs —the reproduction of crops, of animals, and of the race itself. Aeschylus, it seems to me, so modelled the end of the *Oresteia* that it would appeal to that primeval religious feeling too, besides appealing to the more modern type of mentality among his audience; to the old tribal consciousness as well as to the New Learning in that hectically changing community which was the Athens of his last years.

It would be a bold man—certainly a bolder man than I am—who flatly asserted that the finales of the *Suppliants*-trilogy and of the *Prometheia* must have shared the Old Comic character of the *Eumenides*. Yet three considerations certainly point strongly in that direction. First, few who consider the extant material will doubt that those two trilogies must have ended in harmony, in a synthesis of the antitheses expounded in their first two plays. Second, the great *Danaides* fragment, quoted and discussed above, shows that the last play of the *Suppliants*-trilogy moved into the same ambit—fertility —as the *Eumenides* does; a subject which otherwise is the province of comedy, not tragedy. Third, one notes with great interest the theory already mentioned, that the *Prometheus Pyrphoros* culminated with the founding of the Promethean torch-races. Torchlight at the end of the play, with its symbolism of triumph and marriage, would again link the *Prometheia* to the *Oresteia*, and at the same time distinguish the pair of them from any other Attic drama whatsoever *except Old Comedy*; where torches appear towards the end more commonly than not, and in which three of the eleven extant finales actually consist of torchlight processions.

The last characteristic feature of the late group which I am going to speak of can be dealt with more briefly because the individual facts involved have long been recognized. There is a number of passages in the plays of Aeschylus which are so close to doctrines known to have been under discussion by contemporary pre-Socratic philosophers that mere coincidence seems ruled out. What is not so easily recognized, but is (I believe) true, is that all the reasonably certain instances of this sort of allusion are found in the plays of the late group.[11] They are not specially obtrusive in their dramatic contexts, but if one reflects on them as a whole they add up to a certainty: that in his last years Aeschylus was, at least, *aware* of the philosophical move-

---

[11] Summarily: (1) *Suppliants* 556ff. implies a theory of the risings of the Nile otherwise attributed to Aeschylus' younger contemporary Anaxagoras (Anaxagoras, Fragment A42; cf. J. Vürtheim, *Aeschylos' Schutzflehende*, 79ff.). (2) *Danaides*, Fragment 125 Mette, seems closely related to passages in Empedocles (Empedocles, Fragments B71–73; cf. *Phoenix* 17 [1963], 195n.). (3) Apollo's "biology" in *Eumenides* 658ff. abruptly introduces almost the sole Athenian reference to a problem known to have been under discussion by six non-Athenian philosophers and medical men in the middle years of the fifth century (evidence collected by A. Perretti in *Parola del Passato* II [1956] 241ff.). (4) *Prometheus* 88ff. (allusion to the Four Elements, and perhaps to Empedoclean thinking? Compare, e.g., *Phoenix* 17 [1963], 18off.). (5) *Prometheus*, 459f., on the excellence of arithmetic (evidently a Pythagorean notion; cf. G. Thomson, note on lines 475f. in his edition of the play).

ments that were gathering in strength across the Greek world (especially in Sicily, which Aeschylus knew well in the last two decades of his life, and where, in fact, he died)—a rising hurricane which, by the end of the following generation, was to have swept away the structure of archaic thought and religion. How much does that awareness have to do with the new shape and new tendencies of the late trilogies? Are the late trilogies a sort of response by an enquiring, but still essentially religious late-archaic mind, to the coming of philosophy?

The answer to that may become clearer a little later. Meanwhile, to sum up on what has been said so far, I suggested at the beginning of this paper, first, that these three trilogies stood close together chronologically. That belief was reached in the first instance from external and technical considerations, but I hope that what has been said since may reinforce it; thematically too, and compositionally, they seem to belong together. Second, I suggested that they were in fact so different from anything called "tragedy" before or after them that they practically constitute an art-form of their own, a very short-lived art-form that flourished, at the outside, for a decade, and was never revived. One of the trilogies concerned does not even *begin* like a conventional tragedy; the stock complaint, and a well-justified complaint, about the *Suppliants* is that it is not "tragic." And while the *Oresteia* may seem to begin like tragedy of the older type— the *Agamemnon* in many ways reads like a maturer draft of the *Persians*[12]—it is, taken as a whole, almost a denial of tragedy. To seek a name for the new form would be pointless; "tragicomedy," which might have served, is already in use for something quite different. But one may look for a parallel to it, and I do not think it too fanciful to find that parallel centuries later and in a sphere far from Athens: in Dante's *Comedy*. Dante, by the way, would have called the *Oresteia* too a "comedy" without hesitation, if we can trust the views put forward about his own work in the letter to Can Grande: *a principio horribilis et fetida quia Infernus; in fine prospera, desiderabilis, et grata, quia Paradisus . . . et sic patet quare comedia dicitur.*[13] But perhaps it is better not to quibble over names; I see more than a superficial likeness between the *things*, between Dante's Hell, Purgatory, and Paradise and Aeschylus' *Agamemnon, Choephori,* and *Eumenides*. In both the tripartite works there is a similar movement, a gradual climb from torment, through testing, into the light. Indeed, if Headlam's and Thomson's ideas about the Orphic symbolism of the *Oresteia* are anything like correct, there is not only a likeness but—at a vast distance—a historical connection. For there exists a

[12] Noticed at least as early as 1663 by Stanley (quoted by E. Fraenkel in his edition of the *Agamemnon,* I, p. 43), and often since.
[13] Paragraph 10, ed. Arnaldo Monte, *Le Lettere di Dante* (Milan 1921).

certain underground current of mystical belief which flows for ever, calmly ignoring frontiers and religions.

But to come back to that troubled decade, 466–456 BC. Another of the suggestions made at the beginning of this paper was that once these three trilogies were firmly grasped as being a unique group, produced within a short period under a single impulse, they would throw considerable light on each other, and especially on the *Prometheus*. It will be worth while to end by outlining the way in which the grouping might help towards the understanding of that most problematic of all the characters in Aeschylus: Zeus.

The great argument here for the last century or more has been, of course, that the tyrant-Zeus of the *Prometheus* will not fit—that he is irreconcilable with the sublime Zeus known elsewhere in Aeschylus' work. Does he really not fit? The question is worth reconsidering.

Throughout the series *Suppliants*-trilogy, *Oresteia*, *Prometheia*, I trace two new and even more urgent preoccupations, which I believe, must explain each other. A preoccupation with the split in the cosmos; and a preoccupation with the possibility that Zeus may emerge from the chaos as the ultimate authority, *panaitios, panergetas,* all-responsible, all-worker (to quote the Chorus of the *Agamemnon*, 1486). I think we need have little hesitation about the significance of the cosmic split in these late trilogies. When archaic man runs head-on into classical free enquiry, when a tradition of static authoritarianism in politics and religion finally comes face to face with classical democracy (and it happens that the emergence of full-blown democracy, both in Athens and in Sicily, coincides very closely with the last ten years of Aeschylus' life)—when these confrontations occur all at once, the world will in fact seem to split; from the microcosm of the mind, through the state, to the divine macrocosm itself. It is almost a matter of indifference at which of those levels you think of the cleavage. Though Aeschylus (characteristically) chooses in these plays to show it primarily in its aspect of cosmic cleavage, one might think that the struggle in the *Eumenides* makes almost equal sense if you take it as the struggle between the Olympian *ego* and the infernal *id,* or, more prosaically, as that between liberal and conservative. Certainly, for our time as well as for that of Aeschylus, it seems to mean more than a momentary disturbance among fading pagan gods. It is a deadly feud from which not one of us is free.

Aeschylus, it is true, did not have so gloomy an opinion, for in these same plays, as a possible healer of the cleavage, stands Zeus. Lately an assault has been launched against the idea, so popular in the nineteenth and early twentieth centuries, that Aeschylus was the founder of a new and sublime Zeus-monotheism, and it has been held instead that all the difficulties can be swept away by assuming that his Zeus

is quite primitive (that is the word used) throughout; no more developed than the Zeus of the epic poets.[14] I am coming to wonder
whether this assault does not go too far and simplify too much. It has
done valuable work by questioning some hardened prejudices. But
even apart from the difficult question of its method (the rigidly posi-
tivist interpretation of Aeschylus' language gives me pause, because
poets of all people, almost by definition, do not and cannot use words
positivistically), do its results perfectly fit the phenomena?

There is, indeed, a primitive Aeschylean Zeus, no advance on the
Zeus of Homer and Hesiod (or, come to that, on the woman-and-boy-
chasing Zeus who appears on early fifth-century vase-paintings), but
I suspect that he belongs to the dramas of the phases earlier than 466
BC. This is the Zeus who is cursorily mentioned, with no special emphasis, in the *Persians* and the *Seven*; perhaps the fully anthropomor-
phic Zeus who was actually brought on the stage—on the only occasion we know of in fifth-century Attic tragedy—in Aeschylus' *Psycho-
stasia*; certainly the Zeus who mated with a cow-formed Europa in the
play called *Kares ē Europe,* and who is roundly abused by Danae
(whom he has seduced in the golden rain) in the satyric *Diktyoulkoi*
(lines 774–84). But Aeschylus certainly knows of at least one other
Zeus, who has nothing to do with Homer or Hesiod, or any writer
earlier than his own day: the Zeus of that stupendous couplet from the
lost *Heliades (The Daughters of the Sun)*: "Zeus is Aither, Zeus is
earth, Zeus is heaven; Zeus is all, and whatever is beyond the all."

The dramatic context of these words is unknown, and the play to
which they belong is undated. But even as they stand, even if the play
should be rediscovered and it should prove that they were qualified
or denied in the next line, they surely constitute complete proof that
the poet's mind was at least open to more than the epic and archaic
view about Zeus. For a brief and shattering moment they let us
glimpse a universe in which the orthodox polytheism and anthro-
pomorphism simply cannot exist—in that respect strikingly similar
to the universe implied in the writings of Aeschylus' senior contemporary Xenophanes (whom, so far as dates and known movements go,
he could quite well have met at the court of Hieron in Sicily).

If, to Aeschylus, the concept "Zeus" was as malleable as the *Heliades*
fragment suggests, there now seems nothing to forbid the conjecture
that in these last three trilogies we see a series of experiments, not
only with the idea of a cosmic split, but with the idea of Zeus as the
possible answer to the new and chaotic condition of heaven and earth.
The experiments will be open-minded and honest, though there will
underlie them a basic faith, inherited from archaism, in the simple

[14] H. Lloyd–Jones, "Zeus in Aeschylus," *JHS* 76 (1956) 55ff.; compare D. Page
in his and J. D. Denniston's edition of the *Agamemnon* (Oxford 1957), xixff.

power of the archaic supreme god. In the process of the experiments, Zeus will gradually and naturally move nearer to the centre. The same critic who has assaulted the concept of a sublime Aeschylean Zeus has also objected to the idea (likewise popular in the nineteenth and earlier twentieth centuries) of an "evolving" Zeus, which is often brought in to solve our problems. I think he is justified, and I have learned from him not to believe in an evolving Zeus, either. But I do believe, as the whole of this paper has suggested, in an evolving Aeschylus. From that point of view I take a final look at the late group of trilogies.

The *Suppliants* was always famed for its majestic and moving Zeus-hymns.[15] And even in the days, not so long ago, when the play was commonly dated in the 490's or 480's BC, they were customarily compared with the equally splendid Zeus-hymn of *Agamemnon* 160–183, "Zeus, whoever he may be . . ."—without anyone's feeling much embarrassment, apparently, about the almost total absence of such august language from what would then have to be the intervening plays, the *Persians* and the *Seven*. Now that the *Suppliants* seems to be brought down within perhaps as little as five years of the *Agamemnon,* that difficulty, at least, vanishes. But what is still perhaps not enough noticed is that in both these trilogies the Zeus-hymns occur fairly early in the first play, and are placed, of course, in the mouth of the chorus. One would naturally incline to take them within rather than outside their dramatic context: as intuitive hopes by the helpless girls and the old men respectively, rather than, at that stage, as definite statements by the poet. And in fact, in the *Oresteia* we have to wait very long indeed before that intuitive hope is justified. Not only does unnatural murder have to be done, but the universe has to be parted in two, with Apollo and the Furies (and behind them, offstage, Zeus and the Fates respectively) as opposing partisans. And during the middle section of the *Eumenides* we are to have visions of a universe from which all authority has gone, leaving only that mindless and pitiless chaos across which Euripides, later on, was to move consciously all his life. (But that was after the philosophic revolution was complete.) It is only at the very end of the *Oresteia* that the gash is healed, and the original intuitions fulfilled; but it has been touch and go. We cannot know about Zeus's part in the later stages of the *Suppliants*-trilogy, for obvious reasons. The immense importance, however, that is attached to him in the extant play, suggests that he must have been heavily involved at the end also. And the *Danaides*-fragment makes it almost certain that the cosmic cleavage was there.

---

[15] *Suppliants,* 86–103, 524–99.

In almost every way, even down to minor technical and metrical details, the *Prometheia* takes a stride beyond the *Oresteia*. Here the trilogy *begins* on the cosmic level, instead of rising to it from humanity, and *begins* with a total cleavage on that level. And here Zeus, instead of being kept on the periphery of the actual struggle—instead of being the remote object of human hopes—has moved into the eye of the storm. If there was to be anything beyond the *Oresteia*, it probably had to be this. The two preoccupations, with the cosmic split and with Zeus, fuse into one, and the last question is being asked: can the archaic god survive as a viable force in the new world? We only see, now, one side of the debate, not the response. But this much seems likely. In the *Prometheus Bound* Aeschylus fearlessly and honestly shows, through the eyes of Io and Prometheus, a picture of the archaic power-god which is not really too exaggerated a caricature of the Zeus known to Homer and Hesiod, except that it has taken on political overtones. It apparently includes even Zeus the seducer, the Zeus of the *Europe* and *Diktyoulkoi,* here shown at his worst with Io. There are hints, however, both in the prophecies of the *Bound* and in the fragments of the *Unbound* itself, that in the second play a different aspect of Zeus began to be uncovered: the Zeus who freed the Titans, who at least did not prevent the coming of Prometheus' savior Herakles, who—almost unbelievably—*pitied,*[16] and who in the end came to terms with the intellectual, the *sophistēs,* Prometheus.[17]

Anything said about the final synthesis in the last play of the *Prometheia* is bound to be a guess, but here is one. Those who have claimed that the Zeus of the *Prometheia* is irreconcilable with the Zeus of Aeschylus' other works have always pointed to the great Zeus-hymns near the beginning of the *Suppliants* and the *Agamemnon,* and the absence of anything of the sort in the *Prometheia*. The guess is that when the Day of Judgment comes and all vanished Greek literature is unrolled before us, we shall find that missing Zeus-hymn —in the finale of the last play of the *Prometheia,* the *Pyrphoros*. And that it will be a hymn of joy.[18]

---

[16] *Prometheus Unbound,* Fragment 326 Mette (199 Nauck, Murray).

[17] *Prometheus Bound,* 186–92.

[18] See also *Phoenix* 17 (1963) 236–43, where some reasons are put forward for suspecting, not only that such a hymn once existed, but that echoes of it may still be heard in the solemn finale of Aristophanes' *Birds*.

Some Versions of Aeschylus:

A Study of Tradition and Method in Translating Classical Poetry

by Peter Green

I

Nearly every discussion of translation begins, or tries to begin, with a general definition. There is the word; the word implies a concept; the concept must be definable. Classical scholars in particular, nurtured at a tender age on Plato's Theory of Ideas, persist in imagining that somehow, somewhere, there is to be found the Perfect Translation, of which all their laborious versions partake in some degree. To such an optimist the history of translation—especially verse translation—in his own field cannot but present a depressing spectacle. The theorists, like Gibbon's Byzantine heretics, contradict each other at every turn; and what is worse, they show the most lamentable discrepancies between theory and practice. As Dryden acidly observed, "many a fair precept in poetry is, like a seeming demonstration in the mathematics, very specious in the diagram, but failing in the mechanic operation." In the circumstances it is little wonder that the one point over which everyone seems agreed is that the Perfect Translation is an unattainable will-o'-the-wisp. Nothing, it has been suggested, improves by translation except a bishop.

Translation is not, at any level, an ideal art; it is a crutch for human infirmity, a technique to improve various sorts of communication. Any artistic merit it may have in its own right is purely secondary. Furthermore, we cannot cover it with a single blanket definition. It may be used to interpret at an International Court, to disseminate a scientific treatise, to enable Finnish poetry or Chinese philosophy to spread beyond their immediate linguistic frontiers. . . .

It is generally agreed that the whole concept of what translation means, and the laws or principles governing its practice, have undergone a radical change during the last few years. Just what has brought this metamorphosis about is not so clear. In this essay I propose to deal, more or less exclusively, with the *Agamemnon* of Aeschylus. On this thread it may be possible to hang one or two more widely-framed conclusions about the problems of translating poetry in general, and classical poetry in particular. By working out just what the various translators of the *Agamemnon* were at, we may also come to understand the revolution in method which is apparent when we examine some of the most recent versions.

There are over fifty English translations of the *Agamemnon*. This fact is not, I think, an entirely disinterested tribute to Aechylus' poetic genius. By far the greater number of these versions seem to have served as a prop on which the scholarly poet *manqué* could peg up his own threadbare Muse. Such an ungenerous conclusion is supported by the unfailing way in which each version reflects the borrowed light, not so much of Aeschylus, as of whatever poet was in fashion at the time of writing. In the eighteenth century the great choruses of the *Agamemnon* speak with Dryden's voice; they seem begging to be set to music by Purcell. In the nineteenth, the Romantic Revival is faithfully reflected: Scott, Tennyson, and Shelley usurp their original. Towards the *fin de siècle* we recognize the accents of Swinburne, Patmore, Francis Thompson, even Austin Dobson. The conclusion one is tempted to draw is that the history of Aeschylean translation—indeed, of classical translation generally—has been a subtle process of self-flattery, modifying itself according to changing fashions from one generation to the next. But this would, perhaps, be an oversimplification. . . .

II

The first translator of Aeschylus, Robert Potter, is an intriguing figure; partly because he *was* the first, and also because his version held the field undisputed for fifty years and more. It appeared in 1777, and ran into countless editions; it was still being reprinted in 1892, when there were twenty-five rivals jostling for the lead. Potter, like many translators, was a divine and a schoolmaster. His Aeschylus was followed by versions of Sophocles and Euripides, all of which he sedulously dispatched to Lord Thurlow, the Lord Chancellor. His reward was "the second canonical stall in Norwich Cathedral, which he held till his death. . . . Thurlow, in giving the stall, observed.

'I did not like to promote him earlier for fear of making him
indolent.' "

Despite the great popularity of his translations, Dr. Johnson stoutly
dismissed them *en bloc* as "verbiage," a verdict with which the modern
reader may be tempted to concur. Here, for the first but by no means
the last time, we find that flaccid, colourless blank verse, without character or distinction, beneath which Aeschylus' superb iambics have so
often been buried. The Chorus addresses Clytemnestra:

> With manly sentiment thy wisdom, lady,
> Speaks well. Confiding in thy suasive signs,
> Prepare we to address the gods; our strains
> Shall not without their meed of honour rise . . .

When we turn to the Choruses, we see that Gray and Dryden have
been there before us. Here is Potter's version of the *kyrios eimi,* that
magnificent opening choral strophe:

> It swells upon my soul; I feel the pow'r
> To hail the auspicious hour,
> When, their brave hosts marching in firm array,
> The heroes led the way.
> The fire of youth glows in each vein
> And heav'n-born confidence inspires the strain. . . .

This stupefying bromide, as I have said, held the field for half-a-
century. On its own terms it obviously satisfied the customers. . . .
The first protest was raised in 1829 by James Kennedy, who wrote, in
the preface to his own translation:

> The expression of the ancient has either been marred by diffuseness
> or his meaning obscured by dullness, or his spirit evaporated amidst
> the display of overwrought diction. Too often has the unity . . . been
> sacrificed to a passion for ornament and variety; thoughts not his own
> are incorporated into the body of his composition; a species of intel-
> lectual ingraftment, which produces the direct opposite effect to that
> of the gardener's art, infecting the parent stem without deriving from
> it vigour and nutriment.

Unfortunately Kennedy neutralized the sting of the rhetoric by producing a version as permeated with dullness, overwrought diction,
evaporation of spirit, and intellectual ingraftment as his predecessor:
but he did print, above his own translation, the German rendering by
J. H. Voss. This latter is a remarkable achievement in that at one
stroke it achieves both modernity and equivalence: Voss turns iambics
into Alexandrines, and his choral passages catch the exact rhythms

of their original. Here are the first two lines of the play, the Watchman's appeal for relief from his vigil, as Voss rendered them:

> *Gebt, Götter, fleh'ich, dieser Mühn Erledigung,*
> *Der Hut, ein Jahr an Länge, da gelagert ich, etc.*

That is the rhythm and accent of Aeschylus; and Voss also has the honour of seeing that the first line of the *kyrios eimi* Chorus is, and can be rendered as nothing other than, a hexameter:

> *Macht ist mir zu erhöhn † bahnglückliche Stärke der Männer . . .*

In Germany, if not in England, a point had been reached by the eighteen-twenties where the original—not translator, public, or contemporary fashion—was the most important thing. The point was raised over here during the next few years, and argued at length in scholarly periodicals. One translation embodying Voss's principles appeared in 1839, and was a failure. In 1848 the famous scholar John Conington produced an *Agamemnon* which put the clock back to Potter; but he did have one pertinent observation to make in his preface—which, as so often, contained much more of value than his text:

> There are some measures now tolerably congenial to our language [he wrote] which our fathers would have regarded as unnatural and affected; and the breaking up of conventional forms of phraseology, which has been for some time past going on under the influence of such writers as Mr. Carlyle, will allow us to hazard many expressions which could not have been used twenty years ago.

Substitute T. S. Eliot or Dylan Thomas for Thomas Carlyle, and the same verdict, word for word, could be applied to translations of Aeschylus today. This, partially, is what Mr. Day Lewis meant when he said, apropos his version of Virgil's *Georgics,* that if a classic is worth translating at all, it must be translated afresh every fifty years. Translation is a substitute, an inadequate substitute at the best, for original literature: the requirements of each generation from a version will be bound to differ.

But Conington's words implied something more. Fashion, we have seen, changes from age to age: yet the text of Aeschylus (*pace* our more enthusiastic textual critics) does not. Every translator is conditioned by his own assumptions and dogmas, the literary conventions of his time, what he sees as the restrictions of the medium in which he is working. Therefore there are elements in Aeschylus—not always the same elements—which successive generations of translators will be bound to ignore, or transmute into something else. As long as the translator believes that Aeschylus must be turned into English poetry or English drama, with all the associations that such terms imply, this is inevitable. One generation will be unable to digest his startling metaphors and polysyllabic compound adjectives; another may jib at the apparent obscurity of his thought and imagery. Rhyme is in the very fibre of English verse, and Aeschylus is rhymeless: something has to give way, and it is not usually the translator's patriotism. Aeschylus, we are told, must be presented to the English reader in a recognizable English dress, on the grounds—or so it is still sometimes alleged—that the first business of a translator is to catch readers. It might be argued that this savours of the confidence trick: the hungry sheep look up, and are fed with spurious matter. Like the proverbial mean farmer, the translator equips his sheep with green-tinted spectacles, and proceeds to offer them straw.

At first, as I have suggested, this did not matter; the audience was an informed audience, and never supposed that Aeschylus was a spiritual ancestor of the English Augustans. But as the nineteenth century advanced, and the reading public increased, there was a growing demand for enlightenment and interpretation over the great classical authors. It is interesting to speculate what notion the Greekless layman must have formed of Aeschylus from the versions offered him: I have recently perused every single English translation of the *Agamemnon*, and, with honourable exceptions, a more depressing experience could hardly be conceived by the mind of man.

The overall impression gained must have been that Aeschylus was a limp, third-rate hack versifier, the very worst kind of Poet Laureate, who had somehow managed to stumble on a really powerful theme. This theme he then proceeded to obliterate with every stultifying *cliché*, verbal or prosodic, known to the English language. It is hard to explain the proliferation of these versions; during the latter half of the Victorian period a new one appeared almost every year, virtually indistinguishable from its predecessors.

It might be argued that this was due to most translation being done, not by poets but by scholars, yet when we turn up the two nineteenth-century poets who did have a shot at the *Agamemnon*, we find that they are, if anything, worse than the rest. Edward Fitzgerald achieved, certainly, what no one else has done before or since: he made Aeschylus *coy*:

> Not beside thee in the chamber,
> Menelaus, any more;
> But with him she fled with, pillow'd
> On the summer softly-billow'd
> Ocean, into dimple wreathing

> Underneath a breeze of amber
> Air that, as from Eros breathing,
> Fill'd the sail, and flew before . . .

As for the famous, or notorious, "Browning Version," it went, in theory, to the other extreme: Browning announced his intention of being "literal at every cost save that of absolute violence to our language." Unhappily, he took the word "literal"—as many a schoolboy has done before or since—to mean a word-by-word construe. This notion, which outrages every law of linguistics, has played havoc with otherwise well-intentioned translators.

It was in 1878, a year after the Browning Version, that one isolated translator took a leaf out of Voss's German book and produced what is, to all intents and purposes, the first English rendering of the *Agamemnon* which is recognizably Aeschylean. He was not a poet by calling, but the author of that abominable Latin Primer still inflicted on schoolboys learning the rudiments of grammar: Benjamin Kennedy. Open his version at the first page, and the Watchman begins to speak in accent and rhythm about as near to Aeschylus as any translator had hitherto come:

> Still have I asked the Gods deliverance from these toils
> throughout my long year's watch, whereto I lay me down
> upon the Atreidae's roof, arm-rested, like a dog,
> and know by heart the congress of the nightly stars,
> with those which bring to men winter and summer-tide . . . &c.

That is the last time we see the Alexandrine in an English translation of Aeschylus till Mr. Louis MacNeice introduces it, somewhat sparingly, into his 1936 version. Though heavy in vocabulary, clumsy in versification, and baffled by the complexities of the Aeschylean chorus, Kennedy still contrived to get nearer the heart of the matter than Potter and his imitators. But Kennedy's reward was the indifference of scholars and public alike, who would not be ready for nearly fifty years to digest the innovations (paradoxical that they should be so) which Kennedy had adopted.

Meanwhile poetic fashions were changing in England, and Aeschylus, as usual, moved with the times. By the turn of the century Swinburne and the Nineties had brought their roses and raptures to the long-suffering choruses; and England's discovery of the virtues inherent in French drama shackled swift-moving iambic speeches in the elegant straitjacket of the heroic couplet—a perversion hitherto largely confined to such authors as Homer or Ovid. In 1829 James Kennedy had referred in passing to "the rhyming couplets of the French School, a style of versification so abhorrent to Tragic expression, and over which even the genius of a Dryden failed of achieving a triumph." Both practices obtain in the version by W. R. Paton, published in 1907. Here is the close of the Watchman's speech:

> The rest I speak not; on my tongue a weight
> Lieth; but could these walls articulate
> They'd tell it best. Gladly if one but wot
> I speak; if not, gladly remember not.

And here the truly Swinburnian Chorus addresses Clytemnestra:

> Tell all that thou durst, for the hearts of thy servants are fain
> To be healed, that are sick with the mist of despond, till again
> From the fires of the altars doth gleam sweet hope, and represses
> Thought that thirsts for the corsive [*sic*] of love's caresses.

From here, of course, it is only a step—less than a step, perhaps—to the scholar-translator who has more profoundly influenced the popular conception of Greek Drama than anyone else in this century: the late Professor Gilbert Murray. Now if Professor Murray had lived a hundred, or even perhaps fifty years before he did, no great harm would have been done by his work. His audience would have appreciated exactly what he was at, and applauded his ingenious virtuosity: it is not everybody who can convert a chorus-ending from Euripides into the very accents of "The Garden of Proserpine." But since his charming period-pieces were mostly composed after the First World War, they had a highly unlooked-for effect. Up and down England there were thousands of innocents who very likely went to their graves imagining that this was the way Aeschylus or Euripides actually wrote. They gave the credit for Professor Murray's poetic sensibility to the Greek dramatists on whom he modelled himself; and since Aeschylus was dead, and Professor Murray, with scholarly modesty, refused to take any of the credit, error crept in and persisted. Mr. T. S. Eliot saw the dangers of all this as early as 1920: in a splendidly trenchant article[1] he wrote:

> Greek poetry will never have the slightest vitalising effect upon English poetry if it can only appear as a vulgar debasement of the eminently personal idiom of Swinburne. . . . That the most conspicuous Greek propagandist of the day should almost habitually use two words where the Greek language requires one, and where the English language will provide him with one; . . . that he should stretch the Greek brevity to fit the loose frame of William Morris, and blur the Greek lyric to the fluid haze of Swinburne; these are not faults of infinitesimal significance.

[1] "Euripides and Professor Murray," reprinted in *Selected Essays* (3rd ed. 1951) pp. 59–64. This piece deserves to be read by all students of translation.

Let us take two typical examples from Professor Murray's *Agamemnon*. Late in the play he makes Clytemnestra address the Chorus as follows:

> Woulds't fright me, like a witless woman? Lo,
> This bosom shakes not. And, though well ye know,
> I tell you . . . Curse me as ye will, or bless,
> 'Tis all one. . . . This Agamemnon; this,
> My husband dead by my right hand, a blow
> Struck by a righteous craftsman. Aye, 'tis so.

So much for the iambics: now for the lyrics. A few lines later the Chorus are made to riposte as follows:

> Thy thought, it is very proud;
> Thy breath is the scorner's breath;
> Is not the madness loud
>   In thy heart, being drunk with death?
> Yea, and above thine eye
>   A star of the wet blood burneth!
> Oh doom shall have yet her day,
>   The last friend cast away,
> When lie doth answer lie,
>   And a stab for a stab returneth.

It requires, so far as I am concerned, a very great effort of imagination to put oneself in the place of the scholar who offers this kind of thing to posterity. Human nature is frail, and the possibility that my own favourites may suffer a similar fate fifty years hence does nothing to alter my prejudice. . . .

There is, then, a radical split between the old and new ideas of what a poetic translation of Greek drama should aim at and achieve. For our ancestors it was adaptation or pastiche; for us it is imitation, *mimesis* in the fullest sense of the term. These two attitudes, incidentally, reflect a much wider and more general change in ethical attitudes. Earlier generations were interested in incorporating an ancient poet as a kind of guest member in the Athenaeum of English literature. We are more concerned with hearing him talk about his own tradition—through an interpreter, of course, but one who does his best neither to soften the words he hears, nor to overlay them with false associations. For forty years and more now there has been an increasing number of people who wanted to know—not knowing in any way—what Aeschylus actually said, as near as could be, and the texture of his poetic imagery; people who looked to a translator to use his Golden Bough, his double tongue, to pass them into the ancient world.

Now this, whatever its other merits, the old kind of translation did not: though as an exercise in English parody or pastiche it had undoubted value. Its virtues were those of the prize composition; and this was nowhere more apparent than in its synthetic, conventional archaisms. The principle followed was the same as that in the worst kind of historical novel. This is an archaic work, therefore it must be given a flavour of antiquity. The historical provenance of that antiquity is unimportant. Malory for Herodotus? Shakespeare or William Morris for Sophocles? Ingenious, and very tasteful. It did not occur to these translators—indeed, why should it, in their day and age?—that a translator's real business, almost his moral duty, is what Mr. J. B. Leishman pointed out in his essay on Horace: not to "recall" an original, by some vague semi-parallel, to those who knew it already, but to reproduce something utterly unknown for those who have no notion of it at all.

III

This was the situation after the First World War; and it was in fact then that the modernist movement in translation began. Coincidence, I suspect, played a large part in the revolution: the coincidence that at this precise moment new trends in English poetry came closer to the form and spirit of Greek drama than ever before. Ezra Pound, T. S. Eliot, Wyndham Lewis, the Imagists—all these swept away the lingering prejudice against so-called *vers libre* and the absence of rhyme. The toughest bastion was thus stormed almost by accident. It is significant that the first type of classical poetry to receive adequate translation—formally, aesthetically, and rhythmically —was the Greek choral strophe. H. D.'s versions from the *Iphigeneia in Aulis* and the *Hippolytus* actually appeared a year before Professor Murray's *Agamemnon,* but at a time when forward-looking English poets were bursting out into free verse, and the dissemination of Hopkins' methods made experiment with choral rhythms, compound adjectives, and Aeschylean metaphor highly attractive. Then in 1928 Sir Maurice Bowra and Professor Wade-Gery produced a felicitous version of Pindar's *Pythian Odes* on similar lines; and there followed a succession of complete tragedies—Aldington's *Alcestis* in 1930, MacNeice's *Agamemnon* in 1936, Fitzgerald's *Oedipus Coloneus* in 1941, and so through to the contemporary works by Rex Warner and Professor Richmond Lattimore.

But not all forms came as easily as the choral lyric; it was not till 1944, for example, that Mr. Warner took the step (which looks simple in retrospect) of turning to a variable English Alexandrine instead of traditional blank verse to represent the Greek iambic trimeter. Since the Alexandrine is an exact stress-equivalent, it seems fair to assume that Mr. Warner's predecessors were still working empirically rather than from any *a priori* principles. . . . Nor was it till 1940 that Mr. Cecil Day Lewis found a way of dealing with that most intractable of verse-forms, the hexameter. Here as nowhere else the difficulty of transposing a line governed by accentual metre into one dependent on stress rhythm seemed almost insurmountable. Robert Bridges' attempts at an *accentual* equivalent merely did unnatural violence to English: only Calverley, in his fragment of Book I of the *Iliad,* came anywhere near to making even a regular stress-hexameter sound like a natural growth. The inevitable effect, despite such desperate devices as almost line-by-line *enjambement,* was one of flat and unrelieved monotony, as any reader of H. B. Cotteril's *Odyssey* will testify.

Nevertheless, the problem could not be abandoned to the doubtful mercies of blank verse or the heroic couplet. The hexameter, as Matthew Arnold pointed out, is a precipitate, *falling* line: whereas in the iambic line so often and so dubiously used as an equivalent the reader painfully plods uphill with Sisyphus. Mr. Day Lewis employed "a rhythm based on the hexameter, containing six beats in each line, but allowing much variation of pace and interspersed with occasional short lines of three stresses." This at once provides the rushing dactylic movement so essential for the free flow of the hexameter, and avoids the deadly monotony of a regular English line of this type. In 1952 Mr. Day Lewis followed up his *Georgics* with a more ambitious version of the *Aeneid,* and the same year saw the appearance of Professor Lattimore's *Iliad* in the same style and rhythm.

So far, so good: but attributes, as Socrates pointed out, are not the same as definitions. What is the theory behind the method? One can fairly easily isolate certain translators—Mr. MacNeice, Mr. Warner, Mr. Day Lewis, Mr. Leishman, perhaps above all Professor Lattimore —who might, perhaps, be said to form a "modern" school; yet it is almost impossible to find an exposition of the basic principles— conceptual, emotive, linguistic, prosodic, semantic—on which they have worked. A good deal has, indeed, been written on translating Greek and Latin poetry; but little of it by successful translators (Mr. Leishman honourably excepted) who, I suspect, most often arrive at the right method by instinct, without consciously formulating any principles at all. On the other hand, much of the scholarly criticism available is useless where not downright misleading; it fails either through initial errors of principle, or (when the principle itself is sound) by illogical application in practice, and arbitrary concentration on one or two aspects of what is essentially a multiple problem.

One of the few enlightening statements of guiding principle published by a practising modern translator is perhaps the article Mr. MacNeice wrote in connexion with his version of Goethe's *Faust*. His ideal hypothetical verse translation, he declared, would have to satisfy the following conditions: a balancing of masses, a broad pattern equivalent to the original; conceptual accuracy—all "prose" meanings to be brought out without addition or subtraction; connotative faithfulness—all poetic colour and suggestiveness to reappear in identical shades without loss of lustre; an equivalent line-for-line rendering; the order of words to correspond in general, and the imagery in particulars; the original rhythm-patterns and rhyme-patterns to be preserved; the phonetic texture to remain unaltered. It is of course, as Mr. MacNeice admitted, impossible to satisfy all these conditions completely. But that is no reason why critics should condemn the method *in toto* for only achieving partial success. . . .

The concepts governing this methodology—the first comprehensive and logical attempt to come to grips with real rather than ideal problems in translation—had already been touched on by Miss D. C. Woodworth and Sir Harold Idris Bell. The former made a clear distinction between conceptual sense, affective symbolism, and formal significance, stressing the importance of considering all three in any translation; the latter, echoing this argument in slightly different terms, and adding some shrewd comments on the semantic difficulties incurred by a translator attempting exact conceptual equivalents of such words as *Geist* or *numen,* concluded with the round declaration that "in all true poetry meaning and expression, content and form, are an indivisible whole, neither having any substantive existence apart from the other." If these conclusions are valid, the effect will be to condemn, either wholly or partially, the bulk of existing translations from the classical poets—or at least to relegate them to the status of paraphrase or meta-poem.

Confirmation appeared in 1953 from Mr. John MacFarlane, whose article "Modes of Translation" deserved a wider circulation than that afforded by the *Durham University Journal.* . . . Mr. MacFarlane explodes the fallacious concept of the so-called "literal" translation, in which many who rightly aimed at interpretative fidelity (such as Browning) bogged down hopelessly. A word, as he points out, acquires meaning only in a concrete linguistic and situational context. He further demolishes the notion of "pure conceptualism"—that is, words as information alone: there is always an apparatus of referential symbolism present. All language, as Russell observed, is vague; no precise equivalent between precise symbols can ever be reached. Mr. MacFarlane confirms Bell and Miss Woodworth, in greater detail, to maintain that sound and sense are structurally united and essentially indivisible.

This trend toward multiple representationalism is bound to have been affected by the new public for which classical translations cater today, and which is hinted at by the phenomenal success of the Penguin Classics. Discussing Mr. Day Lewis's *Aeneid* (to which he came, he admits, "with all the prejudice of my classical convention") Professor R. G. Austin writes:

> Mr. Day Lewis's audience, and his readers, differ from any public that any other translator has written for, a public in general less familiar with the original than any other has been. . . . He was bound to ignore all the accreted influence of four-and-a-half centuries of translators, and start afresh. Mock-Tudor or mock-Georgian or mock-anything was unthinkable . . . *there had to be nothing intermediate between Mr. Day Lewis and Virgil.* [Italics mine.]

The translator today has, as he never had before, a moral responsibility towards his readers. They rely on him absolutely: they have no valid check on his activities. He can no longer, if he is honest, indulge in poetic dilettantism, turning his original into some fashionable form of English verse. He can no longer make specious excuses about the letter killing the spirit, or the essence of a translation being lost by over-fidelity. The old jeer that his work is bound to be either a bad translation or bad poetry has lost its point.

Perhaps the most immediately effective factor in modernist theory is its concept of translation as a practical science rather than an idealistic art. It establishes recognized criteria from all the fields involved, against which any translation can be tested. This is an enormous step forward. It also means that it is better for a version to succeed partially along the right lines than to achieve a perfection irrelevant to translation properly considered. Compare, for instance, Housman's version of Horace, *Odes* 4.7 with that by Mr. Leishman:

> *Housman.* But oh, whate'er the sky-led seasons mar,
> Moon upon moon rebuilds it with her beams:
> Come *we* where Tullus and where Ancus are,
> And good Aeneas, we are dust and dreams.
>
> *Leishman.* While, though, waning moons can mend their celestial losses,
> we, when we've fallen to where
> pious Aeneas and richest Tullus and Ancus have fallen
> linger as shadow and dust.

Traditionalists may say that Housman's version is fine poetry, while Leishman's is not, and that is all that matters. But Leishman's version has its poetic quality, and it is more essentially Horatian than Housman's. Leishman preserves the First Archilochian metre in a stress-equivalent: it is no argument at all to say that this metre is unfamiliar to English readers. Texture, rhythm, and verbal usage are all far closer to their original. Housman's rhymed quatrain sets up emotive responses in the reader's mind which have nothing to do with Horace at all: it suggests an English, not a Roman tradition. . . .

Today, to introduce inappropriately modern notions or diction into one's interpretation of ancient literature has become a cardinal crime. Nothing can be taken on trust. . . . The translator today is, literally, the last link binding modern readers to the ancient world. It is his duty to refrain from interposing himself, insofar as is humanly possible, between us and the great dramatists who lived in that other, remote world. As Louis MacNeice wrote:

> And how one can imagine oneself among them
>   I do not know;
> It was all so unimaginably different
>   And all so long ago.

IV

Then there are the permanent, inherent difficulties which confront any translator of Aeschylus. Let us assume our translator to be in accord with modern representational theory: how, without being either unintelligible or plain ludicrous, is he fully to convey the sense, rhythm, and texture of his original? Aeschylus presents special problems. He indulges, as I have already remarked, in violent metaphors and compound adjectives which provoked unkind attention even in Aristophanes' day. The pattern of his plays is stiff and ritualistic; it has as much meaning as, but little more movement than, the pattern on a Bokhara carpet—which it also resembles in texture. Over and above these idiosyncrasies are the problems common to all Greek drama—the use of language which strikes an English ear as mere padding or tautological repetition (though we accept it in Isaiah or the Psalms); the curious, almost to us comic understatement; the forced antitheses; the solemn enunciation of the obvious.

All this was brilliantly brought out by Housman in one of the subtlest parodies in the English language. He called it, simply, *Fragment of a Greek Tragedy*; and it is aimed as much at the pedants who attempt an over-literal "construe" as at Aeschylus himself. Those who are interested may identify the quotations he has worked into the text;

taken literally, the parody is hardly a parody at all. The Chorus begin by questioning Alcmaeon:

> O suitably-attired-in-leather-boots
> Head of a traveller, wherefore seeking whom
> Whence by what way how purposed art thou come
> To this well-nightingaled vicinity?

After a brisk exchange of dialogue the Chorus then soliloquises, in choral strophes:

> In speculation
> I would not willingly acquire a name
> For ill-digested thought;
> But after pondering much
> To this conclusion I at last have come:
> *Life is uncertain.*
> This truth I have written deep
> In my reflective midriff
> On tablets not of wax,
> Nor with a pen did I inscribe it there
> For many reasons: Life, I say, is not
> A stranger to uncertainty.

After a good deal more of this, the unlucky Eriphyla, inside the house, utters a cry which any reader of the *Agamemnon* will at once recognize; and indeed the closing lines of the parody all have a horrid familiarity:

> *Er.* Ah, I am smitten with a hatchet's jaw,
>   And that in deed and not in word alone.
> *Ch.* I thought I heard a sound within the house
>   Unlike the voice of one that jumps for joy.
> *Er.* He splits my skull, not in a friendly way
>   Once more: he purposes to kill me dead.
> *Ch.* I would not be reputed rash, but yet
>   I doubt if all be gay within the house.
> *Er.* O, O, another stroke! that makes the third!
>   He stabs me to the heart against my wish.
> *Ch.* If that be so, thy state of health is poor;
>   But thine arithmetic is quite correct.

Now this type of idiom presents a formidable obstacle to the translator. He cannot draw on familiar English patterns to reassure his audience, because that would be to give them a false impression; on the other hand, if he indulges in pseudo-literalism, he is liable to produce unintentionally ludicrous effects. Even Greek-based deriva-

tive words are liable to shift their meaning perilously in the course
of the centuries, as the late Francis Cornford pointed out in his
preface to Plato's *Republic*—of which he made a superlatively good
translation:

> Many key-words, such as "music," "gymnastic," "virtue," "philoso-
> phy," have shifted their meaning or acquired false associations for Eng-
> lish ears. One who opened Jowett's version at random and lighted on
> the statement that the best guardian for a man's "virtue" is "philoso-
> phy tempered with music," might run away with the idea that, in order
> to avoid irregular relations with women, he had better play the violin
> in the intervals of studying metaphysics. There may be some truth in
> this; but only after reading widely in other parts of the book would
> he discover that it was not quite what Plato meant.[2]

This business of the "meaning" of the words assumes a twofold difficulty when we are dealing with a poet—especially a poet so complex
and allusive as Aeschylus. For many years those scholars who interpreted his text—and also were largely responsible for translating him
—worked on the dogged assumption that everything he wrote had
one single, finally ascertainable meaning, without overtones, am-
biguities, or referential symbolism. They treated him, in fact, as if he
were an historian, scientist, or grammarian; they credited him, as
critics and scholars will, with their own habits of thought and un-
spoken assumptions. Thus when they wanted to elucidate his meaning,
which they supposed could be separated off from the texture of his
poetry as cream is separated from milk, they translated him into
prose—a practice which led to much unnecessary puzzlement. Bold
metaphors and pregnant symbolism were obelized as corrupt, or
emended into comforting, comprehensible common sense; and much
time and ink were wasted in arguing whether Aeschylus meant A or B,
when he probably implied both—with C, D, and E thrown in associa-
tively.

These prose translations of the *Agamemnon* are among the comic
curiosities of literature. They veer between the incomprehensible and
the bureaucratic: in 1823 H. S. Boyd made the Chorus ask Clytemnestra: "What intelligence having received, induced by what annuncia-
tion, in divers places hast thou scattered fragrance?" In 1950 Professor
Fraenkel, in his titanic three-volume edition, is still at it: "Like base
bronze, when rubbed and battered, so he becomes indelibly black
when brought to justice; for a boy runs in chase of a flying bird after
bringing an intolerable affliction upon his people." When we read

---

[2] Nevertheless Cornford himself was capable on occasion of blurring Plato's meaning in order to achieve linguistic clarity: in philosophical translation some quaint-
ness of phrase may have to be retained. See the sensible remarks of Mr. D. J. Furley,
Aspects of Translation (1958) esp. pp. 57ff.

this, we realize (if we did not do so before) that to translate a poet into prose is a completely meaningless act, which implies a gross conceptual fallacy in the translator's mind as to the very nature of poetic expression and poetic logic. At the best a good half of the poetry's significance is lost; at the worst we are led straight into Jabberwocky Land.

The only tolerable prose version known to me (which, it might be argued, was not really prose at all, certainly not in the choruses) was that made in 1911 by Arthur Platt, Housman's friend and colleague at University College, London. He translated the *Agamemnon* into the English of the Authorized Version, and made the lyric passages sound surprisingly like Jeremiah at Babylon:

> In the home also of every man is mourning;
> Their hearts are melted as water,
> Much anguish pierces them to the soul.
> For those whom they sent forth they know,
> But there returns to them no more a living man,
> But dust and ashes in a little urn . . .
> My spirit broods over these things in the darkness,
> Awaiting to hear that which shall come.
> For the gods are not regardless of the man of blood,
> But the grim Fury finds him after many days.

Such a method has its advantages. It catches something of the original's ritual and lyric intensity. It avoids rhyme. Above all, it presents Aeschylus's antiphonies and repetitions in a guise which the English ear, through long familiarity, is prepared to accept. Nevertheless, combined with pseudo-theological interpretation, it has done Aeschylus more harm than good. The associations it carried virtually identified the Greek dramatist with the Hebrew prophets in moral purpose; and Professor Hugh Lloyd–Jones has shown us just how misleading *that* notion can be.[3]

Translating ancient poetry, then, is neither impossible, nor, *per contra,* the soft option so many people once believed it to be. It bears very little relation to turning out a set of elegiacs for a college prize, and demands several talents very seldom united in one person. Ancient poetry is proportionately harder to translate than modern; the language is more stubborn, the allusions less familiar, the forms totally alien. A much greater co-operative effort is also required of the reader, even supposing the translator to perform his task adequately. But the reader, acclimatized by tradition to Greek poetry which apparently resembles English, may shy away from the effort of adapting

[3] [The reference is to Professor Lloyd–Jones's article, "Zeus in Aeschylus," *Journal of Hellenic Studies,* 76 (1956), 55–67—Ed.]

himself to the unfamiliar; therefore he must be helped—yet not mis-directed in the process. To cap it all, drama is notoriously the hardest branch of Greek poetry in which to succeed, and Aeschylus the most intractable dramatic poet. Throughout much of his work scholars still argue as to what his corrupt text says, and when that is decided, the interpretation still frequently eludes them. A classical scholar who is also a creative poet, yet with enough sense of Delphic self-abnega-tion to let another poet use him as a mouthpiece—where is such a paragon to be found? Certainly they are rare; but there can be no doubt that Louis MacNeice, Rex Warner, C. Day Lewis, and Professor Lattimore are to be numbered among them.

A favourite climate had, of course, already been established when Mr. MacNeice came to write his version of the *Agamemnon* in 1936. Two poets—both of them, be it noted, deeply soaked in the classical tradition—had made it possible for Aeschylus to come straight through to an intelligent public: Gerard Manley Hopkins and Mr. T. S. Eliot. Hopkins' sprung rhythm and compound adjectives, his massy richness and roughness of line, his pregnant complexity and multiplicity of symbolism, his cosmic, hierarchic religious sense—all these have Aeschylean affinities. They attune our ears to the great thorny, striding choruses, with their breath-taking metaphors—so queerly modern today, so outlandish to our grandfathers—which form the backbone of the *Agamemnon*.[4] As for Mr. Eliot, he thoroughly domesticated the entire structure of Greek tragedy, so to speak, by borrowing its trappings wholesale for his two early plays, *Murder in the Cathedral* and *The Family Reunion*. Anyone who has assimilated these plays, formally and thematically, should not have the slightest difficulty in appreciating Aeschylus.

Half the trouble in the past has been the *unfamiliarity* of the Greek pattern—the convention of the Chorus, half in the play, half out of it, declaiming what to us, with our less ritual tradition, may seem ponderous truisms; the blatantly stylized set speeches; the faintly ludicrous exchange of single-line dialogue, or *stichomythia*, which Housman parodied with such relish. The English stage tradition is one of conventional realism, just as the English poetical tradition—at least as the general public conceived it till very recently—is one of romantic rhymed lyrics. It requires an effort of the imagination to move out and meet a new concept half-way, to accept its conventions at their own value. Here is where the more cautious traditionalists make their basic mistake.

They remind us, in the first place, that the *Agamemnon* was a play,

---

[4] There is another much-loved poet who springs to my mind when I read Aeschylus: if only Dylan Thomas could have translated the *Oresteia* or the *Prometheus*—or, best of all, Euripides' *The Bacchae!*

written for performance before an audience: and this point we may readily concede. It is, indeed, something more than a play; though it is misleading to compare Greek drama to oratorio, nevertheless the music, dancing, and recitative were integral to the playwright's total effect, since he himself was responsible for them. Any translation must aim, ultimately, at being *performed,* before a live audience. But, say the traditionalists, you cannot expect an audience to digest these thorny unfamiliarities: they must be given something they can both understand and recognize. This is both to insult the modern audience and do a disservice to Aeschylus. After all, an Athenian audience was not daunted by his notorious difficulties: why should their modern counterparts be spoon-fed? Secondly, the conservative translator is depressingly anxious to find a good excuse for dodging hard work. "The rhymeless metres of Greek," Mr. F. L. Lucas declares, "are too remote from English for successful imitation." This today is simply untrue.

Let us turn back for a moment to Professor Fraenkel's conundrum of base bronze and flying birds. Mr. MacNeice's version makes no concessions to popular intelligibility or prosaic glossing; but by matching his original image for image, he produces an effect which is strange, indeed, but very far from ludicrous—and which remains, most important consideration, *poetry:*

> But the mischief shines forth with a deadly light
> And like bad coinage
> By rubbings and frictions
> He stands discoloured and black
> Under the test—a boy
> Who chases a winged bird
> He has branded his city for ever.

That is an almost literal translation; it catches the exact cadence of the original; and it could never have been written by an English poet. Yet it is immediately striking to an English reader. The same firm mastery of Aeschylean rhythm and metaphor is apparent in the very first lines of the play, with the surging Alexandrines catching Aeschylus' iambics as never before:

> The gods it is I ask to release me from this watch
> A year's length now, spending my nights like a dog,
> Watching on my elbow on the roof of the sons of Atreus
> So that I have come to know the assembly of the nightly stars
> Those which bring storm and those which bring summer to men,
> The shining Masters riveted in the sky—
> I know the decline and rising of those stars.

And now I am waiting for the sign of the beacon,
The flame of fire that will carry the report from Troy . . .

This century has seized on Aeschylean themes with peculiar avidity, as a perusal of French literature no less than English at once reveals. *The Family Reunion,* indeed, with its pursuing Furies and obsession over blood-guiltiness, is simply the old Orestes-myth retold in a modern romantic setting. . . . In *Murder in the Cathedral*—which is Mr. Eliot's *Agamemnon,* just as *The Family Reunion* is his *Eumenides*—the Chorus catch just that note of agonized involvement which we note in Aeschylus:

A rain of blood has blinded my eyes . . .
How how can I ever return, to the soft, quiet seasons?
Night stay with us, stop sun, hold season, let the day not come, let the spring
     not come.
Can I look again at the day and its common things, and see them all smeared
     with blood, through a curtain of falling blood?
We did not wish anything to happen.
We understand the private catastrophe,
The personal loss, the general misery,
Living and partly living . . .

Those were the women of Canterbury; and here are the old men of Argos, after Agamemnon's death. The translation, again, is Mr. MacNeice's:

> I am at a loss for thought, I lack
> All nimble counsel as to where
> To turn when the house is falling.
> I fear the house collapsing crashing
> Blizzard of blood—of which these drops are earnest.
> Now is Destiny sharpening her justice
> On other whetstones for a new affliction.
>   O earth, earth, if only you had received me
>   Before I saw this man lie here as if in bed
>   In a bath lined with silver.

Despite the similarity of tone and texture between these two passages, the second could not be anything but Greek in origin, and the first, despite its obvious borrowings and allusions, is quintessentially English. The value of their correlation—the general aid which Mr. Eliot's plays bring to our appreciation of Aeschylus—is in the main the dispersal of this unfamiliarity I have mentioned. Modern lyrics, modern verse dramas have no *real* identity with ancient tragedy; but through them the modern reader and playgoer has a stepping-stone back to the past. The transition is made that degree easier. And of course the translator is helped too: he no longer has to fight against the sheer grain of contemporary taste. He has an audience which is prepared to accept a version of Aeschylus much nearer in form, feeling, and imagery to the original than was possible half a century ago.

Yet I do not believe that the position now reached is entirely the result of a fortunate but fortuitous literary coincidence. This is an age of self-criticism. We are no longer sublimely convinced that what is right for us—whether in politics, morals, literary taste, or anything else—is necessarily right for everyone. Whereas the Augustans and Victorians assumed unhesitatingly that the proper way to deal with an ancient author was to stamp him into modern dress, we are more likely, as a first reaction, to say: "How can we bring out the foreignness, the *otherness*, of this author?" We are no longer, on the whole, interested in the irrelevant business of producing something to flatter the translator's creative personality. His personality is at a discount; he now aims, or should aim, at being a kind of transparent communicating vessel for his original. The result may be odd by traditional English standards; but that is not its proper criterion. If it evokes something of the rhythm and usage of that alien, unknown poet—not a comfortably familiar adaptation transposed into contemporary terms—then the bounds of knowledge have been truly extended, the frontiers of darkness pushed back.

Chronology of Important Dates

525 BC	Birth of Aeschylus, son of Euphorion of Eleusis, near Athens
510–508	End of Pisistratid rule in Athens and establishment of democracy
490	Battle of Marathon
484	Aeschylus wins his first tragic victory
480	Battles of Thermopylae and Salamis
479	Battle of Plataea
472	Production of *Persians*
468	Sophocles wins his first tragic victory
467	Production of *Seven Against Thebes*
463?	Production of *Suppliant Women*
458	Production of *Oresteia* (*Agamemnon, Libation Bearers, Eumenides*)
456?	Production of *Prometheus Bound*
456	Death and burial of Aeschylus at Gela in Sicily

Notes on the Editor and Contributors

MARSH H. MCCALL, JR., editor of this volume, is the author of *Ancient Rhetorical Theories of Simile and Comparison*. He is Associate Professor of Greek and Chairman of the Classics Department at The Johns Hopkins University.

The late SIR MAURICE BOWRA, Warden of Wadham College, Oxford, numbered among his many works studies of Homer, epic poetry, Greek elegiac and lyric poetry, Pindar, and Sophocles. He was the editor of the Oxford text of Pindar.

JOHN H. FINLEY, JR., Eliot Professor of Greek at Harvard University and formerly Master of Eliot House, has written studies on Thucydides and, most recently, *Four Stages of Greek Thought*. He is preparing a book on the *Odyssey*.

ROBERT F. GOHEEN, author of *The Imagery of Sophocles'* ANTIGONE, is President of Princeton University.

PETER GREEN, Professor of Classics at the University of Texas, has written most recently *Xerxes at Salamis* and *Alexander the Great*. He has translated several works of French and Italian authors.

N. G. L. HAMMOND, Professor of Greek at the University of Bristol, is the author of *A History of Greece to 322 BC* and numerous studies in Greek history, literature, archaeology, and topography.

C. J. HERINGTON, Professor of Classics at Stanford University, has written *Athena Parthenos and Athena Polias: A Study in the Religion of Periclean Athens*. He is engaged in a series of studies on Aeschylus including the recently published *The Author of the Prometheus Bound*.

RICHMOND LATTIMORE, Paul Shorey Professor of Greek Emeritus at Bryn Mawr College, is the author of *The Poetry of Greek Tragedy, Story Patterns in Greek Tragedy*, and well known translations of Greek epic, lyric, and dramatic poetry.

The late GILBERT MURRAY, Regius Professor of Greek at Oxford, was the editor of the Oxford texts of Aeschylus and Euripides, the author of works on Greek literature and religion, and an influential translator of Greek drama.

THOMAS G. ROSENMEYER, Professor of Greek and Comparative Literature at the University of California, Berkeley, has written most recently *The Green Cabinet, Theocritus and the European Pastoral.*

GEORGE THOMSON, Professor of Greek at the University of Birmingham, has edited, with commentary, the *Oresteia* and *Prometheus Bound* and has written studies of Greek culture and society.

Selected Bibliography

Dawe, R. D. "Inconsistency of Plot and Character in Aeschylus," *Proceedings of the Cambridge Philological Society* IX (1963) 21–62.

de Romilly, Jacqueline. *Time in Greek Tragedy*. Ithaca: Cornell University Press, 1968. Contains a good chapter on Aeschylus.

Dodds, E. R. "Morals and Politics in the *Oresteia*," *Proceedings of the Cambridge Philological Society VI* (1960) 19–31.

Dover, K. J. "The Political Aspects of Aeschylus' *Eumenides*," *Journal of Hellenic Studies* LXXVII (1957) 230–237.

Earp, F. R. *The Style of Aeschylus*. Cambridge: Cambridge University Press, 1948. Includes lists and statistics.

Else, Gerald F. *The Origin and Early Form of Greek Tragedy*. Cambridge, Mass.: Harvard University Press, 1965. Discusses Aeschylus and Thespis as the creators of tragedy.

Fowler, Barbara H. "The Imagery of the *Prometheus Bound*," *American Journal of Philology* LXXVIII (1957) 173–184.

Golden, Leon. *In Praise of Prometheus. Humanism and Rationalism in Aeschylean Thought*. Chapel Hill: University of North Carolina Press, 1966.

Havelock, E. A. *The Crucifixion of Intellectual Man*. Boston: Beacon Press, 1950. A provocative interpretation of the *Prometheus Bound*.

Jones, John. *On Aristotle and Greek Tragedy*. Oxford: Oxford University Press, 1962. Contains a perceptive section on the *Oresteia*.

Kirkwood, Gordon M. "Eteocles Oiakostrophos," *Phoenix* XXIII (1969) 9–25. Interpretation of the *Seven Against Thebes*.

Kitto, H. D. F. "The Idea of God in Aeschylus and Sophocles," in *La notion du divin depuis Homère jusqu'à Platon*. ("Entretiens pour l'étude de l'antiquité classique, I"). Geneva: Fondation Hardt, 1954.

————. *Form and Meaning in Drama. A Study of Six Greek Plays and of* HAMLET. London: Methuen, 1956. The *Oresteia* provides three of the plays studied.

————. *Poiesis: Structure and Thought*. Berkeley and Los Angeles: University of California Press, 1966. The first two chapters center on Aeschylus, particularly the *Persians*.

Kuhns, Richard. *The House, the City, and the Judge: The Growth of Moral Awareness in the* ORESTEIA. Indianapolis: Bobbs-Merrill, 1962.

Lesky, Albin. "Decision and Responsibility in the Tragedy of Aeschylus," *Journal of Hellenic Studies* LXXXVI (1966) 78–85.

Lloyd–Jones, Hugh. "The Guilt of Agamemnon," *Classical Quarterly* XII (1962) 187–199.

McKay, A. G. "A Survey of Recent [1947–54] Work on Aeschylus," *Classical World* XLVIII (1954–55) 145–150, 153–159.

———. "Aeschylean Studies 1955–1964," *Classical World* LIX (1965–66) 40–48, 65–75.

Murray, Robert Duff, Jr. *The Motif of Io in Aeschylus'* SUPPLIANTS. Princeton: Princeton University Press, 1958.

Otis, Brooks. "The Unity of *Seven Against Thebes*," *Greek, Roman, and Byzantine Studies* III (1960) 145–174.

Owen, E. T. *The Harmony of Aeschylus*. Toronto: Clarke, Irwin, 1952.

Peradotto, John J. "The Omen of the Eagles and the *Ethos* of Agamemnon," *Phoenix* XXIII (1969) 237–263.

Podlecki, Anthony J. *The Political Background of Aeschylean Tragedy*. Ann Arbor: The University of Michigan Press, 1966.

Smyth, H. Weir. *Aeschylean Tragedy*. Berkeley: University of California Press, 1924. A solid general work.

Solmsen, Friedrich. *Hesiod and Aeschylus*. Ithaca: Cornell University Press, 1949.

Whallon, William. "Why is Artemis Angry?," *American Journal of Philology* LXXXII (1961) 78–88.

Winnington-Ingram, R. P. "The Danaid Trilogy of Aeschylus," *Journal of Hellenic Studies* LXXXI (1961) 141–152.